JN309130

図録 原爆の絵 ヒロシマを伝える

広島平和記念資料館 編

図録
原爆の絵
A-bomb Drawings by Survivors

ヒロシマを伝える

岩波書店

はじめに

　被爆から60年以上が経過した今日でも、原爆はヒロシマの人々の心から消え去ることはありません。

　広島平和記念資料館では、被爆者が体験にもとづいて描いた「市民が描いた原爆の絵」を所蔵しています。絵の作者は1,200人を超え、作品は約3,600枚に及びます。これらの絵はまさに消し去ることのできない記憶であり、1枚1枚から、広島で起こった筆舌に尽くし難い情景が、生々しくよみがえってきます。そして、絵を見る人の心に強い衝撃を与えます。

　今もなお、地球上には数万発の核兵器が存在し、人類はその脅威にさらされています。「市民が描いた原爆の絵」は、ヒロシマの被爆体験を単に記録するだけではなく、こうした状況に警告を発するとともに、後世に伝える証言としての役割を担っています。

　本書では、広島平和記念資料館が所蔵するすべての絵を掲載することはできませんが、できる限り多くの絵を掲載しました。市民が体験した原爆とはどんなものだったのか、被爆者がどのような思いで絵を描いたのか、読者の皆さんに知っていただきたいと思います。

　最後に、絵を描かれた皆さんに改めて感謝を申し上げるとともに、編集に当たりご協力いただきました関係者の皆様、監修の先生方に心からお礼と感謝を申し上げます。

2007（平成19）年3月
　　　　　　広島平和記念資料館

Introduction

　More than 60 years later, the atomic bombing lives in the hearts of the people of Hiroshima.

　The Hiroshima Peace Memorial Museum collects A-bomb drawings by survivors that are based on personal experiences. We now have roughly 3,600 drawings by over 1,200 witnesses. Each drawing represents a persistent memory of the atomic bombing and evokes a searing image that someone witnessed in the city, scenes that defy the power of words to convey. Each work delivers a powerful shock to the viewer.

　Humanity remains threatened by tens of thousands of nuclear weapons stockpiled on our planet. Beyond recording the Hiroshima A-bomb experience, drawings by survivors play an important role in conveying truths about the bombing to future generations and warn us that as long as these weapons exist, they threaten us all.

　Though unable to include in this book every drawing in the Hiroshima Peace Memorial Museum collection, we present as many as possible. We hope they will help readers understand the nature of the atomic bombing suffered by the people of Hiroshima and what the survivors felt as they drew these pictures.

　We would like to offer our heartfelt gratitude to the creators of these drawings, the editorial supervisors and all who assisted in the editing process.

March 2007
　　　　　　Hiroshima Peace Memorial Museum

目　次
Contents

はじめに
Introduction

原爆被害の概説 1
Overview of Atomic Bomb Damage

絵の収集経緯 5
The Collection Process

凡例 7
Explanatory Notes

「原爆の絵」と向き合うということ ················ 浅井 基文 ············ 9
Confronting A-bomb Drawings　　　　　　　Motofumi Asai

第1章　きのこ雲の下で 13
Chapter 1　Under the Mushroom Cloud

生と死の分岐点──防火水槽をめぐって ········ 横山 昭正 ············ 47
The Turning Point between Life and Death—Looking at Fire Cisterns　　Akimasa Yokoyama

第2章　き ず な 53
Chapter 2　Bonds

絵筆に込められた想い ···································· 直野 章子 ············ 77
Emotions Carried by the Brush　　　　　　　Akiko Naono

第3章　い の ち 81
Chapter 3　Life

広島市街地図 124
Map of Hiroshima City Neighborhoods

作 品 一 覧 127
Other A-bomb Drawings in the Museum Collection

特別寄稿　歴史、記憶、そして「原爆の絵」という遺産 ········ ジョン・W・ダワー ············ 167
　　　　　History, Memory & the Legacy of *Hibakusha* Artists　　John W. Dower

監修者紹介 174

翻訳＝(有)トランズネット

装丁＝後藤葉子

原爆被害の概説

1945（昭和20）年8月6日、人類史上初めて原子爆弾が広島に投下された。街は一瞬にして廃墟と化し、多くの人々の生命が奪われた。かろうじて生き残った人も心と体に大きな痛手を受け、多くの被爆者がいまなお苦しんでいる。

【被爆前の広島】

広島は江戸時代に城下町として栄え、明治以後は高等師範学校が開校するなど学都として、また、陸軍の施設が集中する軍都としても発展していた。

被爆当時、広島市には約35万の人々がいたと推定されている。

被爆前の広島県産業奨励館（現在の原爆ドーム）：広島平和記念資料館蔵　絵はがき

【原子爆弾の開発から広島への投下まで】

1942（昭和17）年8月、アメリカは原子爆弾製造計画「マンハッタン計画」に着手した。太平洋戦争末期、アメリカは戦争終結のため原爆の使用を決めた。これによりソ連の影響力がアジアに広がるのを防ぎ、また膨大な経費を使った原爆開発を国内向けに正当化できると考えたからである。1945（昭和20）年7月16日、初めての原爆の爆発実験に成功。7月25日、広島、小倉、新潟、長崎いずれかへの投下命令が下された。8月2日、攻撃日を6日、第1目標を広島とする命令が出された。8月6日午前8時15分、原爆搭載機B29エノラ・ゲイから原爆が投下され、広島市の中心部の上空600メートルで炸裂した。

Overview of Atomic Bomb Damage

On August 6, 1945, Hiroshima fell victim to the first atomic bombing in history. The city was instantly reduced to rubble, and vast numbers of residents lost their lives. Those who survived suffered terrible physical and emotional trauma. Many still suffer today.

【Hiroshima before the Bombing】

During the Edo Period (1603-1867) Hiroshima flourished as a castle town. The Meiji Period (1868-1912) saw Hiroshima develop as an academic city with the founding of Hiroshima Higher School of Education and other institutions of higher learning. Gradually, a growing concentration of military facilities turned Hiroshima into a military city as well.

Estimates put the number of people in Hiroshima at the time of the bombing at around 350,000.

【The Atomic Bomb: From Development to Use in Hiroshima】

In August 1942, the United States launched the Manhattan Project to manufacture an atomic bomb. In the last days of the Pacific War, the U.S. decided to use atomic bombs to end the war. The intent was to block the Soviet Union's attempts to increase its influence in Asia and to justify to the American people the huge expense of developing the atomic bomb. The first atomic bomb test conducted on July 16, 1945 was successful. On July 25, an order was issued to use the bomb on one of the following cities: Hiroshima, Kokura, Niigata, or Nagasaki. On August 2, a field order was issued that specified August 6 as the day of attack and Hiroshima as the primary target. At 8:15 a.m. on August 6, the B29 bomber Enola Gay dropped an atomic bomb that detonated 600 m in the skies over central Hiroshima City.

Hiroshima Prefectural Industrial Promotion Hall before the bombing (now, A-bomb Dome): Picture postcard (Hiroshima Peace Memorial Museum collection)

【原子爆弾の被害の概要】

　原子爆弾の爆発の瞬間、強烈な熱線と放射線が四方へ放射されるとともに、周囲の空気が膨張して超高圧となり、強烈な爆風が発生。これらが作用し大きな被害をもたらした。原爆による被害の特質は、大量破壊、大量殺りくが、瞬時に、かつ無差別に引き起こされたこと、放射線による障害が長期間にわたり人々を苦しめることにある。

　原爆によって死亡した人の数は、現在も正確につかめていない。これまで推定の数字がいくつか公表されているが、広島市では、急性障害が一応治まった1945（昭和20）年12月末までに、約14万人（誤差±1万人）が死亡したと推計している。

　原爆が市街地のほぼ中心で爆発したことと、市内の全建物の85％が爆心地から3キロメートルの範囲内にあったことから、被害は市の全域に及び、建物の90％以上が破壊または焼失した。

被爆前の空撮　1945（昭和20）年4月13日：米軍撮影

■ 熱　線

　爆発と同時に爆発点の温度はセ氏100万度を超え、空中に発生した火球は、1秒後には直径280メートルの大きさとなり、約10秒間輝いた。

　この火球から四方に放出された熱線は、爆発100分の1秒後から約3秒間、地上に強い影響を与え、爆心地周辺の地表面温度はセ氏3,000～4,000度にも達した。強烈な熱線を浴びた人々は重度のやけどを負い、死亡する人も多かった。やけどは、熱線に直面していた部分にのみ生じており、爆心地から3.5キロメートル離れたところでも、衣服を着ていなかった人はやけどを負った。

【Summary of Atomic Bomb Damage】

In the moment of explosion, intense heat rays and radiation were emitted in all directions. As the surrounding air expanded, super-high pressure created a tremendous blast. These three forces inflicted enormous damage. An atomic bombing is characterized by massive, instantaneous destruction and indiscriminate mass slaughter, accompanied by radiation damage that continues indefinitely to cause human suffering.

The precise number that perished in the bombing is still unknown, but several figures have been made public. Hiroshima City estimates that by the end of December 1945, when acute effects had subsided, roughly 140,000 (±10,000) persons had died.

Because the bomb exploded near the city center and 85% of all city structures were located within a 3 km radius, the entire city was damaged. Over 90% of all buildings were collapsed and/or burned.

Aerial photo of Hiroshima before the bombing (April 13, 1945)
Credit: US Army

被害のようす　1945（昭和20）年8月9日：米軍撮影
Hiroshima after the bombing (August 9, 1945)　Credit: US Army

■ Heat Rays

At the moment of detonation, the temperature at the burst point exceeded one million degrees Celsius. The fireball generated in the air expanded to a diameter of 280 m in one second and blazed for roughly ten seconds.

Heat rays were emitted 1/100th of a second after detonation and burned the earth's surface for roughly three seconds. The ground temperature around the hypocenter reached 3,000-4,000 degrees Celsius.

People exposed to the intense heat rays suffered deep burns, and many died. They were burned only on the parts of their bodies facing the epicenter. Bare skin was burned even 3.5 km away.

■ 爆風

　原子爆弾の爆発の瞬間、爆発点は数十万気圧という超高圧となり、まわりの空気が急激に膨張して衝撃波が発生し、その後を追って強烈な爆風が吹き抜けた。

　爆心地から半径2キロメートルまでの地域では、木造家屋はほとんどが倒壊し、鉄筋コンクリート造の建物は、崩壊はしないものの、窓は全部吹き飛ばされ、内部はことごとく焼失するなどの大きな被害を出した。

　爆風により、人々は吹き飛ばされ、失神した人、負傷した人、倒壊した建物の下敷きになって圧死した人が続出した。

爆風でおしつぶされ傾いたビル　1945（昭和20）年10月上旬：林重男撮影
Building crushed and tilted by the blast (early October 1945)
Credit: Shigeo Hayashi

■ 大火災

　強烈な熱線により市内中心部の家屋が自然発火し、続いて市内のいたるところで、倒れた家屋の台所で使われていた火気などを原因とする火の手が上がり、午前10時ごろから午後2〜3時ごろを頂点に、終日、天を焦がす勢いで燃え続けた。

　爆心地から半径2キロメートル以内の地域はことごとく焼失し、焼け跡では、すべてのものが異常な高熱火災により溶けて、まるで溶岩のようにあたりを埋めつくした。

　倒壊した建物の下敷きになって、生きながら焼かれて亡くなった人も数知れない。

■ Blast

At the moment of detonation, burst point pressure shot to several hundred thousand atmospheres. The sudden expansion of surrounding air generated a super-high-pressure shock wave followed by a tremendous blast wind.

Within a 2 km radius of the hypocenter, virtually all wooden structures were destroyed. Concrete buildings remained standing but were severely damaged, their windows blown away and interiors completely gutted by fire. The blast lifted and hurled people, knocked them unconscious, wounded and/or trapped them under collapsed buildings, and crushed them to death.

原爆が投下された翌日の爆心地あたり：岸田哲平提供／岸田貢宜撮影
Hypocenter area (day after the bombing): Photo courtesy of Teppei Kishida
Credit: Mitsugi Kishida

■ Conflagration

The intense heat rays ignited houses and other flammable objects and materials near the city center. Throughout the city, flames spread from released kitchen fires. The flames peaked between 10:00 a.m. and 2:00 or 3:00 p.m. All day the city burned with a ferocity sufficient to "scorch the sky."

All areas within a 2 km radius of the hypocenter burned completely. The abnormally hot fires melted most objects, pouring them over the earth's surface like lava.

Under fallen buildings, countless people were trapped and burned alive.

■ 放射線

　原子爆弾の特徴は、通常の爆弾では発生しない放射線の影響によって、人体に大きな障害が引き起こされたことである。

　爆心地から1キロメートル以内にいた人は致命的な影響を受け、多くは数日のうちに死亡した。被爆直後から短期間には、発熱、吐き気、下痢、出血、脱毛、全身のけだるさなど、さまざまな症状の急性障害が現れ、多くの人が死亡した。

　原爆は、爆発後、長時間にわたって残留放射能を地上に残した。このため、肉親や同僚などを捜して、また救護活動のため入市した人々の中には、直接被爆した人と同じように発病したり、死亡する人もいた。さらに、このような急性障害のほか長期にわたって白血病、ガンなどの後障害を引き起こし、現在も多くの被爆者を苦しめている。

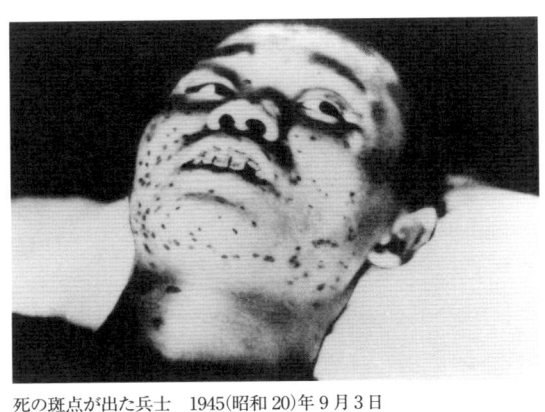

死の斑点が出た兵士　1945(昭和20)年9月3日
：広島原爆被災撮影者の会提供／木村権一撮影
Soldier with "spots of death" (September 3, 1945)
: Photo courtesy of Association of the Photographers of the Atomic (Bomb) Destruction of Hiroshima　　Credit: Gonichi Kimura

■ Radiation

Unlike conventional bombings, atomic bombings are characterized by radiation that inflicts grave damage to human bodies.

Persons within 1 km of the hypocenter absorbed a lethal dose of radiation and most died within a few days. Immediately following the bombing and continuing for a short period, they suffered a variety of acute symptoms, including fever, nausea, diarrhea, hemorrhage, hair loss, and general fatigue. Many perished.

The atomic bombing left residual radiation on the ground for some time. Many who entered the city to search for family members, colleagues, and other acquaintances or to engage in relief activities fell ill with the same symptoms as those directly exposed. Some died. Besides such acute disorders, radiation also caused leukemia, cancer, and other late effects for many years. Even today survivors suffer from their radiation exposure.

絵の収集経緯

【昭和49年 1枚の絵から】

「昭和49年5月のある日、小林岩吉さんという77歳の老人が、下駄ばきの姿で1枚の絵を携え、広島のNHKを訪れました。当時放送中のテレビドラマ『鳩子の海』を見て、原爆当時を思い起こしたという小林さんは、「昭和二十年八月六日午後四時頃、萬代橋付近」と説明書きのある絵を、わたしたちに見せてくださいました。」(日本放送協会編『劫火を見た――市民の手で原爆の絵を』日本放送出版協会、1975年)

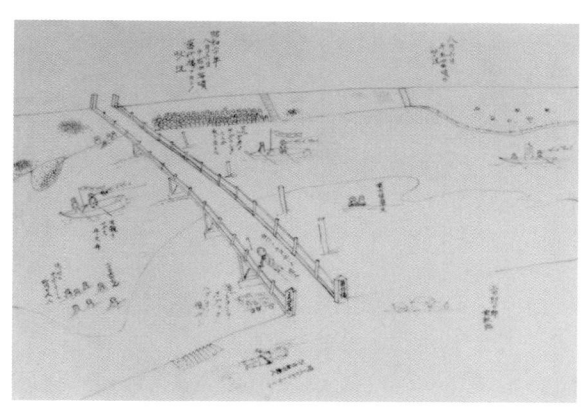

小林岩吉さんが描いた「万代橋フキンノ状況」

この1枚の絵がきっかけとなり、NHKは「市民の手で原爆の絵を残そう」という呼びかけを始めた。反響は大きく、1975(昭和50)年までの2年間で2,225枚の絵が寄せられ、広島平和記念館(現在の広島平和記念資料館東館)をはじめ全国6都市で、巡回展示もされた。

【平成14年の募集】

被爆から57年後の2002(平成14)年、被爆者の平均年齢は70歳を超えた。広島市と長崎市、NHKなどは共同で、「伝えたい…平和の願いを、世紀を超えて」をテーマに、再び原爆の絵を募集した。結果、広島には新たに1,338枚の絵が寄せられた。

The Collection Process

[Launched by a Single Drawing in 1974]

"One day in May 1974, a 77-year-old man named Iwakichi Kobayashi walked into the NHK Hiroshima Broadcasting Station wearing *geta* (wooden clogs) and carrying a drawing. Kobayashi, who told us that watching the TV serial drama *Hatoko no Umi* had reminded him of the atomic bombing, showed us a drawing on which he had written 'The scene around the Yorozuyo Bridge about 4:00 p.m. on August 6, 1945.'" (*Unforgettable Fire—Pictures Drawn by Atomic Bomb Survivors*, edited and published by Japan Broadcasting Corporation, 1975)

"The scene around the Yorozuyo Bridge" by Iwakichi Kobayashi

The appearance of this drawing led NHK to issue a call to create "A People's Pictorial Record of the Atomic Bombing." The call elicited a huge response and by the end of 1975 (in less than two years) the NHK Hiroshima Broadcasting Station had received 2,225 drawings. These were exhibited in the Hiroshima Peace Memorial Hall (now, the Hiroshima Peace Memorial Museum East Building) and traveled to five other Japanese cities.

[Another Call for Drawings in 2002]

In 2002, fifty-seven years after the atomic bombing, the average age of the *hibakusha* was over 70. Hiroshima and Nagasaki cities, NHK, and other entities working together issued another call to "Convey the Desire for Peace Across the Centuries." In response, Hiroshima City received an additional 1,338 drawings.

【今もなお】

2度の収集キャンペーン以後も、「原爆の絵」は描かれ続け、今も広島平和記念資料館に寄せられている。

これらは、常設展や企画展で展示されるほか国内外の原爆展などでも活用され、インターネットで公開されている。

◆掲載している絵について

この図録には、広島平和記念資料館が所蔵する約3,600枚の原爆の絵のうち、本編（第1～3章）と巻末で、約1,200枚を紹介している。巻末には、本編で掲載しなかった作者の絵を1人1点ずつ掲載した。（作者氏名の50音順、匿名は最後）

原爆の絵とともに、作者氏名（敬称は省略）、被爆当時の年齢・絵を描いたときの年齢、情景の日時、爆心地からの距離と場所（当時の町名または施設名）、絵の募集時期を掲載している。

- 「絵のタイトル」は、作者のことばをもとに付した。
- 「作者のことば」は、絵中の文章や添付されていた説明をもとに編集した。表記は可能な限り原文を尊重したが、誤字脱字は訂正し、また読みやすさに配慮するため適宜句読点を補った。
- 文中にある原爆関連の用語などには、注釈を付した。
- 掲載した絵のうち、作者名の後ろに◎印を付しているものは、作者（関係者）の連絡先が不明なものです。心あたりの方は広島平和記念資料館までご連絡ください。
- 募集時期について
  第1回募集（1974・1975年）＝被爆後約30年を経て描かれた絵
  第2回募集（2002年）＝被爆後約57年を経て描かれた絵
  その他＝2回の募集時期以外に寄せられた絵

【Drawings Still Coming In】

Long after the two campaigns, people continue to create A-bomb drawings and send them to the Hiroshima Peace Memorial Museum.

Some are displayed in the permanent exhibition and some in special exhibitions or A-bomb exhibitions in other Japanese cities and overseas. Many of the drawings can be viewed on the Internet as well.

◆ The Drawings

Of the roughly 3,600 drawings held by the Hiroshima Peace Memorial Museum, this book introduces roughly 1,200 in the main text (Chapters 1 to 3) and the appendix. The appendix displays one drawing each by survivors (alphabetized by last name, anonymous last) whose drawings do not appear in the main text.

Each drawing gives: 1) Name of artist (honorifics omitted); 2) Age at time of bombing and at time of drawing; 3) Date and time of the scene depicted; 4) Distance from hypocenter and location (including name of neighborhood at the time or facility); and 5) Drawing solicitation period.

- Title: Titles are based on the artist's comments.
- Artist's comments: Edited versions of the scene descriptions the artists wrote on the drawings themselves or in attached documents. The artist's own words are used as much as possible, but may be modernized or edited.
- Explanations of A-bomb terms, etc.
- The symbol ◎ after an artist's name means that contact information is not available. If you can furnish contact information in such cases, please contact the Hiroshima Peace Memorial Museum.
- Drawing solicitation period
  Call 1 (1974-1975)—Drawings created roughly 30 years after the atomic bombing
  Call 2 (2002)—Drawings created roughly 57 years after the atomic bombing
  Other—Drawings created at times other than above periods

凡　例
Explanatory Notes

❶ 姉さん寒い！　寒い

❷ 今から2時間ほど前、弟を尋ね当てました。「水がほしい！　水がほしい！」といいますので水を与えました。うれしそうに飲みました。「姉さん寒い！　寒い」と言いますので抱いてやりました。弟の体温は次第に無くなり、息を引き取りました。

❸ 8月6日 午後9時頃
❹ 900m ／県立広島病院正門前（10 吉島・舟入・観音）
❺ 田頭 忠之（43 ▶ 72）

❶ "Sister, I'm cold! I'm cold!"

❷ About two hours before the scene in this picture, she found her younger brother. He had cried, "I want water! I want water!" so she gave him some. He drank it happily. Then, he said, "Sister, I'm cold! I'm cold!" and she cradled him. His body gradually grew colder, and he died.

❸ August 6, around 9:00 p.m.
❹ 900m / in front of the gate of Hiroshima Prefectural Hospital (10 Yoshijima・Funairi・Kan-on)
❺ Tadayuki Tagashira (43 ▶ 72)

```
2 - A - ◎
↑   ↑   ↑
❻   ❼   ❽
```

- ❶ 絵のタイトル
- ❷ 作者のことば
- ❸ 絵に描かれた情景の日時
- ❹ 爆心地からの距離／絵に描かれた場所
  （　）内は、124-125ページの地図にある12の地区のどこに当たるかを示している
- ❺ 作者氏名（被爆当時の年齢▶絵を描いたときの年齢）
- ❻ 「作者のことば」が、1 抜粋、2 要約、3 書籍等からの引用のどれに当たるかを示す
- ❼ 絵の募集時期を示す
  Aが第1回（1974・1975年）、Bが第2回（2002年）、Cがその他
- ❽ 作者の連絡先が不明なものは◎印で示す

- ❶ Title of drawing
- ❷ Artist's comments
- ❸ Date and time of the scene depicted
- ❹ Distance from hypocenter / Location of scene
  The neighborhood in (　) refers to the map on page 124, 125.
- ❺ Artist's name (age at time of bombing ▶ age at time of drawing)
- ❻ Artist's comments are either 1) Excerpted, 2) Summarized, or 3) Quoted from a document
- ❼ Period of drawing solicitation
  A = Call 1 (1974-1975), B = Call 2 (2002), C = Other
- ❽ ◎ No contact information is available for the artists.

「原爆の絵」と向き合うということ

浅井 基文

　私が原爆の絵に出会ったのは、正直言って、そんなに古い過去ではない。確かテレビの番組の中で取り上げられた絵を見たときがはじめてだった。その時に受けた印象は言葉にならない強烈なもので、私は激しいショックに襲われた。それからの私は、「いつかはもっと正面から原爆の絵に向き合わなければならない」という自分をむち打つ思いと、「しかし、自分にそれだけの精神的な強じんさがあるだろうか」という弱気になる気持ちとの間で揺れ動いてきた。そんな矛盾した気持ちに整理がつかないために、2005年4月に広島に住むことになってからも、この重い宿題は1日延ばしになっていた。

　そうしたときに、『図録　原爆の絵　ヒロシマを伝える』の出版企画に参加する機会を与えられた。私は、正直に告白するが、かなり動揺した。企画の趣旨から、かなりの数に及ぶ原爆の絵を丹念に見た上で、その監修言を書くということが私に課される役割であることを伝えられたからである。しかし、一瞬ためらった後、この機会を逃したら、私はこれからも原爆の絵から逃げ続けることになってしまうだろう、むしろこの機会を思い切ってとらえ、原爆の絵と正面から向き合ってみるべきだ、と決断した。

　しかし、図録に収められる予定の絵を納めたCD-ROMが手渡された後、思い切ってパソコンの画面に映し出すまでにはやはり葛藤が続き、かなりの時日を必要とした。絵の数々を凝視する精神的強じんさがあるかどうか、私は相変わらず確信がなかったからである。しかし、ある日、ついに意を決して立ち向かうことにした。1枚1枚の絵の強烈さは、私の覚悟をはるかに上回って私の気持ちを締め付け、押さえ付けた。あえぐような感じでようやくすべての絵を見終えた後、私はしばらくただ茫然となって、思考停止になっていた。ショック状態というのは、こういうことを言うの

Confronting A-bomb Drawings

Motofumi Asai

　Frankly, it was not so long ago that I first encountered A-bomb drawings by survivors. I believe I was watching a TV program on the subject. I was powerfully struck in a way I cannot put into words—stunned. After that, I vacillated between stern admonishments to myself: *You're going to have to face up to A-bomb drawings one of these days*, and sheer cowardice: *I'm not sure I have the psychic strength*. Even after I moved to Hiroshima in April 2005, I kept postponing my weighty homework.

　Then, I had the opportunity to join the project to publish *A-bomb Drawings by Survivors*. I confess that I became pretty flustered when I learned that my assignment was to carefully study, according to the goals of the project, a great many A-bomb drawings and then write a supervisor's essay. After a moment's trepidation, I realized that if I ran away from this opportunity, I would probably indefinitely flee from A-bomb drawings. I decided to instead embrace the challenge—to dare to look at A-bomb drawings straight on.

　However, after I was given a CD-ROM that contained the drawings for inclusion in *A-bomb Drawings by Survivors*, I struggled for quite a while before I could get myself to pull the drawings up on my screen. I still lacked the confidence that I had the emotional fortitude to gaze on all those drawings.

　One day I summoned the will. The intense experience of looking at each drawing in succession overwhelmed all my psychic preparation—it strangled, constricted my emotions. Though I was practically panting by the end, I got through them all and sat there in a daze, my mind blank. I must have been in something like shock.

　Looking back at that state now that I have calmed down, I was paralyzed by the overwhelming weight of the reality shown to me. "This is atomic bombing." "This is what happens if you are A-bombed." Each drawing inevitably provokes such reactions. Because they represent

だろうと思う。

　いまようやく冷静さを取り戻した中で考えれば、「これが原爆だ」「被爆する、とはこういうことだ」という圧倒的な事実の重みに、私はうちひしがれていたのだ。1枚1枚の絵は、見るものをしてそんな気持ちに追い込まずにはおかない。それはまさに、原爆地獄に突き落とされた人々の網膜に焼き付いた紛れもない真実であったがゆえに、無機質な写真をはるかに超える迫真力で、見るものの五官を麻痺させるのだと思う。

　第1章の「きのこ雲の下で」は、原爆投下で地獄と化した広島と人々の姿を時間の経過を追って示す形をとっている。あのきのこ雲の下で襲いかかった惨状がどんなものであったのかを、私たちは身の毛もよだつ思いをしながら確認することになる。第2章と第3章は、それぞれ「きずな」及び「いのち」という共通項で結ばれる絵がまとめられている。きずなといのちこそは、人間存在の中心的要素である。そのきずなといのちが原爆によってどんなにむごい目にあったのか、1枚1枚の絵は無言の圧力で私たちに語りかける。

　いま私は、この図録を一人でも多くの人に是非とも見てほしいと願う。この図録を見たら、核戦争が二度とあってはならないことを誰もが素直にうなずくに違いないからだ。そして、被爆した日本の人々の共通の訴えである「ノーモア・ヒロシマ　ノーモア・ナガサキ　ノーモア・ウォー」の持つ意味が、実感として我がものになるとも思うからだ。「ノーモア・ヒロシマ　ノーモア・ナガサキ　ノーモア・ウォー」の訴えが我がものになれば、「戦争する国」に向かってまっしぐらに進んでいる今の日本の国としてのあり方に強い疑問がわき上がってくるだろう。核攻撃に備える？　核攻撃まで予想しなくてはならない戦争に備える？　何のため？　誰のため？　次から次へと疑問が積み重ねられるはずだ。図録の描き出した地獄が再び現実になることを正当化するような戦争なんてあるはずがない。

　つまり、図録は私たちに正気を取り戻させてくれる。人類は、広島、長崎の体験を二度と繰り返してはならない、という原点に私たちを引き戻してくれるのだ。そのことを通して、「ノーモア・

the unvarnished truth burned onto the retinas of those thrown into the hell of atomic bombing, we feel their reality far more potently than we do that of mechanical photos. They paralyze our senses.

Chapter One, *Under the Mushroom Cloud*, shows people at different stages of time in the hell that Hiroshima became after the dropping of the bomb. We learn with hair standing on end what horrors occurred under that mushroom cloud. Drawings in Chapter Two develop the theme of *Bonds* and those in Chapter Three that of *Life*. Bonds and life are the core elements of human existence.

With a wordless pressure, each drawing presses down on our minds the cruel fates awaiting bonds and life in the atomic bombing.

I want as many people as possible to see this book. Anyone who does will immediately agree that we can never have nuclear war again. Then, when the A-bombed Japanese cry, "No more Hiroshima! No more Nagasaki! No more war!" everyone will understand and internalize the plea.

Anyone who makes his or her own the cry "No more Hiroshima! No more Nagasaki! No more war!" will deeply question the Japanese government's headlong rush to become a "war-making country." Prepare for nuclear attack? Prepare for war, which cannot be considered apart from nuclear attack? For what? For whom? The questions pile onto one another. No war can justify the reemergence of the hell depicted in *A-bomb Drawings by Survivors*.

In the end, this book returns us to sanity. It pulls us back to our starting point—determination to prevent humanity from repeating the experience of Hiroshima and Nagasaki. What needs to happen is for the passion behind the cries "No more Hiroshima! No more Nagasaki! No more war!" to again spread around the nation and impel the Japanese government to return to a stance befitting the description "peaceful country."

This leads me to another point. It is often said that the A-bomb experience is fading away. The harsh reality that the Japanese are no longer united behind the cry "No more Hiroshima! No more Nagasaki! No more war!" has

ヒロシマ　ノーモア・ナガサキ　ノーモア・ウォー」が再び全国民的な認識・訴えとなって、日本を再び平和国家の名にふさわしい存在によみがえらせてくれるだろう。

　この図録にかかわって、さらに述べておきたいことがある。
　被爆体験の風化ということが言われるようになっている。「ノーモア・ヒロシマ　ノーモア・ナガサキ　ノーモア・ウォー」が全国民的な認識・訴えとは言えなくなっている厳しい現実があるのも、被爆体験の風化ということと無関係ではないと思う。
　また、被爆体験の継承の難しさが危機感を持って指摘されるようになった。被爆者の平均年齢が73歳を超え、被爆体験の継承が今後ますます困難になっていくことは避けられない。被爆体験が風化し、継承されないということは、被爆した歴史が失われるということである。そのことは、私たちの主体的な立場で言えば、被爆体験の歴史を学ぶことを放棄するということだ。
　「過去(歴史)を振り返らないものは、その過去(歴史)を繰り返す」とは、古今東西を問わない真理である。「ノーモア・ヒロシマ　ノーモア・ナガサキ　ノーモア・ウォー」がかつてのような説得力を持ち得なくなっている現実は、まさにこの真理を物語っている。
　被爆体験を風化させないために、また、被爆体験の継承の難しさに対処するために、さまざまな試みが行われている。私たちは、ありとあらゆる創意工夫を持って取り組むことが求められている。
　この図録は、被爆体験を風化させず、その継承を考える上で、きわめて重要な役割を担っていると考える。図録を真剣な気持ちで見るものであれば(図録を手に取るだけで、誰もが粛然とした気持ちにならざるを得ないはずだ)、被爆を全神経を集中して追体験せざるを得ない。被爆体験を風化させるなんてとんでもないことだと実感するに違いない。そしてその時、その人は確実に被爆体験を継承していることになる。

　　　最後に、『図録　原爆の絵　ヒロシマを伝える』

something to do with the fading of the A-bomb experience.

We are warned that inheriting the A-bomb experience is a difficult task. With the average age of *hibakusha* now 73 and climbing, inheriting their stories can only become more difficult. The difficulty of inheriting the experience aggravated by the inevitable fading over time means that this history will be lost. To say it from our subjective perspective, we are throwing away the history of the atomic bombing.

"To forget the past (history) is to repeat it." This truth transcends time and place. The loss of the persuasive power of the cry "No more Hiroshima! No more Nagasaki! No more war!" reinforces this truth.

Various efforts are underway to prevent the fading of the A-bomb experience and overcome the difficulties of inheriting it. We must bring all our ingenuity and creativity to this task.

A-bomb Drawings by Survivors will play an extremely important role in slowing the fading and facilitating the inheriting process. Simply taking the book into one's hands elicits awe. All who gaze at the pictures straight on find their senses concentrated on reliving the bombing. This reliving builds the conviction that the experience cannot be allowed to fade away. When this passion takes hold, one has inherited the A-bomb experience.

Finally, I wish to speak of the issue of abolishing nuclear weapons, the often forgotten central theme of this book.

Only a handful of people in the A-bombed country of Japan could possibly reject the assertion that "Nuclear weapons are an absolute evil." However, in response to the question, "Do you think nuclear weapons will go away?" most Japanese, even in Hiroshima, think not. This assumption reveals that considerable ambiguity controls the nuclear issue in Japanese society.

The majority of Japanese who believe that nuclear weapons must be eliminated cannot fail to see the contradiction between that desire and Japan's dependence on U.S. nuclear deterrence.

The majority of Japanese who adhere to the "Three Non-Nuclear Principles" (used to describe the policy of not possessing, not producing, and not permitting the

の隠された中心テーマである核兵器廃絶の課題について述べておきたい。

「核兵器は絶対悪だ」という認識に対して、首を横に振るものは、被爆国・日本においては圧倒的少数だろう。しかし、「核兵器はなくなると思うか」という質問に対しては、広島においてもかなりの人が「そうは思わない」と答える現実がある。このことは、日本社会に核問題に関してかなりの曖昧さが支配している状況を反映している。

核兵器は廃絶されるべきだという多くの日本人が、アメリカの核抑止力に依存する政策をとることに大きな矛盾を感じていない。「持たず、作らず、持ち込ませず」の非核三原則は堅持するべきだというこれまた多くの日本人が、実は「持ち込ませない」という原則は守られていないとうすうす感じながら、しかしその曖昧さに安住している。核廃絶の課題は現実的政策課題であるはずなのに、その実現を無限のかなたの目標とすりかえる「究極的核廃絶」という言葉が持ち込まれてきても、多くの日本人はほとんどまったくと言っていいほど目くじらを立てない、等々。

私は、核兵器廃絶という課題を実現するために私たちが本気で取り組む気持ちを養う上でも、この図録はかけがえのない教材であることを保証する。図録を見た誰もが、核兵器廃絶という課題について曖昧さは許されない、という認識を我がものにするに違いない、と確信する。

entry of nuclear weapons into Japan) have also long suspected that the principle "not permitting the entry of nuclear weapons into Japan" is being violated but nevertheless settle for this ambiguity. Though abolishing nuclear weapons should be Japan's actual policy, even this goal has been replaced with that of "*ultimate* abolition of nuclear weapons." Though it has become a goal meant to be always out of reach, most Japanese have no complaints.

I guarantee that *A-bomb Drawings by Survivors* is an essential tool for cultivating the will to seriously work for nuclear abolition. I am convinced that this book will rid anyone who encounters it of ambivalence about the need to free ourselves of nuclear weapons.

第 1 章
Chapter 1

きのこ雲の下で
Under the Mushroom Cloud

1945(昭和20)年8月6日午前8時15分、原爆投下。
爆発後に出現した巨大なきのこ雲は高度約1万メートルにまで達した。
垂れた皮膚をかばい逃げる負傷者、
多くの半死半生の重傷者、折り重なる遺体……。
きのこ雲の下は、血の海と化した地獄絵図だった。

August 6, 1945, 8:15 a.m., A-bomb drop.
Giant mushroom cloud rises roughly 10,000 meters.
Protecting burnt, peeling skin, victims flee.
Many serious injured, all but dead. Piles of corpses . . .
Under the mushroom cloud, inferno turns to sea of blood.

1945(昭和20)年8月6日 原爆投下約1時間後のきのこ雲：米軍撮影
Mushroom cloud taken one hour after the atomic bombing on August 6, 1945　Credit: US Army

原子爆弾の投下
The Dropping of the Atomic Bomb

何かを落とした

「アッ……B29が……何か白いものを落とした」という声に窓から上空を見ると、機影とそれらしきものが目に映った。次の瞬間、濡れた革のむちで思いきり叩かれたような痛みを覚えた。

8月6日 午前8時過ぎ
2,300m／倉敷航空機株式会社広島製作所（10 吉島・舟入・観音）
渡邉 昭惠（17 ▶ 74）

It dropped something.

"Oh! The B29 dropped something white," said someone, and I looked up through the window to see a plane and something falling from it. Just then — a terrible pain, as if I had been struck by a wet leather whip.

August 6, just after 8:00 a.m.
2,300m / Kurashiki Aircraft Corporation, Hiroshima Plant（10 Yoshijima・Funairi・Kan-on）
Akie Watanabe（17 ▶ 74）

2-B

B29
アメリカが第2次世界大戦中に開発し、使用した長距離大型爆撃機。
The long-range, heavy bomber that the U.S. developed and used during World War II.

第1章　きのこ雲の下で

異様な閃光

思わず頭を下げた瞬間、突然全身が異様な閃光につつまれる。

8月6日
1,100m／富士見町の自宅（5 国泰寺・千田）
石谷 龍司（17 ▶ 74）

A strange flash of light

The instant I instinctively lowered my head, a strange flash of light engulfed my whole body.

August 6
1,100m / at home in Fujimi-cho（5 Kokutaiji・Senda）
Ryuji Ishigai（17 ▶ 74）

1-B

オレンジ色の太陽

「キャー」「ウワー」の絶句に舎外に目を向ければ、オレンジ色の太陽が「ボー」という音と共に自分に迫り来た。

8月6日 午前8時13分
500m／広島第一陸軍病院
（4 基町・白島）
内田 栄一（20 ▶ 50）

An orange sun

Amid wordless screams and cries, I looked outside the hospital. An orange sun surged toward me with a great roar.

August 6, 8:13 a.m.
500m / Hiroshima First Army Hospital
（4 Moto-machi・Hakushima）
Eiichi Uchida（20 ▶ 50）

2-A

巨大な溶鉱炉

閃光、熱線。瞬間、建物疎開作業中の私たち70名の生徒は巨大な溶鉱炉にすっぽりと投げ込まれた。

8月6日
1,650m／鶴見橋西詰
(8 比治山・仁保)
森下 弘(14 ▶ 71)

A giant blast furnace

The flash, the heat ray. For an instant, it was like we 70 students were thrown into a giant, red-hot blast furnace.

August 6
1,650m / west end of Tsurumi Bridge (8 Hijiyama・Niho)
Hiromu Morishita (14 ▶ 71)

2-B

校舎が浮き上がった

投下約10秒後、強烈な爆風によりあたり一面暗くなり、校舎が浮き上がった。

8月6日 午前8時15分
2,200m／県立広島商業学校
(9 皆実・宇品)
平野 貞男(12 ▶ 69)

The school building rose into the air.

About ten seconds after the drop, a huge blast turned everything dark and lifted the school building into the air.

August 6, 8:15 a.m.
2,200m / Hiroshima Prefectural Commercial School
(9 Minami・Ujina)
Sadao Hirano (12 ▶ 69)

1-B

第1章　きのこ雲の下で

煙の柱がぐんぐん昇り

巨大な煙の柱が上空にぐんぐん昇り、入道雲がもくもくと重なりあいつつ大きくなり、その間からオレンジ・赤・青などの稲光りに似た光が四方に散り、異様な形を成して巨大化し、キノコ形のものになっていきました。

8月6日 午前8時17分から18分頃
10km ／似島検疫所
後藤 利文（19 ▶ 76）

The pillar of smoke rose rapidly.

A giant pillar of smoke rose rapidly into the sky, creating a thundercloud that piled on itself as it spread. Within its billows, orange, red, blue sparks shot in all directions like streak lightening. As this bizarre configuration expanded, it shaped itself into a mushroom.

August 6, around 8:17-8:18 a.m.
10km / Ninoshima Quarantine Station
Toshifumi Goto（19 ▶ 76）

2-B

練兵場　Drill grounds
軍隊が戦闘のための訓練などを行う場所。広島には基町の西練兵場と二葉の里の東練兵場があり、広大な土地に多くの被爆者が避難した。爆心地近くに位置した西練兵場は軍関係の施設が集中しており、甚大な被害を受けた。
Fields where the army engaged in battle training. Hiroshima had the Western Drill Ground in Moto-machi and the Eastern Drill Ground in Futabanosato. Many *hibakusha* fled to these large open areas. Because of their proximity to the hypocenter, army facilities concentrated around the Western Drill Ground were completely devastated.

雲の縁が舞い降りて来る

モクモクと拡大を続ける雲の縁が舞い降りて来るように思えたので、逃げました。雲はふくらみ続け、ピンク、銀色、青色に変化していました。

8月6日
2,300m／東練兵場
（7 牛田・広島駅周辺）
指田 勢郎（13 ▶ 70）

The edges of the cloud billowed lower and lower.

As the cloud expanded, its edges billowed lower and lower, so I ran away. As it ballooned, it changed colors — pink, silver, and blue.

August 6
2,300m / Eastern Drill Ground
（7 Ushita・Hiroshima Station）
Seiro Sashida（13 ▶ 70）

2-B

直 後
Immediately after the Bombing

四方は火の海

私は母、妹、弟と舟入から横川行きの市電に乗った。十日市電停発車まもなく真っ暗闇になり、何がなんだかわからない。車内は大混乱。「出して」「戸を開けろ」押し合いもみ合ううちにうす明るくなり、われがちに外に出た。四方火の海、赤熱の地獄である。

8月6日 投下直後
750m／十日市交差点北側（6 十日市・中広）
松本 政夫（11 ▶ 41）

Sea of fire in all directions

My mother, younger sister, younger brother, and I were on a streetcar from Funairi bound for Yokogawa. Just as the streetcar was leaving the Tokaichi stop, everything turned completely black. I had no idea what was happening. Inside the streetcar was chaos and panic, pushing and shoving, cries of "Let me out!" and "Open the door!" When it got lighter, we forced our way out. Everywhere we turned was a sea of fire, a red-hot hell.

August 6, just after the explosion
750m / north side of the Tokaichi Intersection（6 Tokaichi・Nakahiro）
Masao Matsumoto（11 ▶ 41）

2-A

路面電車　Streetcars
広島では1912（大正元）年に路面電車が走り始め、被爆当時の架線は約100キロメートルに及んでいた。123両のうち108両が被害を受けた。
Streetcars began running in Hiroshima in 1912 and covered roughly 100 kilometers of track at the time of the atomic bombing. Of 123 streetcars, 108 were damaged or destroyed by the atomic bombing.

第1章　きのこ雲の下で

重傷者を踏んで逃げ出す

原爆炸裂直後、重傷者を踏んで逃げ出す。

8月6日 投下直後
1,300m ／白島線縮景園前
（3 銀山・幟）
山本 節子（14 ▶ 43）

I stepped on the injured to get out.

Just after the atomic explosion, I stepped on the injured to get out.

August 6, just after the explosion
1,300m / at the Shukkeien-mae streetcar stop on the Hakushima Line
（3 Kanayama・Nobori）
Setsuko Yamamoto（14 ▶ 43）

1-A

国民学校　Elementary schools
1941（昭和16）年、戦時体制のもと、小学校は国民学校へ名を変えた。6年の初等科と2年の高等科からなる。国民学校は、国のために、心身を鍛える場とされ、子どもたちは、年少の国民「少国民」とされた。
In 1941, the war regime changed "elementary schools" to "national schools." National schools comprised a six-year elementary lower school and a two-year upper school. The war regime considered them places for training the minds and bodies of "little citizens" to serve the country. (For ease of understanding, "national schools" are referred to as "elementary schools" in this book.)

血だるまになり泣きながら走る女生徒

校庭に走り出た生徒のやけどや流血に、ほどこすすべはなく、ただ少量の給食用の油をバケツに出して、ぞうきんで顔面につけることしかできなかった。

8月6日 投下直後
2,500m ／市立第二国民学校
（10 吉島・舟入・観音）
前田 栄（40 ▶ 69）

Girl students covered with blood, and sobbing as they ran

There was no way to care for the burns and bleeding wounds of the students who ran into the schoolyard. All we could do was put a little cooking oil in a bucket, then dab it on their faces with rags.

August 6, just after the explosion
2,500m / Second Municipal Elementary School
（10 Yoshijima・Funairi・Kan-on）
Sakae Maeda（40 ▶ 69）

2-A

断末魔

夏の朝8時半ごろというのにあたりは暗く、半月の夜の状態。しばらくして軒並みに火を吹き出した。そして火の手は次第に広がり、自分の周辺はことごとく火の海と化した。

8月6日 午前8時30分頃
130m／元安橋
（1 平和記念公園・周辺）
野村 英三（47 ▶ 77）

Death agonies

At 8:30 on a summer morning, it was dark as a half-moon night. In a while, flames began to burst out of buildings. They spread steadily until the area around me was a sea of fire.

August 6, around 8:30 a.m.
130m / Motoyasu Bridge
(1 Peace Memorial Park)
Eizo Nomura (47 ▶ 77)

2-A

爆心地の光景　The scene at the hypocenter
野村英三さんは爆心地から170メートルの燃料会館（現在の平和記念公園レストハウス）で被爆、奇跡的に生き残った。原爆投下直後の爆心地付近の光景を描いたこの絵は、貴重な証言となっている。
Eizo Nomura was exposed but miraculously survived the bombing at the Fuel Hall (now, the Rest House in Peace Memorial Park) 170 meters from the hypocenter. His depiction of the scene in the hypocenter area immediately after the bombing serves as an important record.

原爆絶叫!!

突如として広島市上空に大きな火のたまがゆらゆら揺れ動き、約6〜7秒後、ビシーッという音がして「ウワー！」という広島全市民の絶叫と悲鳴をひとまとめにした声が響いてきた。全市民の悲鳴が！ 断末魔の声が!! 阿鼻地獄の声が!! 原爆絶叫!!

8月6日
9,600m／五日市駅
岡本 兵馬（37 ▶ 66）

Atomic bomb scream!!

A huge fireball was suddenly shimmering in the skies over Hiroshima. Six or seven seconds later, with a whoosh came "Wa-a-ah!" a collective scream from all the people of Hiroshima. The shrieks of the people! The groans of death agonies!! Voices from hell!! The atomic bomb scream!!

August 6
9,600m / Itsukaichi Station
Hyoma Okamoto (37 ▶ 66)

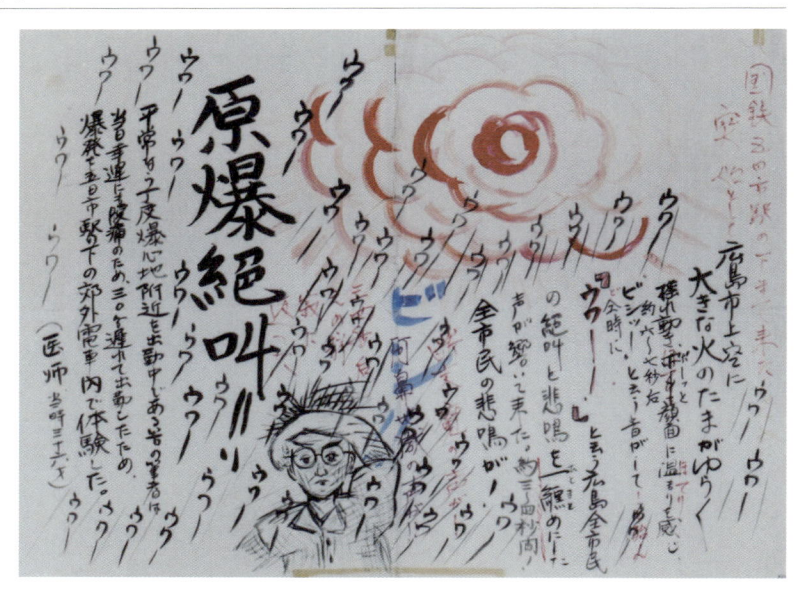

2-A

第1章　きのこ雲の下で

迫り来る炎
Encroaching Flames

燃えさかる猛火に追われて

よけようにも立すいの余地もない人の波。通過跡には何人かの轢死体が。だが、確認できない程人波は続いていた。

8月6日 午前8時40分頃
2,500m／皆実町(9 皆実・宇品)
長峰 忠義(27 ▶ 84)

Chased by the raging, devouring flames

The stream of people was so dense, they could not push through and break free. Corpses lay along the escape route, but I don't know how many because the crowds kept coming.

August 6, around 8:40 a.m.
2,500m ／ Minami-machi（9 Minami・Ujina）
Tadayoshi Nagamine（27 ▶ 84）

1-B

人々を焼き、地獄と化す

火炎はものすごい勢いで人々を焼き、地獄と化す。

8月6日 午前11時
1,300m／天満町付近
(6 十日市・中広)
西田 輝美(33 ▶ 63)

People consumed by fire, the world become hell

The ferocious fires consumed people and turned the world to hell.

August 6, 11:00 a.m.
1,300m ／ near Tenma-cho
（6 Tokaichi・Nakahiro）
Terumi Nishida（33 ▶ 63）

1-A

いたいよ たすけてエー

8月6日
1,650m／鶴見橋
（8 比治山・仁保）
吉山 正子（13 ▶ 43）

"It hurts! Help!"
August 6
1,650m / Tsurumi Bridge
（8 Hijiyama・Niho）
Masako Yoshiyama（13 ▶ 43）

A

橋上の惨事

舟入幸町西側より見た住吉橋上の惨事。

8月6日
1,390m／住吉橋
（10 吉島・舟入・観音）
道田 芳江（30 ▶ 59）

Calamity on the bridge
I saw this calamitous scene on the Sumiyoshi Bridge from the west side of Funairi-saiwai-cho.

August 6
1,390m / Sumiyoshi Bridge
（10 Yoshijima・Funairi・Kan-on）
Yoshie Michida（30 ▶ 59）

1-A

第1章　きのこ雲の下で

どんどん燃えている

自分の頭上目掛けて一発やられたと思っていたが、全市が倒れている。そしてどんどん燃えている。あちらからもこちらからも、助けを求める悲痛なさけび声。

8月6日
1,380m／京橋付近（3 銀山・幟）
石津 一博（37 ▶ 66）

It burned fast!

I thought a bomb had exploded right over my head, but the whole city had tumbled over. And it burned so fast! Voices near and far screamed for help in desperate pain.

August 6
1,380m / near Kyobashi Bridge（3 Kanayama・Nobori）
Kazuhiro Ishizu（37 ▶ 66）

1-A

橋の被害　Damage to bridges
被爆当時、広島市内には、50を超える橋が架かっていた。7つの橋が被爆により焼失あるいは落橋したが、かろうじて渡ることができた橋は重要な避難経路となった。
At the time of the bombing, more than 50 bridges spanned rivers in Hiroshima. Seven burned up or collapsed, but those that victims could make their way across were critical escape routes.

川
Rivers

猛火を逃れて川へ

猛火を逃れてやっと川岸までたどり着いた人たちは、へたへたと崩折れてしまった。目前でもがき苦しみ息絶える人、生き残りはまた対岸に向かって、大きくうねり出した川の中へと入ってゆく。川上の方からはおぼれながら流される人々数知れず、それでも次々に迫り来る火から逃れようと入水する。

8月6日 午前9時頃
1,300m ／縮景園北側の川岸（3 銀山・幟）
菅 葉子（14 ▶ 43）

Escaping the flames into the river

Some managed to skirt the flames to get to the river, only to collapse on the bank. Some writhed in agony and died before my eyes. Those still alive waded into waves, aiming for the other side. Countless victims were swept drowning down the river, while encroaching fires continued to force people into the water.

August 6, around 9:00 a.m.
1,300m / riverbank on the north side of Shukkeien Garden（3 Kanayama・Nobori）
Yoko Suga（14 ▶ 43）

1-A

縮景園　Shukkeien Garden
別名「泉邸」。1620年、広島藩主浅野長晟が別邸の庭園として築いた。原爆によって園内の建物や樹木の大半は失われた。避難先に指定されていたため、被爆直後から多くの被災者が避難してきたが、ここで息絶え、埋葬された者も数多かった。
Another name for Shukkeien Garden was "Sentei Garden." In 1620 Asano Nagaakira, the feudal lord of Hiroshima, built it as a garden for his villa. The structures and most of the trees in the garden were destroyed by the atomic bombing. Because it was a designated place of refuge, the garden was overrun by the injured immediately after the bombing. Many died and were buried there.

第1章　きのこ雲の下で

流れる死体

8月6日　午前10時頃
1,300m ／縮景園北（3 銀山・幟）
佐々木 千鶴子（20 ▶ 50）

Corpses carried by the current

August 6, around 10:00 a.m.
1,300m ／ north side of Shukkeien Garden (3 Kanayama・Nobori)
Chizuko Sasaki（20 ▶ 50）

A

竜巻

竜巻が起こり、同僚と手をとりあったまま巻き込まれて、水をしたたかのみ気絶しました。数刻の後、気が付いたら河原に投げ出されていました。

8月6日
1,300m ／縮景園（3 銀山・幟）
深田 弘子（18 ▶ 48）

Waterspout

A waterspout suddenly gushed up. My co-worker and I were swept into it, still clutching each other. I swallowed a huge amount of water and lost consciousness. When I came to minutes later, I had been dashed down on the riverbank.

August 6
1,300m ／ Shukkeien Garden (3 Kanayama・Nobori)
Hiroko Fukada (18 ▶ 48)

1-A

傷つき、逃げる
Injured and Fleeing

髪が逆立ちに

昔からビックリすると髪が逆立ちになるということを聞いていましたが、本当に見たのは初めてです。髪はまっすぐに上に立ち、うでの上皮がはがれて下にぶらさがっていました。

8月6日 午前9時頃
3,000m ／翠町（9 皆実・宇品）
繁森 アサ（49 ▶ 78）

Hair standing on end

I had heard long ago that astonishment makes people's hair stand on end, but this was the first time I had seen such a thing. The hair on these people was standing straight up, and the skin on their arms had peeled and was hanging down.

August 6, around 9:00 a.m.
3,000m / Midori-machi
(9 Minami・Ujina)
Asa Shigemori (49 ▶ 78)

1-A

この世のものとも思われません

30年前この目で見、この手でふれた当時のさまは余りにもおそろしくて書くことはおろか語ることもさけてきて、今書きながらわいてくる血のにおい、真っ赤にただれた肌、男女の見わけもつかない惨い姿。むけかけの皮がぶらさがり恐怖にゆがんだ表情はこの世のものとも思われません。

8月6日 午前9時
800m ／八丁堀〜縮景園の途中（4 基町・白島）
原田 知恵（18 ▶ 48）

A scene not of this world

It is so horrible to write or speak of what these eyes saw, what these hands and body touched, I have avoided it for 30 years. As I draw now, I smell the blood. I see the wretched figures with burnt skin so red and flayed I cannot tell if they are male or female. Those faces, skin melted off and contorted by terror, were not of this world.

August 6, 9:00 a.m.
800m / on the way from Hatchobori to Shukkeien Garden
(4 Moto-machi・Hakushima)
Chie Harada (18 ▶ 48)

2-A

第1章　きのこ雲の下で

衣服は引き裂け、皮膚はたれさがる

土手の上を、ユーレイのように髪はばさばさ、衣服は引き裂け、皮膚はたれさがり、今の世の人とは思えぬ姿で、負傷者の群れが声もたてず黙々と郊外へ逃げて行く。

8月6日 午前10時頃
4,250m／広島鉄道局広島工機部付近の川土手（7 牛田・広島駅周辺）
吉村 吉助（18 ▶ 75）

Their clothes ripped to shreds, their skin hanging down

On the riverbank I saw figures that seemed to be from another world. Ghost-like, their hair falling over their faces, their clothes ripped to shreds, their skin hanging. A cluster of these injured persons was moving wordlessly toward the outskirts.

August 6, around 10:00 a.m.
4,250m / riverbank near the Hiroshima Machinery Division, Hiroshima Railway Bureau (7 Ushita・Hiroshima Station)
Kichisuke Yoshimura (18 ▶ 75)

2-B

川の中には死体がいっぱい浮かんでいた

川の中には死体がいっぱい浮かんでいた。赤いふんどしは血で染まったもの。よろよろと２本づえであるく兵隊さん。負傷者をはこぶ女学生。

8月6日 午前10時頃
2,320m／工兵橋付近
（4 基町・白島）
石橋 新子（6 ▶ 36）
中桐 春美（29 ▶ 59）

Many corpses floated in the river.

Many corpses floated in the river. A soldier wearing only a loincloth red with blood was tottering on crutches. Girl students carried a wounded person on a stretcher.

August 6, around 10:00 a.m.
2,320m／near Kohei Bridge（4 Moto-machi・Hakushima）
Shinko Ishibashi（6 ▶ 36） Harumi Nakagiri（29 ▶ 59）

1-A

腸がぶら下がったまま

40歳ぐらいの男の人。腸がぶら下がったまま必死で海岸方面に歩いていた。全身やけどで、皮膚が桃の皮のようにムケて下がっている。一点をジッと見つめて、真っ青な顔で目ばかり血走っていた。

8月6日
3,200m／宇品十三丁目電停前（9 皆実・宇品）
初谷 忠曷（34 ▶ 64）

His intestines dangling

The man was around 40 years old. He was desperately walking toward the sea with his intestines dangling from his belly. Burned over his whole body, his skin was peeling like peach skin. His face was completely blue except for bloodshot eyes staring at a fixed point.

August 6
3,200m／in front of the Ujina 13-chome streetcar stop
（9 Minami・Ujina）
Tadakatsu Hatsuya（34 ▶ 64）

2-A

第1章　きのこ雲の下で

黒い雨
Black Rain

黒い雨が降る

家に帰ろうとするが黒い雨にあい、足もとがぬかるんでとても歩きにくい。あちらこちらからわが子を呼ぶ「助けて下さい」という声を聞きながら、母と4歳の弟のいるわが家に命からがらたどり着きました。

8月6日 午前8時40分頃
1,400m ／東観音町二丁目（10 吉島・舟入・観音）
小間 義衛（14 ▶ 71）

Black rain fell.

As I headed for home, black rain fell and wet the ground, making it hard to walk. I heard people everywhere crying out to their children and begging for help. I barely made it home to my mother and four-year-old brother.

August 6, around 8:40 a.m.
1,400m ／ Higashi-kan-on-machi 2-chome（10 Yoshijima・Funairi・Kan-on）
Yoshie Koma（14 ▶ 71）

2-B

黒い雨　Black rain
原子爆弾の爆発後広島市の北西部地域を中心に降った雨。黒く粘質で、放射能を帯びたチリやススなどが多量に含まれていた。
After the bombing, black, sticky rain fell primarily in the northwest sections of Hiroshima City. This rain contained large amounts of radioactive dust and soot.

ぬるぬるとしたものが体中に

黒い雨が原爆投下後降った。雨に油がまじったようなぬるぬるとしたものが、体中についた。空は黒雲におおわれ、逃げまどう人に無気味な不安をもたらした。

8月6日 午前11時頃
4,250m ／庚午町（11 己斐・草津）
吉本 智（13 ▶ 41）

Something slimy covered my body

After the atomic bombing, black rain fell. My whole body was covered by something slimy, like rain mixed with oil. The black clouds covering the sky filled the confused people fleeing the city with an uncanny fear.

August 6, around 11:00 a.m.
4,250m / Kogo-cho (11 Koi・Kusatsu)
Satoshi Yoshimoto (13 ▶ 41)

1-A

水がほしかったのです

くろい くろい雨／大きなつぶの雨／ケガをしながら／ヤケドをしながら／生きていた人達／空にむかつて／その雨をのもうと／口を大きくあけました／あつくて あつくて／からだ中が／火のかたまりのように／なつていたから／水が ほしかつたのです（『被爆体験――私の訴えたいこと（上）』NHK 中国本部、1977 年、244 ページから）

8月6日
260m／住友銀行広島支店前（2 紙屋町・本通）
高蔵 信子（19 ▶ 49）

They wanted water.

Black, black rain. Huge drops. People with injuries and burns. The ones still living craned their faces to the sky and opened their mouths wide to catch the drops. Hot bodies, so very hot, like balls of fire — they wanted water. (Taken from *A-bomb Experiences — What I Want to Say*, Vol. 1; NHK Chugoku Office, 1977, page 244)

August 6
260m / in front of Sumitomo Bank, Hiroshima Branch
(2 Kamiya-cho・Hondori)
Akiko Takakura (19 ▶ 49)

3-A

第1章 きのこ雲の下で

やけどと外傷の体で雨に遭う

三篠橋より太田川の中を歩いてにげているところです。当時私たちは17歳で、看護婦生徒隊におりました。友人とお互いに助け合いながら、やけどと外傷の体で雨に遭いました。

8月6日 午前10時から正午
1,470m／三篠橋（4 基町・白島）
高柴 暖枝

Encountering black rain with burnt, wounded bodies

It was when we were walking along the Otagawa River from the Misasa Bridge. We were 17-year-old members of the Nursing Students Unit. Burnt and wounded, my friends and I were helping each other along when we encountered the black rain.

August 6, 10:00 a.m.-12:00 p.m.
1,470m / Misasa Bridge (4 Moto-machi・Hakushima)
Harue Takashiba

2-A

生徒たち
Students

同級生が叫んでいる

みんな顔や腕、手足、背中などにやけどをしている。大手や家屋の下敷になり、助けを求めて同級生が叫んでいる。川の水は大潮の満潮時で、川岸には人が石垣にしがみついて助けを求めて叫んでいる。

8月6日 午前8時15分から30分
2,150m ／西大橋(10 吉島・舟入・観音)
木村 秀男(12 ▶ 69)

My classmates were screaming.

Burned on their faces, arms, feet, legs, and backs. Trapped under heavy gates and houses, they screamed for help. Some were crying for help from the river, holding onto the stone embankment against the pull of the rising tide.

August 6, 8:15-8:30 a.m.
2,150m / Nishi-ohashi Bridge (10 Yoshijima・Funairi・Kan-on)
Hideo Kimura (12 ▶ 69)

2-B

第1章　きのこ雲の下で

整列したまま

国民学校の校庭に、朝礼中と見える全校児童が整列したまま、一様にうずくまって黒く焼けて死んでいた。

8月6日 午前9時頃
1,000m／大手町国民学校
（5 国泰寺・千田）
世良 戸城（43 ▶ 73）

Still in formation

In the schoolyard, what appeared to be the entire student body at morning assembly was crouched and charred black — still in formation.

August 6, around 9:00 a.m.
1,000m / Otemachi Elementary School（5 Kokutaiji・Senda）
Tojo Sera（43 ▶ 73）

2-A

先生助けてー

折れ重ってたおれた校舎のすき間から、頭と右手を出して、声を限りに助けを呼ぶ生徒がいた。そのまわりにも、何人かの生徒のうめく声がきこえていた。私は助けようとしたが、モルタルの倒壊は私一人の力ではびくともしなかった。「先生助けてー」その声が今も耳元にきこえ、たまらない気持ちだ。

8月6日
1,800m／段原国民学校（8 比治山・仁保）
松村 智恵子（33 ▶ 62）

"Teacher, help!"

From a gap in the pile of school building rubble, a student reached his head and right arm out and yelled for help at the top of his lungs. Around him I could hear other students moaning. I tried to help, but I couldn't budge the collapsed mortar frames by myself. I can still hear them crying, "Teacher, help!" I can hardly bear it.

August 6
1,800m / Dambara Elementary School（8 Hijiyama・Niho）
Chieko Matsumura（33 ▶ 62）

1-A

素裸で逃げる娘

娘は市役所裏で疎開作業中全身やけどをし、素裸で大勢の人と逃げる途中、南大橋で兵隊さんがカーテンの切れ端を拾って下さったのを腰に巻き、吉島飛行場へたどりつき、動けないまま親切な人に上着を着せてもらい、お母さんお母さんと呼びながら3時ごろに死にました。

8月6日
1,750m ／南大橋付近（5 国泰寺・千田）
村上 美佐子（45 ▶ 75）

My daughter fleeing naked

My daughter was doing demolition work behind City Hall when she was burned over her whole body. Naked, she fled in a crowd. At Minami-ohashi Bridge, a soldier found her a curtain fragment to tie around her middle for a little coverage. She made it to Yoshijima Air Field and collapsed. Some kind person covered her with a jacket. Calling "Mother, mother," she died at around 3:00 p.m.

August 6
1,750m / near Minami-ohashi Bridge（5 Kokutaiji・Senda）
Misako Murakami（45 ▶ 75）

2-A

建物疎開　Building demolition

激化する都市への空襲に備え、火災の延焼を防ぐため、あらかじめ建物を取り壊し、防火地帯を作ること。8月6日のこの作業には、国民義勇隊や動員学徒が大規模に駆り出されたため、原爆により多くの犠牲者を生んだ。

As air-raids over cities intensified, cities demolished buildings to create firebreaks to stop the spread of fires. Because the Volunteer Citizen Corps and mobilized students were out in force for this task on August 6, huge numbers perished in the bombing.

第1章 きのこ雲の下で

川になだれ込む

町の道は飛ばされた瓦や材木などで歩けないので、本川に向かって全員にげた。死んだ者は川に流された。

8月6日
650m／本川付近
（1 平和記念公園・周辺）
高原 良雄（34 ▶ 91）

Surging into the river

Streets filled with roof tiles and pieces of wood were impassable, so everyone headed to the river. Some died and were swept away.

August 6
650m / near Honkawa River（1 Peace Memorial Park）
Yoshio Takahara（34 ▶ 91）

2-B

先生が覆いかぶさっている

千田国民学校にて 子どもの上に先生が覆いかぶさっている。

8月6日
1,690m／千田国民学校
（5 国泰寺・千田）
中島 睦男（20 ▶ 76）

The teacher shielded the students with her body.

It was Senda Elementary School. The teacher shielded the students with her body.

August 6
1,690m / Senda Elementary School
（5 Kokutaiji・Senda）
Mutsuo Nakajima（20 ▶ 76）

2-B

水を求めて
Seeking Water

弱々しく訴える母親

子どもはもう立ち上がる力もない。2人ともやけどの火ぶくれが体中にたれ下がり、毛髪はチリチリとちぢれている。母親は「水、水を下さい」と弱々しく通行人に訴える。

8月6日 午後2時
1,500m ／広島赤十字病院前（5 国泰寺・千田）
田坂 元（15 ▶ 45）

A mother feebly begging

The child was too weak to stand. Water blisters sagged the skin all over the bodies of this mother and child. Their hair was singed. Feebly, the mother pleaded to passers-by: "Water, water, please."

August 6, 2:00 p.m.
1,500m ／ in front of Hiroshima Red Cross Hospital
(5 Kokutaiji・Senda)
Hajime Tasaka (15 ▶ 45)

1-A

水 みず ミズ を下さい

橋の上の端から端まで、ヤケドで男女の区別がつかない人が倒れたり、かがみこんでいました。そして息も絶え絶えに、「水・水・水を下さい」と言っています。これは本当の地獄のようでした。

8月6日 午後4時頃
1,750m ／南大橋
（5 国泰寺・千田）
原田 義久（14 ▶ 71）

"Water. Water. Water, please."

People unidentifiable as male or female filled the bridge from one end to the other, lying down or crouching. With what sounded like their last gasps, they cried, "Water. Water. Water, please." It was hell.

August 6, around 4:00 p.m.
1,750m ／ Minami-ohashi Bridge
(5 Kokutaiji・Senda)
Yoshihisa Harada (14 ▶ 71)

1-B

第1章　きのこ雲の下で

死んでもいいから飲ませてください

「水！ 水！ 水！ 水下さーい」の声は、レンガ倉庫に反響してワンワンと鳴った。中学生も女学生も、並べられた顔は風船のようにふくれ、目はみんな糸を引いたように細く、誰の顔もみな同じに見えた。

8月6日
2,670m／広島陸軍被服支廠(9 皆実・宇品)
佐藤 泰子（17 ▶ 74）

"I don't care if I die, just give me water!"

"Water! Water! Water! Water, please!" Voices reverberated through the brick building. The faces of the junior high boys and girls lined up on the floor all looked the same. They were blown up like balloons, their eyes narrowed to slits.

August 6
2,670m / Hiroshima Army Clothing Depot (9 Minami・Ujina)
Yasuko Sato (17 ▶ 74)

1-B

被爆者と水　Hibakusha and water
原子爆弾の爆発により発生した熱線や、その後の火災によるやけどや嘔吐、発熱などにより、多くの被爆者はのどの渇きを訴えた。しかし、水を飲ませたら死んでしまうといわれ、水を飲むことなく亡くなった人が多くいた。
Most *hibakusha* complained of thirst because of vomiting, fever, burns they incurred from the heat ray and the ensuing fires and other problems. Sadly, the common belief that burn victims would die if they drank water left many to die in terrible thirst.

夜
Night

あの空を忘れない

夕方空がまっ赤に焼けて、祖母に「今日ばくだんで死んだ人がたくさん空へのぼっていくんだよ」と言い聞かされた。赤黒いあの空を今も忘れることはなく、あれ以後、あんな空を見たことはありません。

8月6日 夕方
18.8km／呉市
小林 サチ子（7 ▶ 65）

I'll never forget that sky.

The twilight sky burned red. Grandmother said, "The souls of all the people that died from the bomb are climbing into the sky." I cannot forget that red and black sky. I have never seen such a sky since.

August 6, evening
18.8km / Kure City
Sachiko Kobayashi（7 ▶ 65）

2-B

燃え続ける福屋百貨店

8月6日 午後10時
710m／福屋百貨店
（2 紙屋町・本通）
小橋 染春（23 ▶ 53）

Fukuya Department Store, burning and burning

August 6, 10:00 p.m.
710m / Fukuya Department Store
（2 Kamiya-cho・Hondori）
Someharu Kobashi （23 ▶ 53）

A

第1章　きのこ雲の下で

星明かりの中を歩く親子

星明かりの中に見たものは親子3人である。不安定な歩み、荒い呼吸、また立ち止まる。今朝より何か口にしたのだろうか。行き先は山腹の地下壕しかない所である。無事、たどり着けたであろうか。

8月6日 夜
23.6km／呉市広町
齋藤 陽 (19 ▶ 76)

Family walking in the starlight

In the starlight I saw three members of a family. They were tottering along, taking rasping breaths, stopping frequently. Had they eaten anything since morning? Where they were headed was nothing but a bomb shelter dug into the mountain side. I wonder if they made it.

August 6, night
23.6km / Hiro-machi, Kure City
Yo Saito (19 ▶ 76)

2-B

比治山より眺む8月6日の夜

原子の炎光は逃げまどい、焼けただれ、血まみれる地獄絵の中に、なつかしい人々、かけがえのない人々を殺していった。肉親を案じながら放心状態で眺める。

8月6日 夜
1,980m／比治山(8 比治山・仁保)
藤瀬 朝子 (22 ▶ 51)

The night of August 6, we watched from Hijiyama Hill.

In the pandemonium of confused fleeing, burning, and bleeding, the atomic bomb fires killed sweet people, precious people. From Hijiyama Hill, we watched the fires in a daze, wondering what had happened to our families.

August 6, night
1,980m / Hijiyama Hill
(8 Hijiyama・Niho)
Asako Fujise (22 ▶ 51)

2-A

夜が明けて
Morning Breaks

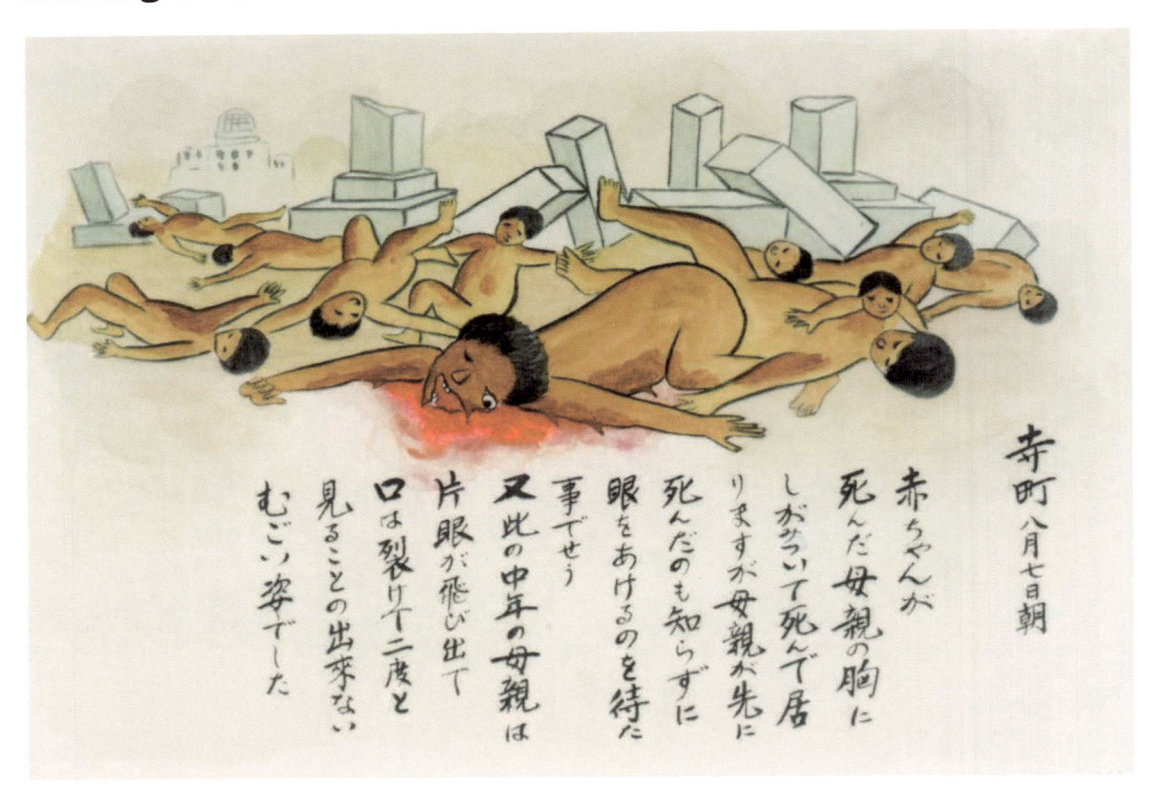

寺町 八月七日朝

赤ちゃんが死んだ母親の胸にしがみついて死んで居りますが母親が先に死んだのも知らずに眼をあけるのを待った事でせう 又此の中年の母親は片眼が飛び出て口は裂けて二度と見ることの出来ないむごい姿でした

片目が飛び出し口が裂けた母親

赤ちゃんが死んだ母親の胸にしがみついて死んでおりますが、母親が先に死んだのも知らずに、目をあけるのを待ったことでしょう。中年の母親は片目が飛び出て口は裂けて、二度と見ることのできないむごい姿でした。

8月7日 朝
1,100m／寺町（6十日市・中広）
中野 健一（47 ▶ 76）

A mother whose eye had popped out and whose mouth was sliced open

A baby had died clinging to its mother's breast. The baby looked as if it did not know its mother was dead and was waiting for her to open her eyes. A middle-aged woman whose eye had popped out and whose mouth was sliced open was too horrible to look at.

August 7, morning
1,100m ／ Tera-machi（6 Tokaichi・Nakahiro）
Kenichi Nakano（47 ▶ 76）

2-A

第1章　きのこ雲の下で

兵隊さんの悲しい姿

8月7日の朝の事です。朝から昨日と同じように暑い暑い日でした。兵隊さんがお化けのような姿で何列にも並んで、水、水、水と言われたあの悲しい姿の絵です。

8月7日 朝
2,100m ／東照宮
(7 牛田・広島駅周辺)
森永 ヨシエ（20 ▶ 77）

Piteous soldiers

It was the morning of the 7th. Like the day before, it was hot early. I drew this to show how piteous they looked, like lines of ghosts saying "Water, water, water."

August 7, morning
2,100m ／ Toshogu Shrine
(7 Ushita・Hiroshima Station)
Yoshie Morinaga（20 ▶ 77）

2-B

新タマネギのような色の内臓

がれきの山で道もなく目印もなく、自分が歩いている所も定かでない。そんな所で異様な物を見つけ、そっと近寄ってギョッとしました。真っ黒焦げの死体なのに、割ばしの先についた目玉、そして新タマネギのような色をした内臓がまるまる胸の上に載っていました。

山中 昭子（17 ▶ 74）

Body organs the color of a new onion

There were no roads or other kinds of landmarks in the piles of rubble. I did not know where I was going. When I saw something strange, I quietly approached for a better look and recoiled in horror. It was a charred black corpse whose popped eyeballs appeared to be standing on the ends of chopsticks. On top of the chest, body organs the color of a new onion lay in a ball.

Akiko Yamanaka (17 ▶ 74)

1-B

カンカン照りの中

娘さんは「どなたをお探しですか」と声をかけてくださった。それでこの人は生きておられるのだなと思った。腕時計が食い込んでいるのでゆるめてあげようと思ったが、さわると手の皮がズルズルむけるので、どうしようもできなかった。日よけをしてあげようにも草も木も無く、壊れたレンガだけである。この人はカンカン照りの中動けないのである。

8月7日 午前11時過ぎ
300m／相生橋付近（1 平和記念公園・周辺）
原田 義諦（16 ▶ 46）

Under the broiling sun

The young girl said, "Are you looking for someone?" That was how I knew she was alive. I saw that her wristwatch was biting into her skin and tried to loosen it, but when I touched the skin on her hand, it slipped off, so I could do nothing for her. At least I wanted to get her out of the sun, but there was no grass, no tree, nothing but broken bricks. She was immobile and helpless under the broiling sun.

August 7, just after 11:00 a.m.
300m / near Aioi Bridge (1 Peace Memorial Park)
Gitai Harada (16 ▶ 46)

1-A

第1章　きのこ雲の下で

市内電車の惨状

7日夕暮に紙屋町付近において目撃した、数十名の客と共に被爆した市内電車の惨状。周辺の山はなお延焼中、市内も余じん猛烈。

8月7日 夕方
200m／紙屋町付近
（2 紙屋町・本通）
横山　正（36 ▶ 66）

Terrible streetcar spectacle

In the Kamiya-cho area at dusk on the 7th, I witnessed the terrible spectacle of a streetcar filled with dozens of victims. The mountains in the area were still aflame, and the city was still burning fiercely.

August 7, evening
200m ／ near Kamiya-cho
（2 Kamiya-cho・Hondori）
Tadashi Yokoyama（36 ▶ 66）

2-A- ◎

人間の炭

焼けて赤くなった電車が天満町に止まり、何かと思えば……。人間の黒焦げが電車の中から点々と外に倒れ、もう炭と言っていい。人間の炭……。

8月7日
1,300m／天満町
（6 十日市・中広）
木原　敏子（17 ▶ 47）

Human charcoal

My eye was caught by a fire-reddened streetcar stopped at Tenma-cho. Inside the car and strewn outside were people actually burned to charcoal—human charcoal.

August 7
1,300m ／ Tenma-cho
（6 Tokaichi・Nakahiro）
Toshiko Kihara（17 ▶ 47）

1-A

材木のように重ねて置かれた遺体

日赤病院の玄関前の丸い花壇の上には、材木のように重ねて置かれた中学1、2年生の遺体がありました。やけどはなく全く無傷のままに息絶えていました。名札には広島二中と書いてありました。

8月7日
1,500m／広島赤十字病院（5 国泰寺・千田）
河野 きよみ（14 ▶ 71）

Corpses piled like lumber

On the circular flowerbed in front of the entrance to the Red Cross Hospital, corpses of first and second-year junior high students had been piled on each other like lumber. They had no sign of injury or burn. Their nametags read "Second Hiroshima Junior."

August 7
1,500m / Hiroshima Red Cross Hospital（5 Kokutaiji・Senda）
Kiyomi Kono（14 ▶ 71）

2-B

広島赤十字病院　Hiroshima Red Cross Hospital
原爆により、鉄筋コンクリート造の本館は大破。隔離病棟などの木造建物は全焼した。収容中の患者約250人中5人と病院関係者69人が犠牲となった。被爆直後から多くの被爆者が救護を求めて集まり、22日間に延べ3万人以上の患者が手当てを受けた。
The large ferro-concrete main building sustained great damage. The isolation ward and other wooden buildings burned to the ground. Five of the 250 hospitalized patients and 69 staff perished. Victims began coming for help immediately after the bombing. In 22 days, the hospital treated more than 30,000 people.

第1章 きのこ雲の下で

水死した被爆者の数知れず

元安川に飛び込んで水死した被爆者の数知れず。8月6日以後、死体は潮の干満により上下して、8日ごろには、目玉は飛び出し、腹の腸は渦を巻いて外に出て化け物の状態でした。

8月8日頃
890m／万代橋（5 国泰寺・千田）
佐々木 正名(37 ▶ 67)

Countless victims had died in the water.

Countless victims had jumped into the Motoyasugawa River and drowned. On the 6th and during the next few days, the corpses drifted in and out with the tide. Around the 8th, their eyeballs popped out and coiled intestines protruded, making them look monstrous.

Around August 8
890m / Yorozuyo Bridge
（5 Kokutaiji・Senda)
Masana Sasaki (37 ▶ 67)

2-A

川に浮く屍

死屍累々とはまさにこのようなものかとしばしあぜんとすると同時に、先夜姉と二人で、屍と知らず流れる死体を手さぐりで押しのけて水浴びをしたので、二重の大ショックでした。

8月9日 朝
2,600m／本川下流(舟入川口町と江波町の境の川岸)（10 吉島・舟入・観音）
榎本 安枝(20 ▶ 50)

Corpses floating in the river

I was dumbfounded by the mass of corpses. I received a double shock recalling the night before, when my sister and I waded in and must have unknowingly pushed them aside to bathe our bodies.

August 9, morning
2,600m / downstream in the Honkawa River (riverbank on the border between Funairi-kawaguchi-cho and Eba-machi)
（10 Yoshijima・Funairi・Kan-on)
Yasue Enomoto(20 ▶ 50)

2-A

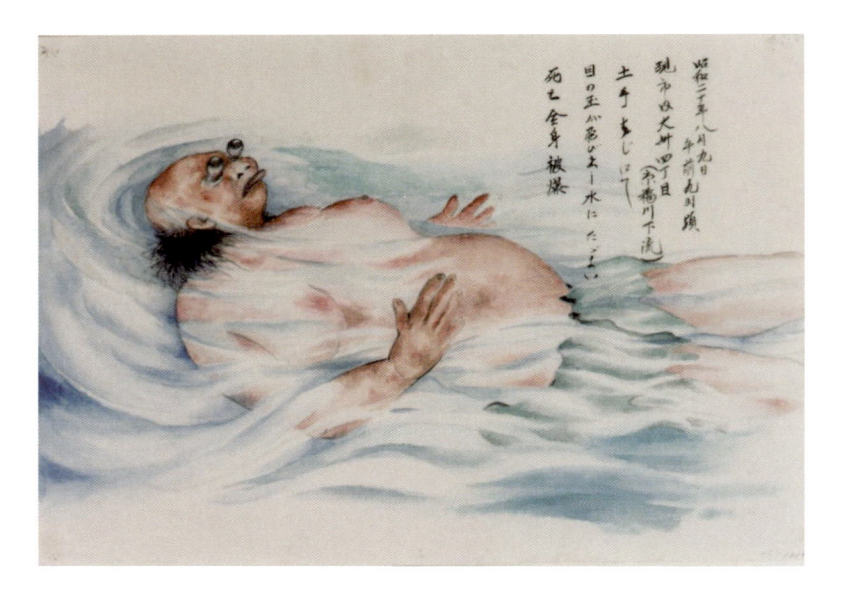

目の玉が飛び出し水にただよう

目の玉が飛び出し水にただよい死亡　全身被爆

8月9日 午前9時頃
大州四丁目 京橋川下流
（7 牛田・広島駅）
古川 正一（32 ▶ 62）

A corpse floating in the river with its eyeballs popped out

A corpse floating in the river with its eyeballs popped out. The whole body had been burnt.

August 9, around 9:00 a.m.
Ozu 4-chome, downstream in the Kyobashigawa River
（7 Ushita・Hiroshima Station）
Shoichi Furukawa（32 ▶ 62）

1-A

川一面の水ぶくれの死体

被爆であまりにも熱いため川に飛び込まれたと思う。向こう岸に軍隊の兵士が多勢と思う。川一面、水ぶくれの状態で浮いて水死されていた。川土手を見ると当時の思い忘れず。

1,290m／横川橋（12 三篠・祇園）
中田 政彦（15 ▶ 72）

Bloated bodies covered the surface of the river.

They must have jumped in the river to escape their suffering. I think many were soldiers. The surface was covered with bloated, floating bodies of people who died in the water. When I look at the riverbank, I can't help but remember how I felt then.

1,290m / Yokogawa Bridge
（12 Misasa・Gion）
Masahiko Nakata（15 ▶ 72）

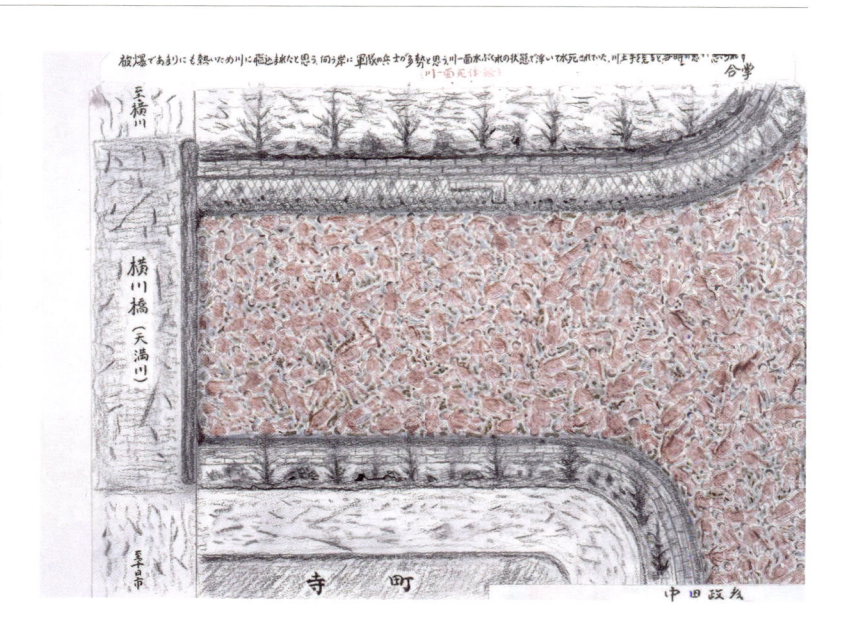

1-B

The Turning Point between Life and Death
— Looking at Fire Cisterns

Akimasa Yokoyama

"Objects" Recalling the Catastrophe

On the 45th anniversary of the bombing, Kenzaburo Oe gave the keynote address at the Forum for Authors and the General Public held by the Asahi Shimbun Company to commemorate publication of the survey report *A-bombed Buildings of Hiroshima* (Asahi Shimbun Hiroshima Office, 1990).[1] He said, "How very important objects are when we remember the past, when we seek to convey the past to the future." Similarly, the victims, streetcars, horses, cows, buildings, bridges, and fire cisterns captured in A-bomb drawings are tangible proof of what occurred.

It is well known that *hibakusha* seeking water inevitably appear in all collections of A-bomb accounts and drawings. Suffering from burns they sustained at the moment of detonation, skirting raging flames on roads hot enough to melt their shoes onto their feet, thirsting terribly under the August sun, countless victims groped their way toward rivers, ponds, pools, ditches, wells, and broken water pipes. They also crowded into the fire cisterns that had been placed all around the city. We know of 156 drawings that show fire cisterns. It is not surprising that so many pictures incorporate a motif that was so much a part of daily life.

Quoting written accounts, I will explain the background and roles of fire cisterns at the time of the atomic bombing. I want the people who see these drawings to understand how critical water was to people hovering between life and death, and the different ways the water in the cisterns served them.

Types of Fire Cisterns

Numbers of fire hydrants and fire cisterns placed around the city just prior to the bombing are as follows:

Category	East Fire Precinct	West Fire Precinct	Total
Fire hydrants	629	1,280	1,909 (5,322)
Fire cisterns	31	80	111 (530)

Numbers in brackets are as of the end of February 1975.
Source: *History of Fire-Fighting in Hiroshima after the Atomic Bombing* (Hiroshima City Fire Services Bureau, 1975)

水槽の数が、被爆前の家屋敷の総戸数 76,327[2] に比してずいぶん少ないが、これは要所に置かれた大型水槽の数を示しているからである。これとは別に、コンクリート製で長方形の中型水槽と小型水槽が各班・各戸に割り当てられ、後者には木製や酒樽型のものもあった。

大型水槽：10 kl〔55.5 石〕以上
中型水槽：1 kl〔5.5 石〕以上
小型水槽：0.1 kl〔5.5 斗〕以上

他に、太田川（河川延長 103 km）の 7 つ（現在 6 つ）の支流が瀬戸内海に注ぐデルタの街・広島の豊かな伏流水を利用する、もっと大がかりな底なしの地下貯水槽も設置された。

小松キクエさん（当時 37 歳）が描いたコンクリート製で酒樽型の水槽はめずらしい（p.106）。2、3 人でいっぱいになる水槽が小型、10 人ぐらい入れるものが中型で、この 2 種類を描いた絵が圧倒的に多い。

防火水槽の働き

原爆炸裂以後、防火水槽が果たした役割は、大まかに分けると次の 6 つになる。それぞれの役割を、絵と証言にもとづいてたどり直してみよう。

1．水を飲む／水をかぶる

中村巌さん（当時 11 歳）は爆心地から 0.9 km の水主町で被爆、住吉橋（爆心地から 1.39 km）の近くへ来ると、「壊れかけた水槽に、数人の人達が頭を突込んでしきりに水を飲んでいる」。のどの渇きと人なつかしさに近寄るが、「あッ」と、後ずさりする。

僕が水槽の中に見たものは、血に赤く染まった水に映っている怪物の顔だった。彼等は水槽にもたれ、水槽に首を突込んで、水をのみかけたまま死んでいたのだ。焼け千切れたセーラー服から女学生だということがわかったけれども、髪の毛は一本もなく、やけただれた顔は血で真赤に染まり、とうてい人間の顔とは思えなかった。

Before the atomic bomb was dropped, the total number of fire cisterns in the city was quite small with respect to the number of housing units: 76,327.[2] This figure represents only large cisterns placed in key locations. In addition, rectangular midsize and small cisterns made of concrete were allotted to neighborhood teams and households. Some of the small cisterns were wooden boxes or sake casks.

Large fire cisterns: 10 kl (55.5 *koku*) or more
Midsize cisterns: 1 kl (5.5 *koku*) or more
Small cisterns: 0.1 kl (5.5 *to*) or more

For larger water sources, underground water storage tanks without bottoms were dug to make use of the plentiful groundwater under this delta city divided by seven (now, six) tributaries of the Otagawa River (103 km long).

The concrete barrel-shaped cistern drawn by Kikue Komatsu (then, 37) is unusual (p. 106). Small cisterns could only hold two or three persons. Midsize cisterns could hold about ten. Drawings that depicted these two types were by far the most numerous.

Roles of Fire Cisterns

After the bomb exploded, the cisterns chiefly played six roles. Based on drawings and eyewitness accounts, let us consider each of these.

1. Drinking the water and splashing it over their bodies

Iwao Nakamura (then, 11) was exposed 0.9 km from the hypocenter at Kako-machi. These are his words about his approach to the Sumiyoshi Bridge (1.39 km from the hypocenter): "Some people had thrust their heads into the broken cistern and were thirstily gulping the water." Pulled by his own thirst and the comforting sight of people, he approached but then, "Ah!" He recoiled.

What I saw reflected in the blood-red water were faces of monsters. They had leaned over the cistern, thrust their heads in, and died in the act of drinking. The burnt, tattered sailor uniforms they were wearing told me that they were girl students, but they had lost every hair on their heads. Their burnt faces were dyed red with blood. It was impossible to see them as human.

Arata Osada, ed., *Children of the Atomic Bomb
—Testament of Boys and Girls of Hiroshima*

(長田新編『原爆の子』岩波書店、1951 年)

彼女らは、木挽町（爆心地から 0.4 km）あたりで建物疎開の跡片付け中に被爆し、逃げてきた市女[3]の 13、4 歳の生徒かもしれない。水を飲む前か、飲んだ後かは不明だが、はたして彼女らは、赤い水に映る無惨な顔が自らの顔と気づいただろうか。もしそうであれば、その顔と向きあったまま息絶えたのは、あまりに痛ましい。しかも、水槽の水は負傷者や死者の血だけでなく、汗と脂と膿に汚れていたはずで、その水を飲むしかなかったのは、むごい。

小川紗賀己さん（当時 28 歳）の絵（p.108）で、中型水槽をぎっしり埋める 12 人ほどの死者はみな真赤である。火傷や裂傷で出血している人々のなかに、応急手当で赤チンを塗られた人がまじっているかもしれない。よく見ると、ほぼ全員が口から黄色い息を吐いている。なぜだろうか。

逃げる被災者はもちろん、救援に駆けつけた人々や消防職員たちが、防火用水をかぶって真夏の暑熱と中心街（爆心地から半径約 2 km 以内）の大火をしのいだという証言は、少なくない。

２．傷口を洗う／内臓を洗う

原田治さん（当時 9 歳）の脳裡には、爆風に吹き飛ばされた兄の姿が焼きついている。

> お兄ちゃんは道路にとばされた。
> ちょうが出ていたので防火用水の中にぼうふらのわいている茶色の水でちょうをあらった。
> そしてシャツでまいておばさんとどこかへ逃げた。

(峠三吉編『原子雲の下より』青木書店、1952 年)

たった 3 行の描写で、凄絶な光景を、50 行の詩、100 枚の小説よりも鮮烈に切り取っている。自らの血まみれの腸を、とっさにボウフラが泳ぐ水で洗う少年の姿が目に浮かぶ。同じように、たいていは血と土、塵埃や灰や燃えさしに汚れた防火用水で、ガラス片がいっぱい刺さった乳房や血の噴き出る幼児の顔を洗ったなどの証言は、いくつも残されている。

(Iwanami Shoten, Publishers, 1951)

The girls may have been 13- or 14-year-old students of First Municipal Girls.[3] They had fled Kobiki-cho (0.4 km from the hypocenter) after being bombed while cleaning up debris from building demolition. It is unclear whether they died before or after they drank. Did they know that the pitiful countenances reflected in the red water were their own? The image of girls dying while encountering their transformed faces is even more painful to contemplate. Beyond that, how cruel to have to drink water soiled not only with the blood of the injured and dead, but their sweat, fat and pus.

A drawing by Sagami Ogawa (then, 28) (p. 108) depicts around a dozen bright red corpses packed into a midsize cistern. Among the bodies burned or bloodied by injuries may be some that were reddened by mercurochrome applied as first-aid. A close look reveals that virtually all are emitting yellowish breath. One wonders what the artist meant to show.

Many reports indicate that fleeing victims, rescuers and firemen braved the midsummer heat and the raging city fires (within a 2 km radius of the hypocenter) by drenching themselves with cistern water.

2. Bathing wounds and organs

Imprinted on the mind of Osamu Harada (then, 9) is the image of his brother thrown by the atomic blast.

> *My brother was thrown into the road. His intestines were bulging out so he washed them with the mosquito-larvae infested tea-colored water in the fire cistern. Then, he bound his middle area with a shirt and escaped with our aunt.*
>
> Sankichi Toge, ed., *Under the A-bomb Cloud*
> (Aoki Shoten Publishing Co., Ltd., 1952)

Those three terse sentences evoke the grim scene more powerfully than a 50-line poem or a 100-page novel. We see a boy moving quickly after the bombing to wash his own bloody intestines in mosquito-infested water. Similarly, many accounts tell of using cistern water mixed with blood, dirt, grit, ash, and burning embers to wash breasts pierced with glass splinters or children's faces opened by wounds gushing blood.

3．水に浸かる／火炎を避ける

避難する道筋に川や池、プールや井戸、巨大な地下貯水槽などがないとき、負傷者が防火水槽に入って炎暑とまわりの猛火から身を守り、死を免れたという証言も多い。

山本節子さん（当時7歳、爆心地から1.15 kmの鉄砲町で被爆）は、母親が倒壊家屋の下敷きになり生きたまま火に焼かれるが、子どもの力では助けられない。母親には先に逃げるようにと急かされ、自分の着物にも火がつき、「お母ちゃん、お母ちゃん」と泣き叫びながら走って逃げる。だが、

> どこまで行ってもまわりは火の海で、もうにげられなくなってしまったので、夢中で用水桶の中にとびこんだ。火の粉がどんどんとんでくるので、トタンの切れはしを頭の上にのせて火を防いでいた。用水桶の水は、まるでお風呂のように熱かった。その中には、私のほかにも四、五人の人が、誰かの名を呼んで泣いていた。
>
> （長田新編『原爆の子』岩波書店、1951年）

これは中型の水槽であろう。山本さんは気を失い、水槽に翌朝まで浸かっていて一命をとりとめるが、「そばを見ると、女の人が水につかったまま、眠ったように死んでいる」。

小野木明さん（当時15歳）の絵（p.107）では、中型水槽に妊婦が全裸で仰向けに浮かび、口から鮮血を流している……。

このように、水槽のなかで死を迎えた人はたくさん目撃されているが、水槽のおかげで生き延びた人も数えきれない。防火水槽は文字通り火と水の接点として、被爆者を生と死に分けたのである。

4．伝言を書きつける

焼け残った電柱や門・塀・板切れなどに、逃げる負傷者も、家族や知人を捜す人々も切実な伝言を書きつけた（p.60）。筆記用具は主に消炭やチョークである。袋町国民学校では、階段に沿った壁などにチョークで書かれた。重く、堅固で、低い位置にあったおかげで数多く残された防火水槽も、

3. Immersion in water to escape the flames

When their escape routes lacked rivers, ponds, pools, wells, large underground water tanks, or other water sources, the injured tell of how they survived by immersing themselves in water cisterns to protect themselves and escape death from the heat and flames.

Setsuko Yamamoto (then, 7; exposed at Teppo-cho, 1.15 km from the hypocenter) reported that her mother was trapped under the family's collapsed house when the flames approached to burn her alive. The little girl lacked the strength to save her mother. Her mother told her to hurry and run away. When her own clothing ignited, she did so screaming, "Mother! Mother!"

> *Every direction was a sea of flames. When I could see no path to safety, I jumped in a fire cistern. Sparks kept flying at my head so I shielded it with a piece of tin sheeting. The water in the cistern was as hot as a bath. Four or five others were in there with me, all of us calling someone's name and weeping.*
>
> Arata Osada, ed., *Children of the Atomic Bomb
> —Testament of Boys and Girls of Hiroshima*
> (Iwanami Shoten, Publishers, 1951)

This cistern was probably one of the midsize cisterns. Yamamoto lost consciousness in the cistern and survived by staying immersed until the next morning, but "Next to me, a woman who appeared to be sleeping was actually dead."

A drawing by Akira Onogi (then, 15) (p. 107) shows a naked pregnant woman floating on her back in a midsize cistern, blood pouring from her mouth.

Indeed, corpses in cisterns were sighted by many people, but cisterns saved countless lives as well. These structures were the convergence point of fire and water, which divided victims into survivors and the dead.

4. Writing messages

People fleeing the city and those searching for their kin or friends wrote urgent messages on remaining telephone poles, gates, walls, pieces of wood, and other surfaces (p. 60). Their writing tools were charcoal, chalk, and the like. Chalk was the tool used for messages scrawled on the basement stairwell wall and other places at Fukuromachi Elementary School. Because they were heavy, solid, and near the ground, unknown numbers of fire cisterns remained intact and became boards for desperate messages.

Heading from Ujina to Hatchobori on the 6th, Tomio

Shibata (then, a private first class of the Army Marine Training Division) saw:

> *Chaotic charcoal scribbles on fences, fire cisterns, wall boards, any place likely to draw the eye, relating to the safety of family members and giving contact information. For example, "XX are safe, waiting for you at XXX, come as soon as you see this." Or "XX is safe. Am searching for XX."*
>
> Record of the Hiroshima A-bomb War Disaster, Vol. 5
> (Hiroshima City Office, 1971)

One wonders how many people found the messages written to them. How many reunited as a result with their loved ones, whether surviving, or—sadly—dead?[4]

5. Quenching fires

Some accounts by people far from rivers or fire hydrants tell of using water from the large cisterns to fight the raging A-bomb fires. But the water soon ran out and the fires had their way. However, firemen pulled many victims out of the flames.

6. Other uses (shelter for the victims, bathing, sterilizing diapers, placing documents for safekeeping)

Yoshio Hashimoto (then, assistant fireman) saved a girl (about third grade) who was trapped under the collapsed auditorium of Dambara Elementary School on the 6th. For her safety, he "put her in a 5.5 *koku* fire cistern on the streetcar road."[5] Several days after the bombing, a fire cistern was used as a bath[6] at the Victims Counseling Center opened by Toyo Kogyo Company at Hiroshima University of Literature and Science.[7] At Hijiyama Elementary School, which became a shelter for orphans on the 8th, staff were using a fire cistern to sterilize diapers soiled by bloody stools.[8] On the 7th, Noboru Mitani (then, working for the Prefectural Office Relief Division) found 50,000 disaster certificates placed inside "an empty cistern on the pond side" in the burnt ruins of the Prefectural Office Building (Kako-machi; 1.4 km from the hypocenter). They divided these into stacks to distribute around the city for survivors.[9] Naturally, these disaster certificates were later used in relief efforts for the survivors.

Questions Posed by the Fire Cisterns

As we have seen, after the bombing cistern water was rarely used for its intended purpose of putting out fires.

に被爆者の援護のために活かされたことはいうまでもない。

防火水槽が問いかけること

　以上みてきたとおり、防火水槽は本来の目的の消火にはほとんど役立っていない。しかし、逃げ惑う被爆者にとっては必死にすがるしかない救いの場であった。だが同時に、防火水槽は数知れぬ負傷者の無残な最期をみとらねばならなかった。皮肉な、しかし悲痛な結末である。具体的な「もの」に刻みつけられたこうした事実を想い描きながら、原爆の絵をあらためてみつめ直したい。そうすれば、原爆投下によるホロコーストの底知れぬおぞましさ、無益な戦争を引き起こした人間の救いようのない愚かさが読み取れるはずである。

1）筆者は執筆メンバーの1人である。
2）1946年8月の広島市の調査による。広島市・長崎市原爆災害誌編集委員会編『広島・長崎の原爆災害』岩波書店、1979年を参照。
3）市立第一高等女学校のこと。現在の舟入高校。541人の全員が死亡。
4）こうした伝言のおかげで尋ね人に出会えたり、肉親の遺骨を引き取ることができたという証言は、いくつか残っている。
5）『原爆広島消防史』広島市消防局、1975年。
6）後の広島大学。
7）末包敏夫編『天よりの声』日本YMCA同盟出版部、1983年。
8）広島市『広島原爆戦災誌4』広島市役所、1971年。
9）広島市『広島原爆戦災誌3』広島市役所、1971年。

However, cisterns saved the lives of many confused, fleeing victims who flung themselves in them. Of course, cisterns also witnessed the piteous final moments of innumerable injured people. Their deaths appear ironic and pathetic. Let us turn again to A-bomb drawings as we hold in our minds the realities engraved onto these concrete objects. We may be able to read from them new truths about the unending horror of the A-bomb holocaust and the hopeless idiocy of the humans who caused that futile war.

1. I am one of the authors of this book.
2. According to a Hiroshima City survey of August 1946. Source: *Hiroshima and Nagasaki—The Physical, Medical and Social Effects of the Atomic Bombings* (The Committee for the Compilation of Materials on Damage Caused by the Atomic Bombs in Hiroshima and Nagasaki, Iwanami Shoten, Publishers, 1979).
3. First Municipal Girls High School; now, Funairi High School. All 541 mobilized students perished.
4. Some accounts indicate that the writer was able to reunite with missing persons or retrieve their remains thanks to such messages.
5. *History of Fire-Fighting in Hiroshima after the Atomic Bombing* (Hiroshima City Fire Services Bureau, 1975).
6. Toshio Suekane, ed., *Voices from Heaven* (National Council of YMCAs of Japan, 1983).
7. Now, Hiroshima University.
8. *Record of the Hiroshima A-bomb War Disaster*, Vol. 4 (Hiroshima City Office, 1971).
9. *Record of the Hiroshima A-bomb War Disaster*, Vol. 3 (Hiroshima City Office, 1971).

第2章
Chapter 2

きずな
Bonds

防火水槽の中で寄り添うように亡くなった先生と生徒、
焦土の中を必死でわが子の名を叫ぶ母親、
亡くなったことも知らず母親に水を飲ませようとする女児……。
一発の原子爆弾は、広島を破壊し尽くした。
それでも家族を励まし、瀕死の友を助け、生徒を守ろうとする
人々の強いきずながあった。

A teacher and students dead and huddled close in a fire cistern.
A mother walking the scorched earth desperately calling her child's name.
A small girl trying to get water past the lips of the mother she does not know is dead.
A single atomic bomb obliterated Hiroshima.
Through it all, family members, friends, and students held tight to each other,
encouraging and protecting each other, even to the brink of death.

共に
Together

妹と私を抱えて

倒壊した家のがれきの下に私と父と2歳の妹は完全に埋没した。時間はどのくらいたったであろうか。見守る母の前で、屋根瓦の一部がむくむくと動き出し、中から父が、私と妹を脇に抱え、仁王立ちになって姿を現した。

8月6日
1,300m ／天満町の自宅（6 十日市・中広）
金近 衛（3 ▶ 59）

Rising up clutching my sister and me

Our house collapsed, completely burying my father, my two-year-old sister, and me. I don't know how much time passed. As my mother watched, a section of roof tiles began to rattle and move. As they parted, my father arose, clutching my sister and me under his arms.

August 6
1,300m / at home in Tenma-cho（6 Tokaichi・Nakahiro）
Mamoru Kanechika（3 ▶ 59）

2-B

第2章 きずな

君が泣くと
僕まで悲しくなるよ

着ている服ははがれ、私は頭から血が出て顔から体から血まみれです。主人は路上で被爆しましたので、顔や手足の皮ははがれ、ぶらさがり、人間とは思えない様子でした。生まれたばかりの子供は、外傷はなかったのですが、原爆症で9月24日に亡くなりました。

8月6日
安部 初子（24 ▶ 81）

When you cry I get sad, too.

My tattered clothes were hanging in shreds. Blood poured from my head over my face and whole body. My husband had been exposed out on the street. The skin on his face, legs and arms was peeling and hanging loose. He did not look human. Our newborn infant showed no sign of injury, but died on September 24.

August 6
Hatsuko Abe（24 ▶ 81）

2-B

おろしたてのブラウス　Brand new blouse
安部初子さんが着ていたブラウスは、その日おろしたてだった。
When the bomb exploded, Hatsuko Abe was wearing this blouse. It was brand new.

友人と一緒に逃げる

私は友人と一緒に逃げた。友人は足の裏をやけどしているので、歩くことができない。四つんばいになったり、私の肩をかしてやったりして逃げた。

8月6日 午前9時頃
2,000m ／山手橋
（12 三篠・祇園）
高橋 昭博（14 ▶ 42）

Escaping with my friend

My friend and I escaped together. He couldn't walk because the soles of his feet were burned. Sometimes he crawled and sometimes I lent him my shoulder.

August 6, around 9:00 a.m.
2,000m / Yamate Bridge
（12 Misasa・Gion）
Akihiro Takahashi（14 ▶ 42）

2-A

防火水槽で亡くなっていた先生と女学生

水槽に熱気を避けてか、思い思いの姿で先生や生徒が入っていました。師を信じて防火用水の汚水の中で、互いに励まし合ったのであろうか。

木挽町から水主町付近（10 吉島・舟入・観音）
川口 シマ子（22 ▶ 50）

Teacher and girl students who died in a fire cistern

Girl students and their teacher had climbed in every which way to escape the heat. In that dirty water, believing in their teacher, they must have encouraged each other.

Between Kobiki-cho and Kako-machi
(10 Yoshijima・Funairi・Kan-on)
Shimako Kawaguchi (22 ▶ 50)

2-A

愛馬の苦痛をやわらげる

この場面が強く私の印象に残った理由は、この主人公が自分も死ぬかもしれないほどの苦痛を耐えて、まず一切の馬具を取除いて、少しでも愛馬の苦痛をやわらげてやろうとの思いやりが感じ取られたからでした。

8月8日 午前
1,320m／横川新橋南詰
（12 三篠・祇園）
沖田 繁一（43 ▶ 73）

Comforting his beloved and suffering horse

What impressed me so powerfully about this scene was the compassion of the main character in the picture. Possibly mortally wounded himself, he bore his own pain to remove his horse's saddle and other gear, doing what he could to alleviate the horse's suffering.

August 8, morning
1,320m / south end of Yokogawa-shinbashi Bridge (12 Misasa・Gion)
Shigeichi Okita (43 ▶ 73)

1-A

永遠の別れ
Eternal Farewell

第2章 きずな

友人との永遠の別れ

川で出会った友人の道子さんと励ましあいながらここまできた私たちはとうとう、悲しい永遠の別れをしなければなりませんでした。

8月6日
1,700m／金屋町
（8 比治山・仁保）
松原 美代子（12 ▶ 69）

My final parting from my friend

After we found each other in the river, my friend Michiko and I came this far together, encouraging each other along. But at this point we sadly had to part forever.

August 6
1,700m / Kinya-cho
（8 Hijiyama・Niho）
Miyoko Matsubara（12 ▶ 69）

1-B

姉さん寒い！ 寒い

今から2時間ほど前、弟を尋ね当てました。「水がほしい！ 水がほしい！」といいますので水を与えました。うれしそうに飲みました。「姉さん寒い！ 寒い」と言いますので抱いてやりました。弟の体温は次第に無くなり、息を引き取りました。

8月6日 午後9時頃
900m／県立広島病院正門前（10 吉島・舟入・観音）
田頭 忠之（43 ▶ 72）

"Sister, I'm cold! I'm cold!"

About two hours before the scene in this picture, she found her younger brother. He had cried, "I want water! I want water!" so she gave him some. He drank it happily. Then, he said, "Sister, I'm cold! I'm cold!" and she cradled him. His body gradually grew colder, and he died.

August 6, around 9:00 p.m.
900m / in front of the gate of Hiroshima Prefectural Hospital
（10 Yoshijima・Funairi・Kan-on）
Tadayuki Tagashira（43 ▶ 72）

2-A-◎

長女を自分で焼く

長女尚子（3歳）を自分で焼く。泣けて泣けて涙が止まらない。「私も行く。先に行っていてくれ」と、手を合わす。だんだん焼けて体の中の油が流れ出る。大変な量だ。元気な子を焼くのだ。かわいそうだ、見ていられない。気が狂いそうだ。これが現世とは思えない。

8月7日 夕方
石風呂 環（35 ▶ 65）

I cremated my eldest daughter myself.

I cremated my daughter Naoko (three years old) myself. I wept and wept, tears without end. "Wait for me, I will follow you." I put my hands together in prayer. As Naoko burned, the oils of her body began to ooze out. A huge amount! What a healthy child! I couldn't stand to watch. I was losing my mind. I could not believe it was happening.

August 7, evening
Tamaki Ishifuro (35 ▶ 65)

2-A

きちんと並べられたお弁当

朝の整列を終え、体操をしていたに違いない。中学生くらいの生徒か。きちんと並べられた弁当の主はいずこへ。お母さんの心のこもった優しさが別れのお弁当になるなんて。

360m／西練兵場（4 基町・白島）
竹内 勇（25 ▶ 82）

Neatly lined up lunch boxes

They must have finished morning assembly and been doing exercises when it happened. Probably junior high students. Where were the owners of the lunch boxes so neatly laid out? Each packed with a mother's tender devotion, the last lunch for her child. . . .

360m / Western Drill Ground
(4 Moto-machi・Hakushima)
Isamu Takeuchi (25 ▶ 82)

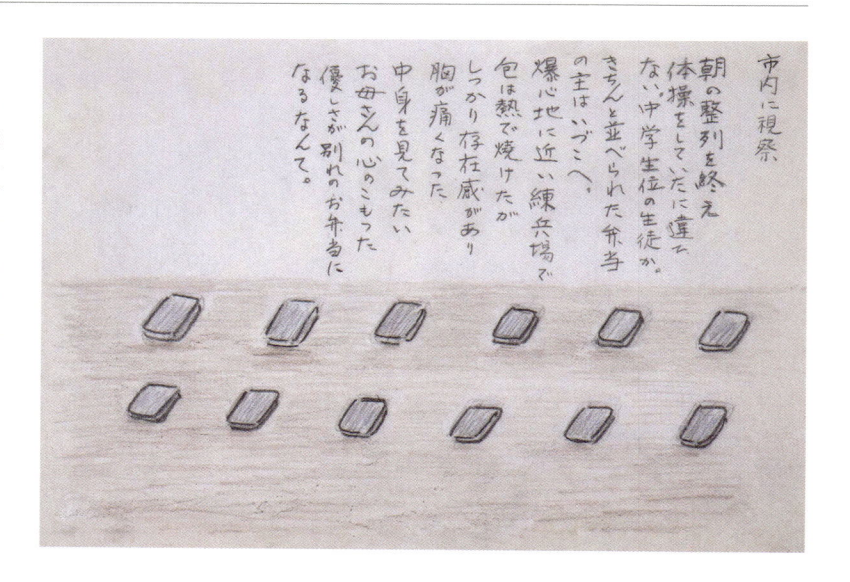

2-B

第2章 きずな

消息を尋ねて
Asking the Whereabouts

橋の上からわが子の名を呼び叫ぶ

このあたりは動員学徒ばかり。13、4歳の背丈も同じような子で、土手も川の中もいっぱいに、死んだ子がさながら大根をながしたごとく浮きつ沈みつ川下に流れて行く。わが子の名を呼びさけんでいる母親がいた。

8月7日 午前9時頃
620m ／新大橋東詰（1 平和記念公園・周辺）
炭本 末子（37 ▶ 67）

Screaming her child's name from the bridge

The dead in this area were mobilized students. The riverbank and the river itself were full of dead children about the same height, 13 or 14 years old. Looking like *daikon* radishes, they floated downstream, slipping under the surface, then bobbing up. A mother was screaming the name of her child.

August 7, around 9:00 a.m.
620m / east end of Shin-ohashi Bridge（1 Peace Memorial Park）
Sueko Sumimoto（37 ▶ 67）

2-A

動員学徒　Mobilized students
1944（昭和19）年8月に発令された「学徒動員令」により、中等学校以上の学生・生徒に対して、軍需産業部門での勤労奉仕が強制された。
The Student Mobilization Order of August 1944 required students in middle school and higher levels to perform labor service in the munitions industries.

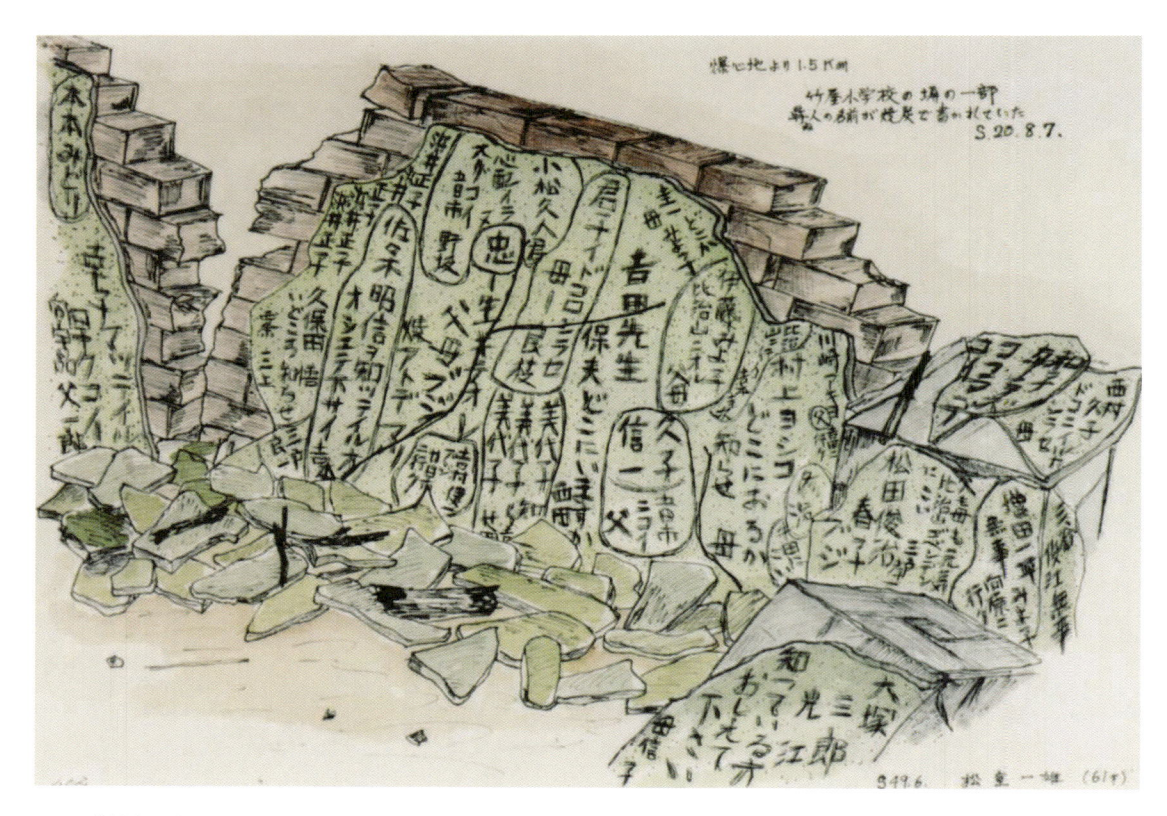

国民学校の塀に書かれた名前

国民学校の塀の一部。尋ね人の名前が焼炭で書かれていた。「西村 久子 ドコニイルカシラセ 母」、「和子 カナラズココマデコイ」など多数。

8月7日
1,280m／竹屋国民学校（5 国泰寺・千田）
松室 一雄（32 ▶ 61）

Names written on a section of elementary school wall

Section of an elementary school wall. Names of missing people were written in charcoal. "Hisako Nishimura, tell me where you are —Mother" "Kazuko, come here." And on and on.

August 7
1,280m / Takeya Elementary School（5 Kokutaiji・Senda）
Kazuo Matsumuro（32 ▶ 61）

2-A

行方不明者を捜して歩く

国民義勇隊の行方不明者を捜して歩く。掲示板に食い入り、みんなため息をついている。

8月12日
3,900m／宇品町東部桜土手付近
（9 皆実・宇品）
下谷 軍一（42 ▶ 72）

Walking the city searching for the missing

I walked the city looking for missing members of the Volunteer Citizen Corps. I saw people staring hard at each notice board, then turning away with a sigh.

August 12
3,900m / near cherry tree-lined bank in east Ujina-machi
（9 Minami・Ujina）
Gunichi Shimotani（42 ▶ 72）

2-A

国民義勇隊　Volunteer Citizen Corps
1945（昭和20）年6月、政府は国民義勇兵役法、国民義勇戦闘隊統率令を制定した。国民義勇隊は、本土決戦に備えて各地に編成されたもので、男子は15歳から60歳まで、女子は17歳から40歳までの全国民が編入された。
In June 1945, the national government enacted the Volunteer Citizen Corps Service Law and the Volunteer Citizen Combat Command Act. Volunteer Citizen Corps were formed around the country in preparation for a "decisive battle" on the homeland. Males from 15 to 60 and females from 17 to 40 were enlisted for the corps.

むしろをめくって

お寺の広縁にずらりと主に子供の遺体が並べられてあり、むしろがかけられてあった。傷ついた母親はむしゃくしゃの顔をして、むしろをめくってはわが子を捜していた。

8月7日 夕方
5,000m／安佐郡祇園町
（12 三篠・祇園）
村田 久子（29 ▶ 58）

Lifting each straw mat

The floor of the temple was lined with the corpses of mostly children, covered with straw mats. An injured, angry-looking woman was lifting each one, looking for her child.

August 7, evening
5,000m / Gion-cho, Asa-gun
（12 Misasa・Gion）
Hisako Murata（29 ▶ 58）

1-A

よく自慢していた見覚えのあるドイツ製の黒皮バンドの時計を目印に、恐らく爆心地近くで被爆したと思われる父を熱さで川にのがれ死んでいる多くの死骸の中などを、私は毎日捜し回った。当時満1歳になったばかりの背中の妹は微かな息をしながら夏の炎天下をよく耐えてくれた。とうとう私は、父を見つけだすことができなかった。

黒革バンドの時計を目印に

黒革バンドの時計を目印に、爆心地近くで被爆したと思われる父を捜す。満1歳になったばかりの背中の妹は、かすかな息をしながら夏の炎天下をよく耐えてくれた。とうとう私は、父を見つけだすことができなかった。

太田川
深町 陸夫（13 ▶ 70）

Looking for a watch with a black leather band

Assuming he had been exposed near the hypocenter, I searched for my father by looking for a watch with a black leather band. My baby sister, just one year old, rode on my back, breathing lightly and withstanding the blazing summer sun. I never found my father.

Otagawa River
Rikuo Fukamachi（13 ▶ 70）

2-B

父親の形見　Keepsake of his father

深町陸夫さんの父親侃さん（当時51歳）は、勤務先に向かう途中で被爆し、行方不明になった。自宅で被爆した陸夫さんが持ち出せたのは、侃さんのかばん1つだけだった。この防弾チョッキはその中にあったもの。

Rikuo Fukamachi's father Kan Fukamachi (then, 51) was exposed on the way to work and disappeared. The only item Rikuo, who was at home, was able to rescue from their collapsed house was his father's briefcase. This bulletproof vest was in the briefcase.

それぞれの再会
Various Reunions

第2章 きずな

ナガヒロのおじさん

母を捜して、一人ずつのぞきこんでは走りまわりました。後ろから声がしたので、振り返ると「ナガヒロじゃ」といいました。家から5軒先のおじさんです。裂けた口から血がタラタラとながれおちました。一瞬の理不尽さにおじさんは怒っていました。

8月6日 午前8時35分頃
1,710m／比治山橋（8 比治山・仁保）
早川 耐子（22 ▶ 79）

"Uncle" Nagahiro, my neighbor

Looking for my mother, I ran around peering into the face of each person. Someone called me from behind, and I turned around to hear a person say, "I'm Nagahiro." The Nagahiro family lived five houses away. Blood was gushing from his mouth, which was slashed wide open. He was furious at all that had happened in an instant.

August 6, around 8:35 a.m.
1,710m / Hijiyama Bridge (8 Hijiyama・Niho)
Taeko Hayakawa (22 ▶ 79)

2-B

オーイ、カヘッタデー

主人は同じ会社の救援隊に助けられ、家の前まで担架で帰り、手の皮をぶらさげて「オーイ、カヘッタデー」とさけびました。私はあまりの姿に目の前は真っ暗になりました。

8月6日 午後2時から3時頃
4,300m／安佐郡祇園町の自宅前(12 三篠・祇園)
中山 清子（28 ▶ 58）

"Hey, I'm home!"

My husband had been rescued by the rescue squad of his company. They brought him home on a stretcher. He called out, "Hey, I'm home!" With the skin peeling from his arms, the sight of him was so ghastly, I almost fainted.

August 6, around 2:00-3:00 p.m.
4,300m / in front of their home in Gion-cho, Asa-gun
(12 Misasa・Gion)
Kiyoko Nakayama (28 ▶ 58)

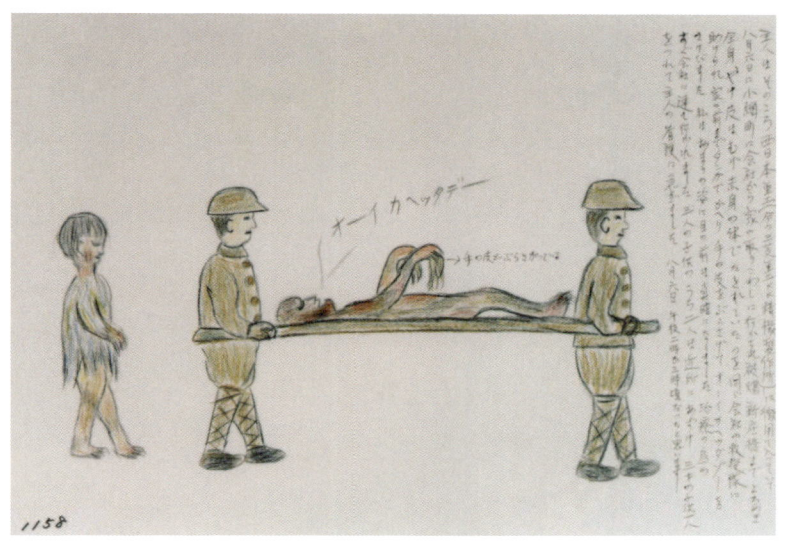

2-A

偶然にも妹だ

２人の女学生とすれ違った。鮮血に染まったユニホーム、頭に鉢巻き、顔面血だらけで髪はバサバサ、赤鬼のような姿に一言声をかけてみると偶然にも妹だ。

8月6日 午後3時30分から4時頃
800m／土橋付近（6十日市・中広）
大田 晴代（18 ▶ 48）

It turned out to be my sister!

I passed two girl students. One looked like a demon with a blood-drenched uniform, bandage-wrapped head, face covered with blood, and singed hair. For some reason I spoke to her and it turned out to be my sister!

August 6, around 3:30-4:00 p.m.
800m / near Dohashi (6 Tokaichi・Nakahiro)
Haruyo Ota （18 ▶ 48）

2-A

息子の硬直した遺体を運ぶ

建物疎開作業中に被爆した息子の硬直した遺体を運ぶ父親

8月7日
900m／小網町
（6十日市・中広）
石田 晟（13 ▶ 70）

Carrying the rigid corpse of his son

This father was carrying the rigid corpse of his son, who died while demolishing buildings.

August 7
900m / Koami-cho
(6 Tokaichi・Nakahiro)
Akira Ishida （13 ▶ 70）

1-B

この革バンドは確かに主人の物です

34、5歳ぐらいの婦人が赤子を背負い、遺体収容所に来られた。どの遺体も肌は真っ黒。「この革バンドは確かに主人の物です。主人の面影も少々あり間違いありません」と、涙の対面をされた。

8月8日
1,290m ／住吉神社境内（10 吉島・舟入・観音）
小笠原 昭道（17 ▶ 74）

"This leather belt is definitely my husband's."

A woman of 34 or 35 carrying a baby on her back came to a place where bodies were being kept. The skin of the corpses was burned completely black. "This leather belt is definitely my husband's. The face is also similar. I'm sure this is him." A tearful reunion.

August 8
1,290m / on the grounds of Sumiyoshi Shrine
（10 Yoshijima・Funairi・Kan-on）
Shodo Ogasawara (17 ▶ 74)

2-B

汚れたハンカチにもらった一握りの骨

似島の収容者名簿の中にただ一人「名不明二中一年生」とあった。多分これかもしれないと思い、一握りの骨を箱の中からもらい、汚れたハンカチに包んだ。この大きな背骨は子供のではないと思うと、涙があふれた。

9月15日
1,020m ／広島市役所（5 国泰寺・千田）
宮地 臣子（34 ▶ 64）

Fistful of bones I took home in a dirty handkerchief

On the list of patients who had been taken in at the relief station on Ninoshima Island, I found only one entry that read: "First-year, Second Junior High, name unknown." Thinking that could be my child, I took a fistful of bones out of the box and wrapped them in a dirty handkerchief. When I realized that the spine was too large to be a child's, the tears flowed.

September 15
1,020m / Hiroshima City Hall
（5 Kokutaiji・Senda）
Tomiko Miyaji (34 ▶ 64)

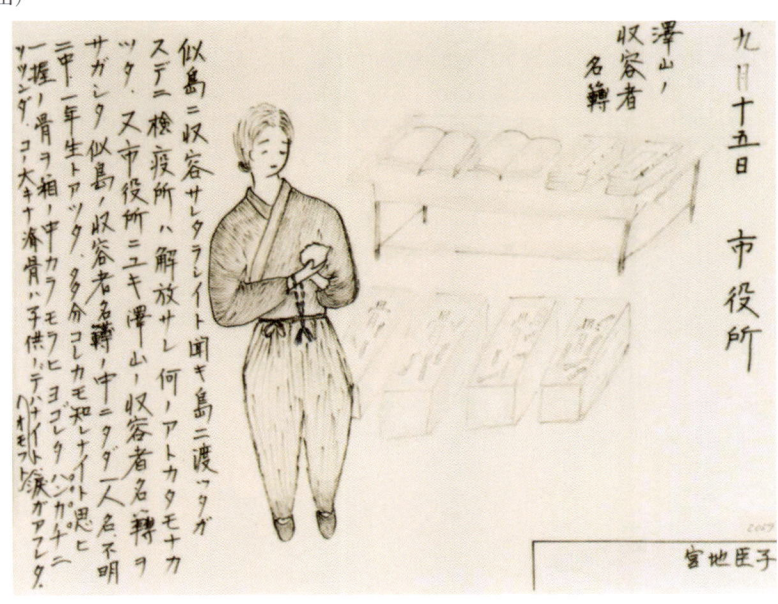

2-A

オトウサン イツニナッタラ カエルノカナ

父は被爆死。妹は5歳。男の人を見ると「ワッ オトウサンガ カエッテキタ。マチガッタ。オトウサン イツニナッタラ カエルノカナ」。父を待っている妹の姿がとてもかわいそうで、今でも忘れられません。

4,400m ／安佐郡祇園町の自宅付近（12 三篠・祇園）
青原 久子（11 ▶ 68）

"I wonder when Daddy will come home?"

Our father died in the bombing. My sister was five. Whenever she saw a man in the street, she cried, "Oh, it's Daddy! ... No, it's not him. I wonder when Daddy will come home?" I can never forget the sight of my poor little sister waiting for our father.

4,400m / near the family home in Gion-cho, Asa-gun（12 Misasa・Gion）
Hisako Aobara（11 ▶ 68）

2-B

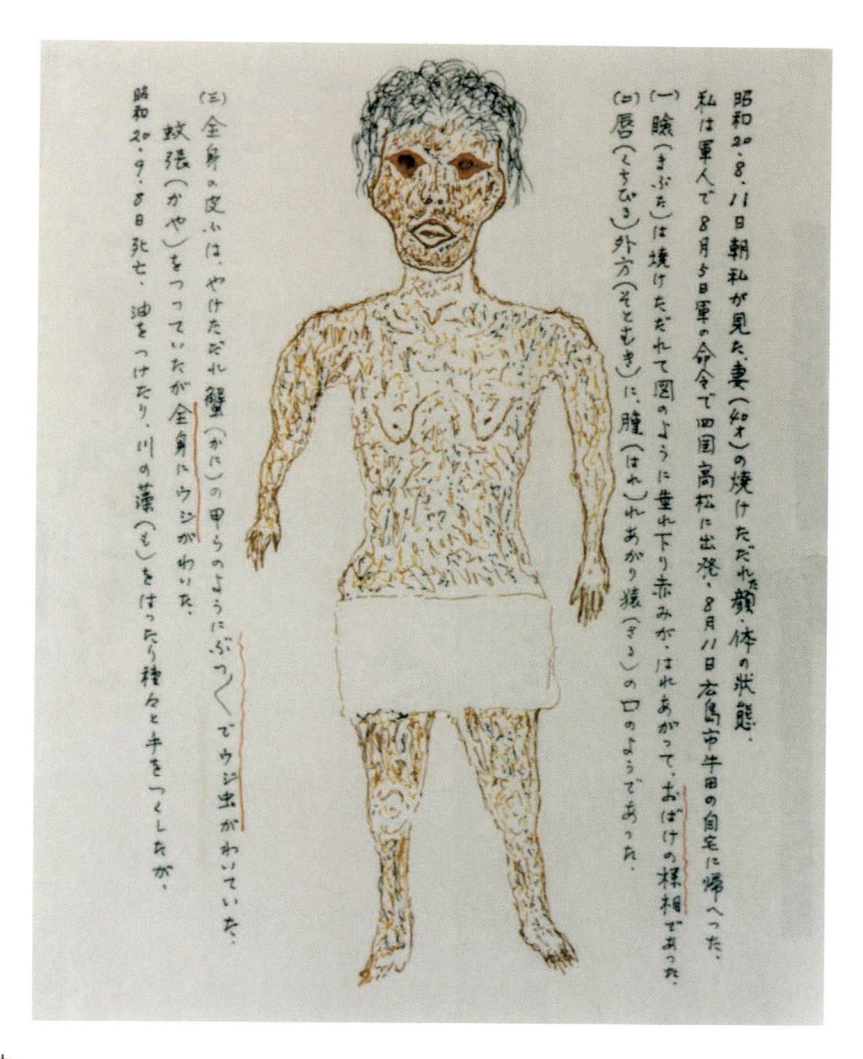

妻の顔と体

妻のまぶたは焼けただれ、おばけの様相だった。唇は外向きにはれあがり、サルのようだった。全身の皮膚はカニの甲羅のようにぶつぶつで、うじ虫がわいていた。手をつくしたが、9月8日死亡。

8月11日 朝
3,500m ／牛田町の自宅(7 牛田・広島駅周辺)
谷峰 房太郎(45 ▶ 74)

My wife's face and body

My wife's eyelids were burned and shredded, making her look monstrous. Her lips were swollen and protruding, like a monkey's. The skin over her whole body was speckled like a crab shell, and maggots were breeding in the wounds. I did my best, but she died on September 8.

August 11, morning
3,500m / at home in Ushita-machi (7 Ushita・Hiroshima Station)
Fusataro Tanimine (45 ▶ 74)

2-A

みとられることなく
Dying Alone

助ける人のないまま

猿猴川において助ける人のないまま息絶えた少女。

8月9日
猿猴川
山下 正人（20 ▶ 49）

No one to help her as she died

A girl had died in the Enkogawa riverbed with no one there to help her.

August 9
Enkogawa River
Masato Yamashita（20 ▶ 49）

2-A

声をかけてさわってみると

一人の男の幼児が門にすがって泣いていた。声をかけてさわってみると、彼は死んでいた。

1,300m ／縮景園の裏門（3 銀山・幟）
作者不明

I called to him and touched him, but . . .

A boy clinging to a gate seemed to be crying. When I called to him and touched him, I found he was dead.

1,300m / Shukkeien Garden's back gate
(3 Kanayama・Nobori)
Artist unknown

1-A- ◎

第2章 きずな

焼けたトタンの上に

焼けたトタンの上に並べられていた被爆死者。

8月15日頃
1,700m／横川駅東寄りの踏切付近(12 三篠・祇園)
寺岡 美樹(15 ▶ 72)

On burnt tin sheets

People killed by the bombing were lined up on tin sheets.

Around August 15
1,700m / near the railroad crossing at the east end of Yokogawa Station (12 Misasa・Gion)
Yoshiki Teraoka (15 ▶ 72)

1-B

シャベルですくい取る

身寄りの一人も来ている様子もなく意識もないようなこの女性は、兵隊さんから手当てを受けていましたが、終戦で兵隊さんが引き上げてしまい、いつの間にか息を引き取ってしまったようです。どろどろに腐敗して、死臭もひどいので、シャベルですくい取っています。

内藤 みさを(31 ▶ 61)

Clearing remains with shovels

No one came for this unconscious woman, so soldiers had been taking care of her. But the soldiers were pulled out at the end of the war, and she died at some point. By the time we disposed of the corpse, it was mushy and smelled horrible. We cleared it away with shovels.

Misao Naito (31 ▶ 61)

2-A-◎

69

母と子
Mother and Child

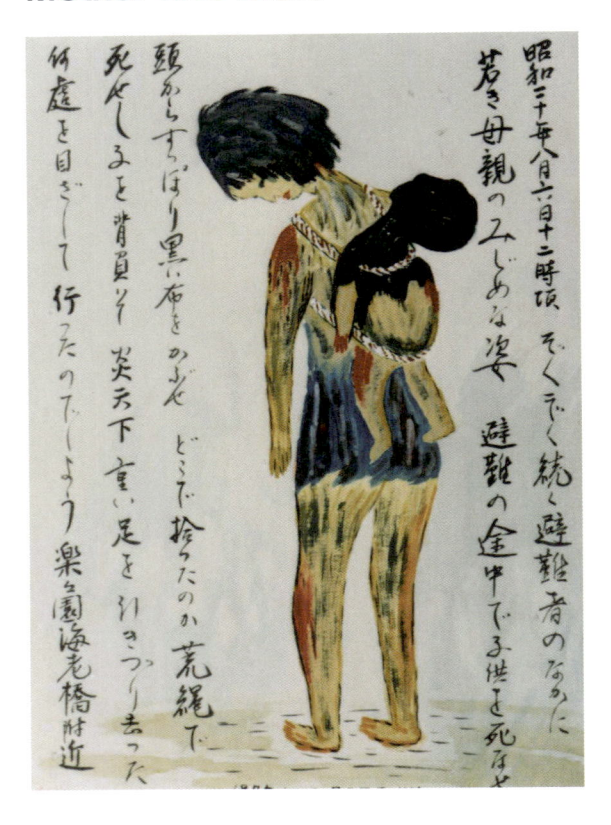

死せし子を背負いて

若き母親は、避難の途中で子供を死なせ、頭からすっぽり黒い布をかぶせ、どこで拾ったのか荒縄で死せし子を背負いて、炎天下、重い足を引きずり去った。どこを目指して行ったのでしょう。

8月6日 正午頃
10km／佐伯郡五日市町海老橋付近
前 カズノ（26 ▶ 56）

Carrying her dead child on her back

The young mother's baby had died as they fled. She had covered it with a black cloth and tied it to her back with a straw rope she found somewhere. She dragged herself along under the scorching sun. I wonder where she was going?

August 6, around noon
10km / near Kairo Bridge in Itsukaichi-cho, Saeki-gun
Kazuno Mae（26 ▶ 56）

2-A

坊やどこどこ

坊やどこどこ。20歳ぐらいの気の狂ったような若い女の方。あちこち血が出て丸裸でした。きれいな目、あいくるしいお母さん、今はいずこに。生きていて幸せであってほしいと祈っています。

8月7日 午前6時頃
1,100m／大手町の電車通り
煙石 二三枝（24 ▶ 54）

"My son, where are you?"

"My son, where are you?" A deranged young woman of around 20 years old. She was completely naked and bleeding here and there. Where is that cute young mother with the beautiful eyes now? I pray that she is alive and happy.

August 7, around 6:00 a.m.
1,100m / streetcar street at Ote-machi
Fumie Enseki（24 ▶ 54）

2-A

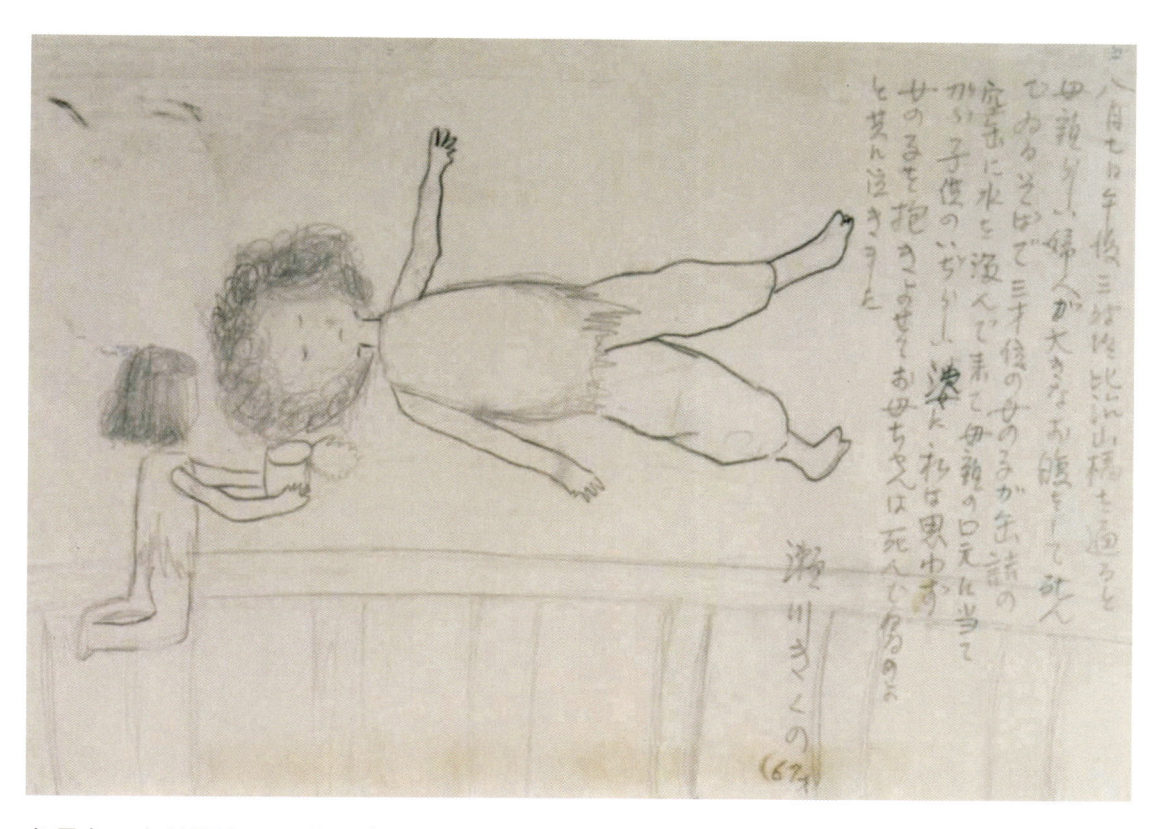

お母ちゃんは死んでいるのよ

3歳ぐらいの女の子が缶詰の空缶に水をくんで来て、母親の口元にあてがう。子供のいじらしい姿に、私は思わず女の子を抱き寄せて「お母ちゃんは死んでいるのよ」と、共に泣きました。

8月7日 午後3時頃
1,710m／比治山橋(8 比治山・仁保)
瀬川 きくの (37 ▶ 66)

"Your mother is dead."

A child of about three had filled an empty can with water and had brought it near her mother's lips. At this piteous sight, I instinctively drew the child into my arms and said, "Your mother is dead." We wept together.

August 7, around 3:00 p.m.
1,710m / Hijiyama Bridge (8 Hijiyama・Niho)
Kikuno Segawa (37 ▶ 66)

1-A

赤ちゃんを抱きかかえたままで

赤ちゃんのはげしい泣き声がするので行ってみましたら、大きな柳の木が立っていました。大木にすがり、お乳を飲ませていたのでしょう。お母さんは、胸をはだけたまま、赤ちゃんをしっかりと抱きかかえて死んでいました。私と母はどうしてあげることもできず、後ろ髪を引かれる思いでそこを離れたのでした。

8月7日
1,650m／鶴見橋付近（8 比治山・仁保）
今中 弘子（20 ▶ 77）

Still holding her child

The sound of a wailing infant drew us to a large willow tree. The woman had probably sought shelter under the tree to nurse her baby. While cradling her child and offering it her breast, she had died. Mother and I did not know what to do. We tore ourselves away from the scene and kept going.

August 7
1,650m / near Tsurumi Bridge（8 Hijiyama・Niho）
Hiroko Imanaka（20 ▶ 77）

2-B

重傷の母に風を送る

重傷の母に風を送る幼女、5歳と3歳ぐらい

8月10日
410m／本川国民学校
（1 平和記念公園・周辺）
進藤 博（33 ▶ 62）

Fanning their seriously injured mother

Two little girls, aged about five and three, fanned their seriously injured mother.

August 10
410m / Honkawa Elementary School
（1 Peace Memorial Park）
Hiroshi Shindo（33 ▶ 62）

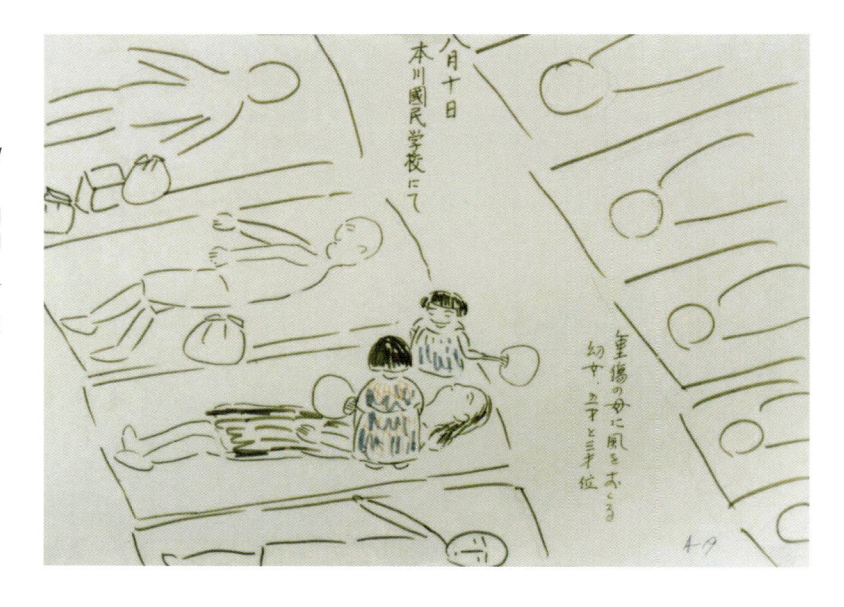

1-A

広島中央放送局前の母と子

我が子を守ろうとした母親の姿は、だれの目にも焼きついていた。中央放送局前にあった真っ黒い親子の死体の絵が10枚描かれており、日時もほぼ一致している。

Mother and child in front of the Hiroshima Central Broadcasting Station

The figures of a mother and the child she tried to protect burned themselves into the eyes of all who saw them. Ten drawings created of the bombing depict a charred mother and child in front of the Central Broadcasting Station. The reported sightings of the two are all close in time.

広島放送局前に来たところ、道路の中央に黒い物体、近づいて見ると黒焦げの女性、よく見ると胸に幼子をだき覆いかぶさる様にして死んでいる母子でした。一瞬母と妹ではないか、家へ急いだ。70m位はなれた我が家、しかしあとかたも無く焼けおちていた。泉邸まで行ってみる。多数の遺体と負傷者、この中に母と妹はいなかった。頭の中をよぎる、母の体形とよく似ていた、確認しよう…。急ぎ場所にもどってみると、すでに遺体は無くあたりを探すも再びその姿に合う事は出来なかった。（広島平和文化センター編『被爆体験記集 国立広島原爆死没者追悼平和祈念館収集分 第39巻』厚生労働省、2003年、69ページから）

8月7日 午前6時30分頃
1,000m／広島中央放送局付近（3 銀山・幟）
安原 義治（17 ▶ 74）

When I passed in front of the Hiroshima Central Broadcasting Station, I saw something black in the center of the road. I approached and saw it was a woman's charred body. I peered closer and saw that she had died covering the body of her infant with her own. I instantly thought it could be my own mother and baby sister, so I rushed to our house about 70 meters ahead. It had burned completely to the ground. I went on to the Sentei Garden, where I saw many corpses and wounded people, but not my mother and sister. I thought of the corpses on the road — the woman was about the size of my mother. I had to go back and check closely. But when I hurried to the spot, the bodies were gone. I searched the area but never found them. (Taken from *A-bomb Memoirs collected by Hiroshima National Peace Memorial Hall for the Atomic Bomb Victims*, Vol. 39, edited by Hiroshima Peace Culture Foundation, published by Ministry of Health, Labour and Welfare; 2003, page 69)

August 7, around 6:30 a.m.
1,000m / near the Hiroshima Central Broadcasting Station （3 Kanayama・Nobori）
Yoshiharu Yasuhara （17 ▶ 74）

3-B

真っ黒焦げになったまぎれもない母子の姿であった。

8月6日 午後5時過ぎ
1,000m／広島中央放送局前
（3 銀山・幟）
井野上 忠夫（35 ▶ 64）

They were burned black, but obviously a mother and her child.

August 6, just after 5:00 p.m.
1,000m / in front of the Hiroshima Central Broadcasting Station
(3 Kanayama・Nobori)
Tadao Inoue (35 ▶ 64)

1-A

お母さんがピカの瞬間、わが子を守るため伏せられたのだと思いました。母の愛の偉大さが天に通じてか、一昼夜にならんとするに二人とも真っ黒のままでくずれていませんでした。涙が出ました。手を合わせました。

8月7日 午前8時頃
1,000m／上流川町の広島中央放送局前の道路
（3 銀山・幟）
植田 貢（34 ▶ 91）

It seemed to me that in the instant of the flash the mother had thrown herself over the infant to protect it. Though burned to char, these two remained intact all day and through the night, as if the power of a mother's love had moved heaven to preserve them in this position. Tears came. I put my hands together in prayer.

August 7, around 8:00 a.m.
1,000m / on the road in front of the Hiroshima Central Broadcasting Station in Kami-nagarekawa-cho (3 Kanayama・Nobori)
Mitsugu Ueda (34 ▶ 91)

1-B

私は異様なものを見てギョッとした。近づいて見ると、赤ちゃんをしっかり両手に抱いた女性らしき真っ黒焦げの片足を上げた走る姿のままの死体。

8月7日 午前8時頃
1,000m／広島中央放送局前の路上（3 銀山・幟）
山縣 康子（17 ▶ 46）

I gasped at a strange sight and approached for a better look. The corpse of a woman cradling her baby, both charred completely black, while the woman remained in running position, one leg raised.

August 7, around 8:00 a.m.
1,000m / on the road in front of the Hiroshima Central Broadcasting Station (3 Kanayama・Nobori)
Yasuko Yamagata (17 ▶ 46)

2-A

第 2 章 きずな

親子ともに黒こげになり、男女の区別もつきませんでした。

8月7日 午前9時頃
1,000m／広島中央放送局付近（3 銀山・幟）
谷本 初登（41 ▶ 71）

Both parent and child were so charred I could not even tell the gender.

August 7, around 9:00 a.m.
1,000m / near the Hiroshima Central Broadcasting Station (3 Kanayama・Nobori)
Hatsuto Tanimoto (41 ▶ 71)

1-A

黒いものがあり、近づいて見ると、幼児を左腕に抱えた母親の遺体だった。

8月7日 午前10時頃
1,000m／広島中央放送局前（3 銀山・幟）
北村 弘（14 ▶ 71）

At the sight of something black, I came closer and saw that it was a mother holding her baby under her left arm.

August 7, around 10:00 a.m.
1,000m / in front of the Hiroshima Central Broadcasting Station (3 Kanayama・Nobori)
Hiroshi Kitamura (14 ▶ 71)

2-B

赤ちゃんを抱えて逃げ遅れたのでしょうか。髪は逆立ち、赤ちゃんを胸の下にかばい、生きている人のよう。目をかっと開き、そのものすごさ、今でも忘れることができません。

8月7日 朝
1,000m／広島中央放送局前（3 銀山・幟）
田口 光子（30 ▶ 60）

Carrying her child, she had probably been unable to outrun the flames. Her hair was standing on end. She still protected her child under her breast, like a living person. Her eyes were open wide. I cannot forget that shocking sight.

August 7, morning
1,000m / in front of the Hiroshima Central Broadcasting Station (3 Kanayama・Nobori)
Mitsuko Taguchi (30 ▶ 60)

2-A

75

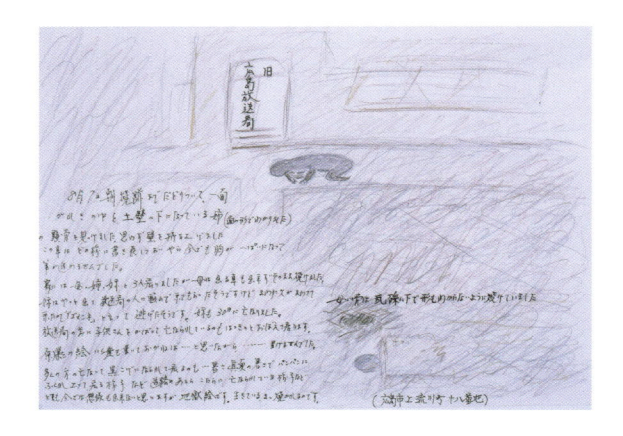

子供さんをかばって亡くなられているのも、はっきりとおぼえております。

8月7日 朝
1,000m ／広島中央放送局前（3 銀山・幟）
波多野 ヤエ子（19 ▶ 76）

I clearly remember the sight of that mother who died protecting her child.

August 7, morning
1,000m / in front of the Hiroshima Central Broadcasting Station (3 Kanayama・Nobori)
Yaeko Hatano (19 ▶ 76)

1-B

死体は蒸し焼きの状態で、頭髪は縮れたままになっていた。

8月7日
1,000m ／広島中央放送局前（3 銀山・幟）
佐々 和英（29 ▶ 58）

The corpse appeared to have been steamed, her hair singed crinkly.

August 7
1,000m / in front of the Hiroshima Central Broadcasting Station (3 Kanayama・Nobori)
Kazuhide Sasa (29 ▶ 58)

1-A

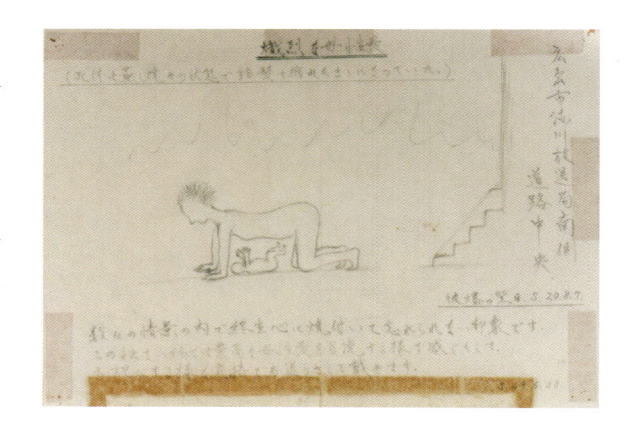

乳のみ児の上におおいかぶさったまま焼死

8月7日
鉄砲町路上（3 銀山・幟）
中野 王吉（34 ▶ 63）

She burned to death while crouching protectively over her suckling child.

August 7
On the road in Teppo-cho (3 Kanayama・Nobori)
Okichi Nakano (34 ▶ 63)

1-A

Emotions Carried by the Brush

Akiko Naono

A-bomb drawings by survivors (hereinafter, "A-bomb drawings") have the power to shock and capture those who view them.[1] Wherever these pictures are shown in Japan and around the world, viewers can be seen gasping, staring intensely, or fighting tears. Some of the drawings are crudely executed, but even these can shock those who encounter them.

Families trapped under collapsed houses, flames bearing down. Victims burned from head to toe, their skin slipping off as they stagger out of the city. Persons near death begging for water. Corpses filling a river. Piles of corpses doused with oil for cremation. A-bomb drawings portray the devastation and death that nuclear weapons wreak. Could such things really have happened? The drawings stop people in their tracks and make them think.

A few winters back, I felt drawn to A-bomb drawings. I spent several months commuting to the basement of the Peace Memorial Museum to record the 2,200-plus drawings that had been sent in response to the first call. I took a photo of each one with a digital camera, printed it, developed a database, and visited about 60 of the artists.[2]

Continuously encountering memories of A-bomb experiences takes considerable physical and emotional energy. Sometimes the content is so brutal and horrific that my chest seizes up. Because A-bomb drawings visually render scenes recalled from immediately after the bombing, they etch themselves into *our* brains as well. We experience the scene vicariously. As I gazed time and again at over the 2,000 images, some began to appear in my dreams. Sometimes I was the one trapped in the flames. Occasionally I felt disoriented, pursued by the stench of death, even though I only encountered the calamity indirectly through the drawings and words of the artists.

それでも私には、逃げ出すという選択肢がある。しかし、ヒロシマに居合わせてしまった人たちは、忘れたいと願ったところで、「生き地獄」の記憶が身体に刻み込まれている。段原国民学校で校舎の下敷になった子どもたちを描いた松村智恵子さん(p.33)は、あの日から30年経っても〈「先生助けてー」その声が今も耳元にきこえてたまらない気持ち〉になると絵中に綴った。観音橋のたもとの火葬場面を絵にした人(匿名、p.109)は、この〈想い出したくない光景〉が、被爆から60年近くの月日が流れてもなお〈時折の夢に出て〉くるという。

　爆心地から700メートルの地点で被爆した原田知恵さん(p.26)も、その直後を表した絵を描きながら、当時を〈まざまざと思いおこし〉た。しかし、それほどの記憶も〈30年間のめまぐるしい社会の変貌〉の中でぼかされて、描ききれないもどかしさを感じたという。被爆の記憶は、「凍りついた記憶」と「薄れゆく記憶」という、相反する2つの方向へと引き裂かれるのだ。時の流れが生々しさを和らげはしただろう。しかし、刻み込まれた「地獄絵」の記憶を消し去ることができたわけではない。30年を経ても〈血のにおい〉が湧いてくるのだから。記憶が薄れたからという面もあろうが、それ以上に、いまだ内に抱える「地獄絵」を表現する術がないため、絵の中に〈うめ様もない空間〉を残すことになる。記憶が焼きついていたとしても、表現できるとは限らないのだ。

　「こんなもんじゃなかった」と描ききれない歯がゆさを感じるだけではない。あの日の記憶と向き合うことは、身を切られるような痛みを引き起こす。筆を取ろうとしてはやめ、ようやく1枚描きあげた人は少なくない。菅葉子さん(p.24)が絵を描こうと思い立ったのは、第1回募集が始まった1974年だったが、完成したのは翌年だった。〈昨年は画を出そうかとは思いましたが、書いているうちに様々なあらゆる場面が鮮明に脳裏に再現し、被爆死した父のこと、大怪我とやけどをした今は亡き母のこと、友人達と、胸がしめつけられる程につらくなるので昨年は見送りました〉と絵の裏にある。絵を破り捨ててしまった人さえいる。原爆に遭った人たちの大部分は、体験を語る

Of course, I can will myself out of that "living hell," but for those who actually went through it, the memories are imprinted in their bodies, however intensely they wish otherwise. Chieko Matsumura, who drew a picture of children trapped under the collapsed Dambara Elementary School (p. 33), wrote in her drawing that 30 years later "I can still hear them crying, 'Teacher, help!'" The artist who drew the picture of the crematorium at the foot of Kan-on Bridge (anonymous, p. 109) tells us that 60 years after the bombing, "This hated memory still appears in my dreams."

As she created her drawing of a scene that took place immediately after the bombing, Chie Harada (p. 26), who was exposed 700 m from the hypocenter, "relived the moment vividly." However, she reports that "the dizzying societal changes in the 30 intervening years" had so faded even her stark memory that she was frustrated by her inability to recall the scene clearly. Two opposing forces work on A-bomb memories: freezing and withering. Though the passage of time blunts their clarity, the memory of experiencing that "hell" never dies. Thirty years later, Harada still "smelled the blood." More is at work here than fading memory. Because no available means of representation can depict that "hell," the drawings inevitably expose "an unbridgeable chasm." Having a memory branded in one's mind does not mean that it is representable.

Many survivors felt intense frustration that their drawings simply don't get their experiences across. Furthermore, the act of drawing forced the artists to face their painful memories. Many picked up the brush and put it down many times before they could finish a single drawing.

The first drawing campaign moved Yoko Suga (p. 24) to start a drawing in 1974, but she could not complete it until the following year. On the back of her drawing she wrote, "I wanted to do this drawing last year, but as I drew, all sorts of scenes reappeared so vividly in my mind—my father, who died in the bombing; my mother, who was badly burned and died later; and my friends. I felt as if my heart were breaking so I decided to put it off." Some people even tore up their drawings and threw

ことなく沈黙したまま逝った。にもかかわらず、1,200人をも超える人たちが絵を届けたのはなぜだろうか。

　アメリカが広島に落とした原爆は、十数万もの老若男女を殺戮し、「モノとしての死」を強いた。しかし絵の作者たちは、無残に殺された人たちをモノとして見たわけでも描いたわけでもない。伝えようとしたのは原爆の残虐性ばかりではないのだ。

　小野木明さん(p.107)は、水を求めて防火用水の中や周りで死んだ人たちに、赤い絵の具を塗るにあたって心が痛んだという。小野木さんと同じく死者を悼む気持ちから、鉛筆で下書きした絵に、忍びないと血の色を塗らなかった作者もいる。救護所を埋め尽くす負傷者の呻き声を、60年近くたっても忘れられないという桃井完二さん(p.91)は、その場の状況をありのまま描くことはできなかった。絵の中には〈もっと悲惨だったが、私の絵筆はすすまなかった〉とある。〈ただただ、鎮魂の祈りをこめて〉桃井さんは筆を進めた。

　平川壽子さん(p.91)も「供養のひとつにでもなれば」と絵筆を握った。女学生だった当時、看護活動にあたった救護所での一場面だ。「毛布をかけた絵にしましたのは、傷あといっぱいウジもわいてたし、暑いときだからなんにもかけない人もいたし、下着やなんかは着てらっしゃるけど上の方は裸んぼうでしょう。それへもって、ウジがわいたりしたのは何となくかわいそうだから、皆ちょっと見えないようにしたげて、絵だけでもせめてね。あんまり辛いのは、あれだからと思ってね」。平川さんは、救護所で横たわる負傷者1人ひとりに、実際にはその場になかった毛布を絵の中でかけてあげた。

　材木のように重ねて置かれた学徒たちの遺体。幼いわが子をその手で火葬せざるを得なかった父親。亡くなった子どもの遺骨さえ胸に抱くことができなかった母親。親を求めながら死んでいった子どもたち……。この上ない悲惨に胸が詰まる。しかし、「原爆の絵」は、惨状をそのまま写し出しているわけではない。

絵筆に込められた想い

them away. After all, most people who experienced the bombing died without ever talking about it. So why did over 1,200 people take up the brush?

The bomb the US dropped on Hiroshima indiscriminately slaughtered hundreds of thousands—the old, the young, male and female—destroying them like objects. But to those who drew the drawings, the cruelly slain victims were not objects. Thus, they had more to express than the cruelty of the atomic bombing. For example, Akira Onogi (p. 107) reported that he found it painful to paint red pigment on the bodies of those whose lives ended seeking water in and around fire cisterns. The desire to honor the dead halted the hands of many as they tried to brush the color of blood into their sketches. Haunted by the groans of injured people packed into a relief station, Kanji Momoi (p. 91), found himself unable to portray the scene as he remembered it. On his drawing he wrote, "The reality was far more dreadful, but I could not bear to draw exactly what I saw. The brush would not move." Only by "ceaselessly praying for the souls of the victims" did he manage to get the brush going.

Similarly, Toshiko Hirakawa (p. 91) painted her picture as a way to comfort the victims. The drawing was a scene from the relief station to which her school had assigned her. "I covered the people in the picture with blankets. Actually, maggots were breeding in their wounds. It was hot and many had nothing on them at all. Some wore underwear or something, but their upper bodies were bare. And on top of it all, maggots were crawling all over them. I felt so sorry I just had to cover them up. I could not bear to draw such cruel scenes the way they were."

Thus, Hirakawa gave each of the victims lying on the floor of the relief station a blanket that never covered them in real life.

Corpses of students stacked on each other like lumber. A father who had to cremate his daughter with his own hands. A mother who could not clasp the bones of her dead child to her chest. Children who died calling for their parents. What could be more heartbreaking than these scenes? But people did not create these A-bomb

瀬川きくのさんの絵 (p.71) は、息絶えた母親に水を飲ませようとしている幼い女の子の姿を通して、原爆がもたらした「人間的悲惨」を描いており、見るものの胸を締めつける。だがそれだけではない。この場面を残すことによって、瀬川さんは、死んだ母親をなんとか生き返らせようとする幼い女の子に寄り添いながら、奪われた命と断ち切られた絆を取り戻そうとしているのだ。瀬川さんの他にも、原爆によって引き裂かれた親子が、せめてあの世でだけでも再びめぐり会えるようにとの願いを絵に込めた作者たちがいる。

100枚以上の「原爆の絵」には、〈合掌〉〈合掌念仏〉など死者を慰める言葉が添えられている。「生き地獄」の記憶に苛まれながらも多くの人が筆を取ったのは、人として死ぬことさえも許されず、弔ってくれる家族や仲間さえも奪われた死者たちが、たしかに生きていたという証しを刻み、その魂を慰めようとしたからだろう。「モノとしての死」を強いられた人たちが安らかに眠れるようにとの想いを、絵筆に込めているのだ。自らの「心の傷」を癒すために、生き残った「うしろめたさ」から解き放たれることを目的として絵を描いたわけではない。死んだ人が生き返ることはありえない。それでも絵の作者たちは、原爆がもたらした破壊と「むごい死」から死者を救い出そうとする。私はそこに、生き残った人たちが、静かに原爆と対峙する姿をみる。

1) 筆者が現在まで第1回募集時の絵について調査研究してきたため、本稿は主にそれらの絵を通しての考察となる。
2) 作者たちが絵筆に込めた想いについては、拙著『「原爆の絵」と出会う』岩波書店、2004年を参照。

drawings only to express the cruelty of the bomb.

Kikuno Segawa (p.71) conveyed the "human tragedy" of the atomic bombing by depicting a small girl trying to get her dead mother to drink water. The image certainly smites the hearts of viewers, but it does more. In leaving this scene to posterity through her drawing, Segawa wanted to give meaning to the girl's attempt to bring her mother back to life and to reunite the two. Segawa was one of many who painted with the hope that parents and children torn apart by the atomic bombing would reunite in the next world.

More than 100 pictures contain "*Gassho*" (hands together in prayer) or "*Gassho nembutsu*" (prayer to Buddha), common expressions used to console the dead. Pained by memories of the "living hell," many *hibakusha* took up the brush to comfort the souls of those who were forced to die as "objects" and robbed of family and friends to mourn their deaths. They wanted to bring to life those killed by reasserting their individuality and the social relations the bomb had taken away. The purpose was not to heal the artists' own emotional wounds or relieve "survivor's guilt." The artists' brushes carried the hope that those forced to "die like objects" might sleep peacefully. The dead would never come back. And yet, the artists who created these drawings were trying to lift the dead out of the ruins and alleviate their cruel suffering. In doing so, these survivors quietly defied the atomic bombing.

1. Because I have been analyzing the A-bomb drawings submitted in response to the first call, the insights in this paper are based primarily on those drawings.
2. I have presented the artists' feelings and thoughts about their drawings in *Encountering A-bomb Drawings by Survivors* [Iwanami Booklet No. 627].

第 3 章
Chapter 3

いのち
Life

人類史上初めて投下された原子爆弾は、
人々を焼き殺し、人間と社会を否定した。
罪のない命が奪われ、人々の耐え難い苦痛と恐怖は極限に達した。
空の一点を見つめたまま硬直した遺体、ハエとウジに襲われた負傷者、
倒れた建物から子どもを助けることができなかった無念な気持ち……。
傷つき、悲しみに暮れ、死におびえながらも、
人々は生きなければならなかった。

The first atomic bombing in history burned and destroyed human beings,
utterly negating human life and society.
Amid the robbing of innocent lives, suffering and terror reached their extremes.
A rigid corpse staring fixedly at a point in the sky, injured persons covered by flies and maggots,
the painful frustration of failing to save a child from burning up in a collapsed house.
Injuries, profound grief, the fear of lingering death—people had to overcome these to survive.

助けて
Help!

わずかにうごめく

全身黒こげ、性別すら分からず、それでもわずかにうごめく。とても正視できずすぐ目をそらしたが、その姿は一生、私の脳裏からはなれ得ぬものとなった。

8月6日 午前
3,600m／広島第一陸軍病院江波分院前（10 吉島・舟入・観音）
山科 兼規（16 ▶ 72）

Weakly writhing

The whole body was so deeply charred that the gender was unrecognizable — yet the person was weakly writhing. I had to avert my eyes from the unbearable sight, but it entrenched itself in my memory for the rest of my life.

August 6, morning
3,600m / in front of the Hiroshima First Army Hospital, Eba Branch（10 Yoshijima・Funairi・Kan-on）
Tomomi Yamashina（16 ▶ 72）

1-B

第 3 章　いのち

目玉を右手にのせて

あの黒い雨の降る中に、丸裸の男の人が飛び出た目の玉を右手のはらにのせて、さも痛そうに立っておられるさまを見ました。実に驚きましたが、私では何とも致しようがなかったのです。

8月6日 午前9時30分頃
1,500m／中広町
(6 十日市・中広)
西田 謹造(50 ▶ 79)

Resting his eyeball on his right hand

Standing there was a naked man being pelted by black rain while he rested his popped-out eyeball on his right hand. He seemed to be in great pain. I was astonished but could do nothing to help him.

August 6, around 9:30 a.m.
1,500m / Nakahiro-machi
(6 Tokaichi・Nakahiro)
Kinzo Nishida (50 ▶ 79)

2-A-◎

耐えられない痛み

中年の女性が「殺してくれ」と大声で叫びながら苦しんでいた。頭を大けがしたのか、髪と顔は血のりがべっとりついていた。苦しい時は「助けてくれ」と言うが、「殺してくれ」と叫ぶのはよほど痛くて苦しかったのでしょう。

8月6日 午前9時頃
2,000m／県立広島工業学校入口
(5 国泰寺・千田)
西岡 誠吾(13 ▶ 70)

Pain beyond endurance

A middle-aged woman in terrible pain was screaming, "Kill me!" She must have had a serious head injury, because her hair and face were a mass of blood. Considering that most suffering people call for help, imagine the pain that would make a person scream, "Kill me!"

August 6, around 9:00 a.m.
2,000m / entrance to Hiroshima Prefectural Technical School
(5 Kokutaiji・Senda)
Seigo Nishioka (13 ▶ 70)

1-B

83

姉ちゃん助かるかね

妹の顔は、まるで地獄から鬼がとび出して来たようでした。十数カ所の傷口からは出つくしたというように、顔にはベットリと血のりがこびりつき、あまりのことに声も出ませんでした。それでもかすかに「姉ちゃん助かるかね」と一言。その声が今でも耳の底に残っています。

8月6日 午前10時過ぎ
3,400m／大内越峠下（7 牛田・広島駅周辺）
三浦 静子（28 ▶ 85）

"Sister, will I make it?"

My little sister's face was like that of a demon that had leapt from hell. Blood oozing from at least ten gashes was caked over her face. I was too shocked to speak, but she managed to faintly ask me, "Sister, will I make it?" I still hear that voice.

August 6, just after 10:00 a.m.
3,400m / foot of Ochigo Pass (7 Ushita・Hiroshima Station)
Shizuko Miura（28 ▶ 85）

2-B

棒が突き立ったまま

廿日市国民学校の校舎にケガ人を収容していたので、広島でヤケドをした何百という人が校門を入っていく。太さ3センチくらいの杭のような棒が、顔の真ん中、目の辺りに突き立ったままのまっ黒になった女の人が、トラックからおりて、よろよろと学校に入っていった。

8月6日 午後
11.7km／廿日市国民学校
林 隆（15 ▶ 72）

A stake stuck in her face

Hatsukaichi Elementary School was taking the injured in, so hundreds of people burned in Hiroshima went through the front gate. A blackened woman with a stake about three centimeters wide sticking into the middle of her face between the eyes got off a truck and staggered into the school building.

August 6, afternoon
11.7km / Hatsukaichi Elementary School
Takashi Hayashi（15 ▶ 72）

2-B

第3章 いのち

班長殿、水をください

一人の兵士が身を起こし「班長殿、水をください。」としきりに叫びます。血に染まった顔ははれ、目は見えぬようです。倒れた兵士たちにまじって頭の毛が茶色で体がひときわ大きい人がいます。裸で後ろ手にされています。外国人に違いありません。

8月7日 午前8時30分頃
980m／広島城入口付近
（4 基町・白島）
森 孝人（22 ▶ 79）

"Captain! Water, please!"

One soldier sat up and shouted, "Captain! Water, please!" His blood-soaked face was so swollen he evidently could not see. Among the fallen soldiers was one larger than the rest. The naked man had brown hair, and his hands were tied behind his back. He was definitely a foreigner.

August 7, around 8:30 a.m.
980m / near the entrance to Hiroshima Castle (4 Moto-machi・Hakushima)
Takahito Mori（22 ▶ 79）

2-B

私をじぃーと見ていました

老若男女を問わずトラックの荷台に山盛りになった状況で、顔や腕、手、足が血だらけの被爆者の方々が、苦しそうな痛そうな姿で私をじぃーと見ていました。

8月7日
11km／可部線梅林踏切付近
浅野 光彦（4 ▶ 61）

They stared at me.

They were jumbled up together on the truck — male, female, the old, and the young. Their faces, arms, hands, and legs were bloody. They stared at me with expressions of pain.

August 7
11km / near the Bairin railroad crossing on the Kabe Line
Mitsuhiko Asano（4 ▶ 61）

1-B

救助する
Rescuing the Injured

水を飲ませる

医師の姿はない。外科、内科、薬局へと行ってみたが、ガーゼ1枚も取り出せず。一度外に出てやっと樋(とい)の角を見つけました。守衛室の水道の水がちょぼちょぼ出ているのを見つけ、水を何回となく運びました。

8月6日 午前9時から10時頃
1,500m／広島赤十字病院玄関広場(5 国泰寺・千田)
池庄司 トミ子 (17 ▶ 47)

Giving them water

I saw no doctors anywhere. I went around to the surgical and internal medicine departments and the pharmacy, but could not lay my hands on a single piece of gauze. One time I made it outside and found a roof gutter corner piece. The faucet at the security station was dripping, so I filled the gutter piece and made countless trips, carrying water to the patients.

August 6, around 9:00-10:00 a.m.
1,500m / entrance to and open area in front of Hiroshima Red Cross Hospital (5 Kokutaiji・Senda)
Tomiko Ikeshoji (17 ▶ 47)

2-A

第3章　いのち

三日三晩飲まず食わずの救護活動

軍医部に採用されてわずか2カ月で、「原爆」を受けたのです。三日三晩飲まず食わずの救護活動でした。

3,800m／陸軍教育船舶団司令部
(8 比治山・仁保)
服部 道子（16 ▶ 73）

Rescuing victims for three days and nights without food or drink

Only two months after I joined the Army Medical Division, the atomic bomb fell. For three days and nights, I rescued victims without food or drink.

3,800m / Army Educational Shipping Command
(8 Hijiyama・Niho)
Michiko Hattori (16 ▶ 73)

2-B

応急手当が始まる

応急手当の治療が開始される時の、集まって来られた方々の様子です。

8月6日 午後2時頃
1,500m／広島赤十字病院（5 国泰寺・千田）
小川 ヨシコ（19 ▶ 76）

First-aid treatment began.

When first-aid treatment began, this is what the crowd that had gathered looked like.

August 6, around 2:00 p.m.
1,500m / Hiroshima Red Cross Hospital (5 Kokutaiji・Senda)
Yoshiko Ogawa (19 ▶ 76)

1-B

まん幕をほうたいがわりに

約1キロの川ぞいの道に1,000人はいるかと思われる。避難してきた人のほとんどが半死半生の状態。紅白のまん幕をほうたいがわりに使い、食用油をやけどにぬって手当てをし、備蓄米をにぎりめしにしてたき出した。

8月6日 午後
2,000m／県立広島工業学校前
（5 国泰寺・千田）
若井 澈（39 ▶ 68）

Using ceremonial curtains for bandages

It looked like about 1,000 people laid out on a one-kilometer stretch of the river. Most of the people who had fled to this spot looked half dead. We used red and white ceremonial curtains for bandages and applied cooking oil to the burns. The neighbors made rice balls for the victims with their spare rice.

August 6, afternoon
2,000m / in front of Hiroshima Prefectural Technical School
（5 Kokutaiji・Senda）
Kiyoshi Wakai（39 ▶ 68）

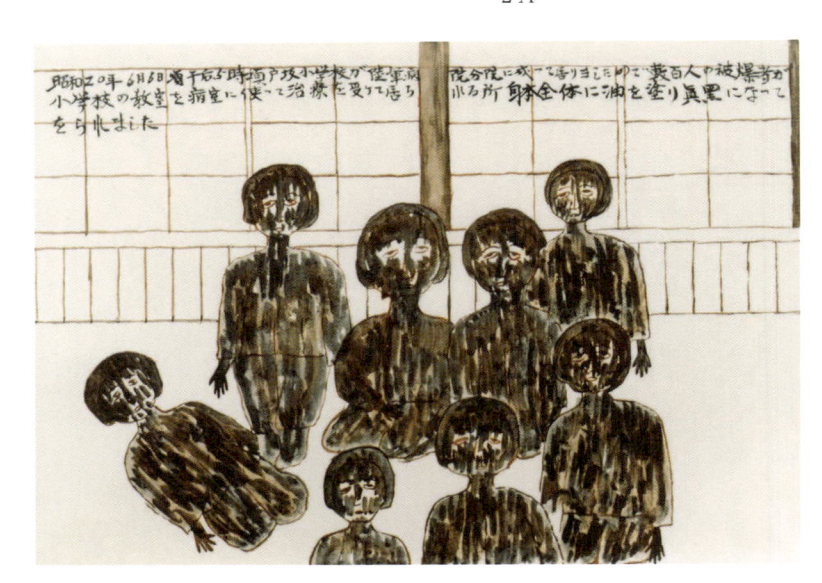

2-A

臨時救護所　Emergency relief stations

被爆当日は、橋のたもとや河原、学校など負傷者が集まった場所がそのまま臨時の救護所となった。その数は市内・郊外合わせて53か所に上り、10月5日までに収容された負傷者は約10万6,000人、外来治療を受けた負傷者は延べ約21万人に達した。

On the day of the bombing, the feet of bridges, riverbeds, schools, and other places where the injured gathered became relief stations. A total of 53 operated in the city and its suburbs. By October 5, the total number of injured people taken into relief stations stood at roughly 106,000, while those receiving outpatient care were roughly 210,000.

真っ黒になった被爆者

数百人の被爆者が国民学校の教室を病室に使って治療を受けておられるところ。体全体に油を塗り、真っ黒になっておられました。

8月6日 午後5時頃
5,100m／戸坂国民学校
平田 德與（36 ▶ 67）

Totally blackened *hibakusha*

Several hundred *hibakusha* were receiving treatment in the classrooms of an elementary school. The oil applied to their whole bodies turned them completely black.

August 6, around 5:00 p.m.
5,100m / Hesaka Elementary School
Tokuyo Hirata（36 ▶ 67）

2-A

第3章　いのち

電車通りの救護所

やけど、裂傷の方がほとんどで、瀕死(ひんし)の重傷でした。日を重ねるにつれ、多くの人が亡くなられ、また身内に引き取られる方もありました。しかし、収容人員が減ることはなく、兵隊さんがどこからか担架で運んでこられ、常に200人ぐらいはおられました。

8月9日から14日
1,200m／神崎国民学校前の電車通り（10 吉島・舟入・観音）
山岡 文子（18 ▶ 47）

Relief station on the streetcar street

Most of the people were near death from their burns and wounds. As the days went by, they died. Some were taken away by their families. And yet, the number of patients never decreased — soldiers continued to carry them in on stretchers from somewhere, maintaining a constant number of around 200.

August 9-14
1,200m / streetcar street in front of Kanzaki Elementary School (10 Yoshijima・Funairi・Kan-on)
Fumiko Yamaoka (18 ▶ 47)

1-A

地獄のような国民学校

被災者の列、死者の山。「アツイアツイ」と、水を求めて力尽きて死んでいった人が多かった。汚物もたれ流しで、異様なにおいが市内をただよった。

8月6日
3,150m ／大河国民学校校庭（8 比治山・仁保）
高田 滿（13 ▶ 43）

An elementary school like a scene from hell

The injured stood in rows, the dead lay in piles. Many cried, "I'm hot! I'm hot!" They pled for water until their strength gave out and they died. Waste ran out of their bodies, emanating a terrible stench throughout the city.

August 6
3,150m / schoolyard of Oko Elementary School（8 Hijiyama・Niho）
Mitsuru Takata（13 ▶ 43）

2-A

第3章 いのち

被爆者のうめき

国民学校は被爆者でいっぱいであった。教室でのこの方々の姿。そのうめきは今も忘れられない。

8月7日 朝
3,050m／己斐国民学校裁縫室
（11 己斐・草津）
桃井 完二（17 ▶ 74）

Groans of the suffering

Victims filled the elementary school. This is how they looked in the classrooms. I cannot forget the groaning.

August 7, morning
3,050m / sewing classroom of Koi Elementary School
（11 Koi・Kusatsu）
Kanji Momoi（17 ▶ 74）

2-B

どうする力もなく

教室の板の間に軍隊用の毛布をしき、その上に休んでおられ、中には体の所々にウジがわいたりハエがとまっていてもどうする力もなく弱っておられた方もある。

8月18日か19日頃
4,800m／草津国民学校（11 己斐・草津）
平川 壽子（14 ▶ 43）

Too weak to do anything

The victims rested on army blankets laid on the wooden floors of the classrooms. Some were too weak to do anything about the maggots breeding or the flies alighting on their wounds.

Around August 18 or 19
4,800m / Kusatsu Elementary School（11 Koi・Kusatsu）
Toshiko Hirakawa（14 ▶ 43）

1-A

竹やぶの救護所

親戚の家の後片付けに行く祖父母について入市し、しばらく市内に通って、祖父に教えてもらいながら原爆の惨状を見た。

8月20日頃
三滝町（12 三篠・祇園）
小尻 勉（4 ▶ 60）

Relief station in a bamboo grove

I went to Hiroshima with my grandparents to clean up their relatives' house. For some days I saw the devastation with my grandfather telling me what was going on.

Around August 20
Mitaki-machi（12 Misasa・Gion）
Tsutomu Kojiri（4 ▶ 60）

1-C

ムスビを配る

家族を尋ねて入市する人、街を逃げ出す人にムスビを配る兵たち

8月7日 早朝
1,390m ／住吉橋西詰（10 吉島・舟入・観音）
原 美味（26 ▶ 82）

Passing out rice balls

Soldiers passed out rice balls to people entering the city to find their family members, as well as those fleeing the city.

August 7, early morning
1,390m / west end of Sumiyoshi Bridge
（10 Yoshijima・Funairi・Kan-on）
Yoshimi Hara（26 ▶ 82）

1-C

似島
Ninoshima Island

広島市の沖合約 4 キロメートルに位置する小島。似島には日清戦争が終わると、中国大陸からの帰還兵のための検疫所が設けられた。似島は原爆による建物の被害がほとんどなかったため、投下直後から、検疫所は負傷者のための臨時野戦病院となった。8 月 6 日から 25 日までの 20 日間に約 1 万人を受け入れたと推定されている。負傷者は被爆当日から次々と亡くなり、死体は、検疫所やその周辺で火葬された。しかし、あまりの多さに火葬が間に合わず、防空ごうなどに埋葬された死体もあった。

This small island was located roughly four kilometers offshore of Hiroshima City. After the Sino-Japanese War of 1894-95, a quarantine station was set up on Ninoshima for soldiers returning from the Chinese continent. Because the buildings on Ninoshima were largely unaffected by the bombing, the quarantine station was immediately turned into an emergency field hospital for the wounded. In the 20 days between August 6 and August 25, the hospital admitted an estimated 10,000 persons. The wounded died and were cremated in a steady stream in and around the quarantine station. When the number of corpses overwhelmed those assigned to cremate them, they were buried in air-raid shelters and other places.

似島臨時救護所へ

宇品桟橋へ負傷者がトラックに積まれて運ばれてくる。似島の臨時救護所へ船で運ぶのだが、桟橋へ着いた者の大部分が息絶えていて、見る見る死体の山が築かれる。船に乗せられた者は、まだ息のあるもので、助かる見込みのある人たちだ。

4,700m ／広島港（9 皆実・宇品）
清水 正明（27 ▶ 84）

Bound for the Ninoshima Emergency Relief Station

Victims were packed onto trucks and brought to the piers at Ujina. Though they were bound for the Ninoshima Emergency Relief Station, most died before they reached the piers. The piles of corpses grew as I watched. The ones carried onto the boats still had breath, some chance of survival.

4,700m / Hiroshima Port（9 Minami・Ujina）
Masaaki Shimizu（27 ▶ 84）

2-B

船尾にえい航される人

船尾よりたらしたロープに体を縛り付けて、水面下をえい航されてきた人もありました。陸揚げする時は死んでいました。出発時から死んでいたか、満員のためにそうされたのか、自身でロープを縛りえい航してもらっている間に死んだのか、どちらかは知りません。

8月6日 投下30分後
10km／似島桟橋
福井 巌（29 ▶ 58）

People towed by boat ropes

Bodies were tied to ropes bound to boat sterns and towed through the water. They were dead when we heaved them out of the water. I don't know if they were dead from the start or towed because the boat was full, or initially grabbed the rope but died along the way.

August 6, 30 minutes after the bombing
10km / Ninoshima pier
Iwao Fukui（29 ▶ 58）

2-A

ぞくぞく被災者が上陸する

広島から似島へ船でぞくぞく被災者が上陸する。

8月6日
10km／似島桟橋
内山 兼武（33 ▶ 63）

Victims landing in a never-ending stream

One after another came the boats carrying victims from Hiroshima to Ninoshima Island.

August 6
10km / Ninoshima pier
Kanetake Uchiyama（33 ▶ 63）

1-A

第3章 いのち

赤鬼のような被爆者たち

次々と死んでいく人を運びきれず、コモをかけておく。やけどの油薬が不足しているので、初めは白の油薬を、次は赤チンを付け、赤鬼のような被爆者たち。

8月7日
10km／似島検疫所
景山 美八重（34 ▶ 64）

Hibakusha with faces like red demons

So many were dying, they could not all be carried out right away. Straw mats were laid on the corpses. When they ran out of burn medicine, the relief workers applied white ointment, then mercurochrome, which made them look like demons.

August 7
10km / Ninoshima Quarantine Station
Miyae Kageyama（34 ▶ 64）

2-A

あふれる負傷者、山積みの死体

仮収容所として、10棟の兵舎にあふれるほど横たわり、「父さん、母さん」と言って泣いている者、「水を」と叫ぶ者、痛みを訴える者、死体となっている者。中庭には死体の山積み。続けざまに死体を運んで焼くところ。

8月10日
10km／似島検疫所
加川 博美（43 ▶ 73）

Overflowing with the injured, piles of the dead

The ten or so army barracks that had been turned into relief stations were overflowing with people lying on the floor crying, "Father, Mother!" or screaming, "Water!" or moaning in pain. Many were dead. The courtyard was piled with corpses. A constant stream of new corpses to burn.

August 10
10km / Ninoshima Quarantine Station
Hakumi Kagawa（43 ▶ 73）

2-A

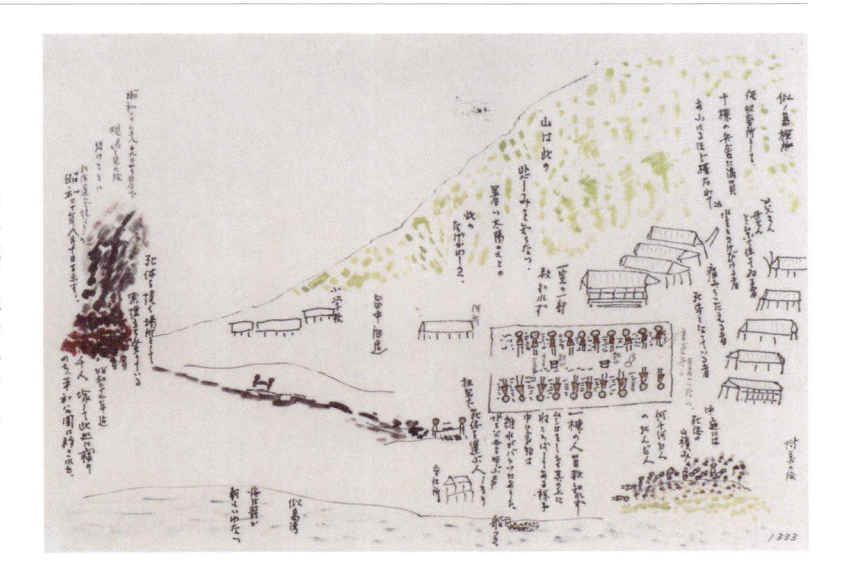

薬もなく
No Medicine

不足する医薬品　Scarce medical supplies
被爆直後、医薬品はすぐに底をつき、やけどには赤チンや油、キュウリやジャガイモのすりおろした汁を塗る程度の治療しか受けられなかった。
After the bombing, medical supplies quickly ran out. Treatments available to burn victims were limited to mercurochrome, oils, and the juice from grated cucumber and potato.

頭の中に埋もれたガラス

まるで子供が母のひざの上に頭を乗せて耳を掃除してもらうようなそんな姿勢で、先生から頭の中に埋もれたガラスの破片をピンセットで取り除いてもらう友。カチャリカチャリと、机の上のシャーレの中で、取り出されたガラスが小さな音をたてて、重なっていった。

8月7日か8日 午前中
10km ／観音国民学校
芳賀 順子（11 ▶ 68）

Glass fragments buried in her head

Assuming the posture of a child lying in her mother's lap to have her ears cleaned was my friend, but it was our teacher extracting glass fragments from her head with tweezers. I laid each piece in a Petri dish on the desk to the small tinkle of glass on glass.

August 7 or 8, morning
10km / Kannon Elementary School
Junko Haga（11 ▶ 68）

1-B

キュウリと大根おろし

白いのはウジ虫。キュウリ、大根おろし、すり鉢

8月9日か10日
3,500m ／牛田町
（7 牛田・広島駅周辺）
小野 勝（41 ▶ 69）

Cucumbers and *daikon* radish grater

The white is maggots. Cucumbers, grater, and mortar.

August 9 or 10
3,500m / Ushita-machi
(7 Ushita・Hiroshima Station)
Masaru Ono（41 ▶ 69）

1-A

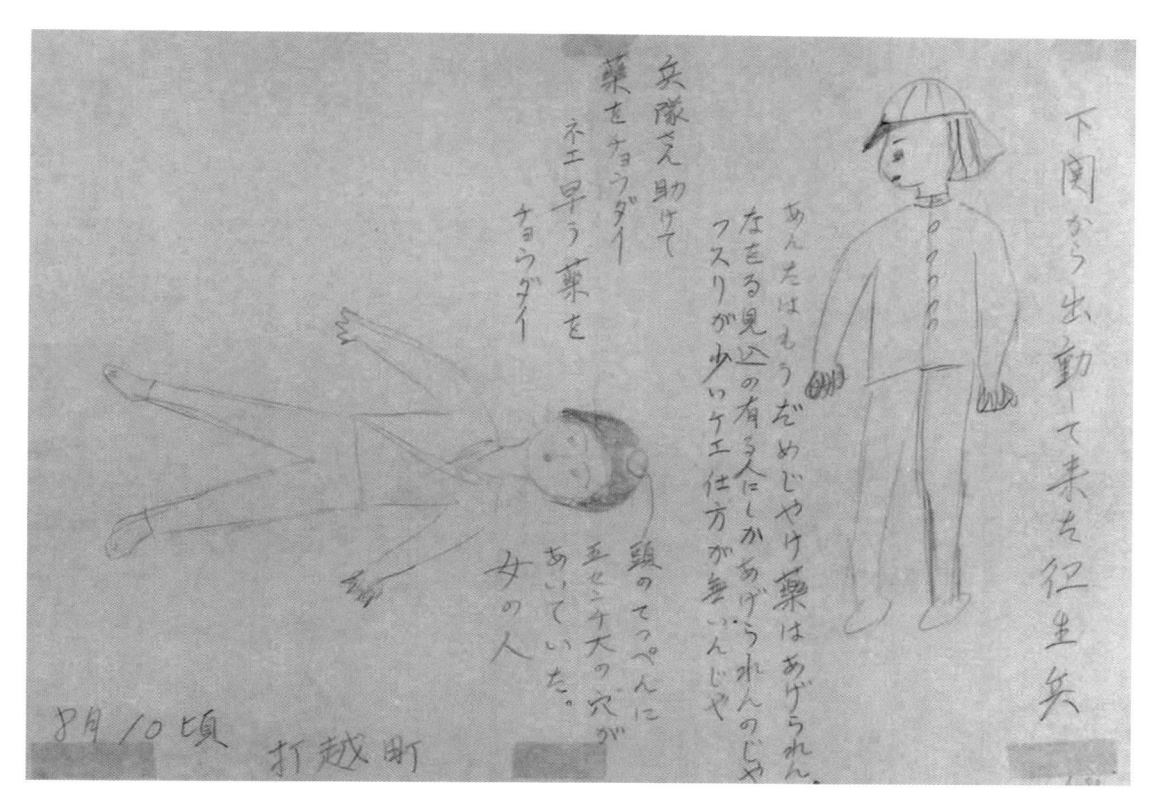

もうだめじゃけ薬はあげられん

衛生兵「あんたはもうだめじゃけ薬はあげられん。なおる見込みのある人にしかあげられんのじゃ。薬が少ないけえ、仕方がないんじゃ」。

8月10日頃
2,200m／打越町（12 三篠・祇園）
山本 忠代（24 ▶ 53）

"It's all over for you, so we can't give you any more medicine."

Medic: "It's all over for you, so we can't give you any more medicine. We can't waste it on people without hope of survival. There isn't enough medicine to go around, that's the problem."

Around August 10
2,200m / Uchikoshi-cho（12 Misasa・Gion）
Tadayo Yamamoto（24 ▶ 53）

1-A

ハエとウジに襲われる
Attacked by Flies and Maggots

数万匹のハエに襲われる

電車のレールを枕にして、悪臭プンプン。破れたむしろで西日を防いでも、数万匹のハエに襲われる。

8月8日 午後
1,300m／江波線の電車通り（10 吉島・舟入・観音）
徳本 トシミ（37 ▶ 67）

Tens of thousands of flies buzzed around them.

They used the streetcar rail for their pillow. The stench was overpowering. Torn straw mats were put up to shelter them from the sun, but tens of thousands of flies buzzed around them.

August 8, afternoon
1,300m / streetcar street on the Eba Line（10 Yoshijima・Funairi・Kan-on）
Toshimi Tokumoto（37 ▶ 67）

2-A-◎

第3章 いのち

頭の膨れたところからバラバラとウジが落ちてきた

中年の男性が、頭がかゆくて三日三晩一睡もできないと訴えておられました。お医者様が、頭の一部が少し膨れた場所をピンセットで引っ張られると、なんとウジがバラバラと何十匹か何百匹か分かりませんが落ちてきました。もう1カ所もでした。

8月8日頃
30km／小方国民学校
正木 鏡子（21 ▶ 77）

Maggots fell out from the swollen place on his head.

The middle-aged man complained that he had not slept for three days and nights for the itching. When the doctor pulled open a swollen spot on the man's head with tweezers, dozens, even hundreds of maggots fell out. The same thing happened with another spot on his head.

Around August 8
30km / Ogata Elementary School
Kyoko Masaki (21 ▶ 77)

2-B

ウジ虫が発生している女の人

病院内の壁にもたれて、肩から腕の裂傷に生きていながらウジ虫が発生している女の人

8月13日頃
1,500m／広島赤十字病院
（5 国泰寺・千田）
平岡 隆（24 ▶ 54）

Woman with maggots breeding on her body

Slumped against a wall in the hospital, the woman was still alive as maggots bred in the gash running from her shoulder down her arm.

Around August 13
1,500m / Hiroshima Red Cross Hospital
(5 Kokutaiji・Senda)
Takashi Hiraoka (24 ▶ 54)

2-A

散乱する死体
Scattered Corpses

5人がかりで死体をトラックへ投げ入れる

体全体がやけどのため皮膚がズルーとむける。そのため、両手に二人、両足に二人、首に一人が手を入れてトラックへ投げ入れる。

8月7日 午後0時30分頃
1,200m ／雑魚場町（5 国泰寺・千田）
原 廣司（13 ▶ 69）

A team of five hoisted corpses onto a truck.

Because their whole bodies were burned, their skin slipped off when they were picked up. It took five soldiers grasping the arms, legs, and head to hoist the body into the truck.

August 7, around 12:30 p.m.
1,200m / Zakoba-cho（5 Kokutaiji・Senda）
Hiroshi Hara（13 ▶ 69）

1-B

第3章　いのち

死体を引き寄せて縄でつなぐ

横川駅前の河岸に出て見ると、水を飲んだ被爆死者が腹を太鼓のように膨らませてプカプカと浮いて流れている。それを警察官と囚人がとび口を使って死者を引き寄せ、河岸に並べて再び流れないように縄でつないでいる。

8月7日
1,400m／横川駅近くの本川
（12 三篠・祇園）
向井 健二郎（7 ▶ 64）

Pulling corpses up and tying them with ropes

When I went out to the bank in front of Yokogawa Station, corpses were bobbing down the river. They had swallowed so much water that their stomachs were swollen like drums. Policemen and prisoners used fire hooks to pull them to shore, then tie them up so they wouldn't float off again.

August 7
1,400m / Honkawa River near Yokogawa Station （12 Misasa・Gion）
Kenjiro Mukai（7 ▶ 64）

2-B

河原に山積みされた死体

8月9日 午後2時頃
2,030m／神田橋下河原
（4 基町・白島）
三浦 高雄（48 ▶ 78）

Bodies piled in the riverbed

August 9, around 2:00 p.m.
2,030m / riverbed under Kanda Bridge
（4 Moto-machi・Hakushima）
Takao Miura（48 ▶ 78）

A

ちぎれる手足

練兵場付近は、兵隊の死体が足の踏み場もないほど倒れている。炎天下なので死体は腐敗し、ブクブクに膨れている。収容するのに腕や足を持ち上げると、ちぎれてくる。

8月8日
360m／西練兵場（4 基町・白島）
辻口 清吉（21 ▶ 78）

Arms and legs breaking off

Corpses of soldiers so filled the Western Drill Ground that it was hard to walk through it. Under the broiling sun bodies were decomposing and swelling. When we tried to lift them up to dispose of them, arms and legs broke off.

August 8
360m / Western Drill Ground（4 Moto-machi・Hakushima）
Seikichi Tsujiguchi（21 ▶ 78）

2-B

ソーセージ色の腸がひょろひょろと出てきた

上向いた真っ黒い死体の腹部の赤黒い色をしたものは何であろうかと思っていたら、「ピューッ」という音が聞こえた。ふり向くと、ソーセージ色をした腸がひょろひょろと出てきた。黒々とした路面をよく見ると、たくさんの死体がいろいろな姿で転んでいた。

8月8日 午後1時
710m／福屋百貨店前（2 紙屋町・本通）
迫 幸一（27 ▶ 56）

Sausage colored intestines twisting out

I wondered about the reddish-blackish things attached to the mid parts of the black bodies of victims lying on their backs. Just then I heard a squishy sound and turned around to see a sausage-colored intestine snaking out of a corpse. When I studied the blackened road more carefully, I could make out corpses twisted into various postures.

August 8, 1:00 p.m.
710m / in front of Fukuya Department Store
（2 Kamiya-cho・Hondori）
Koichi Sako（27 ▶ 56）

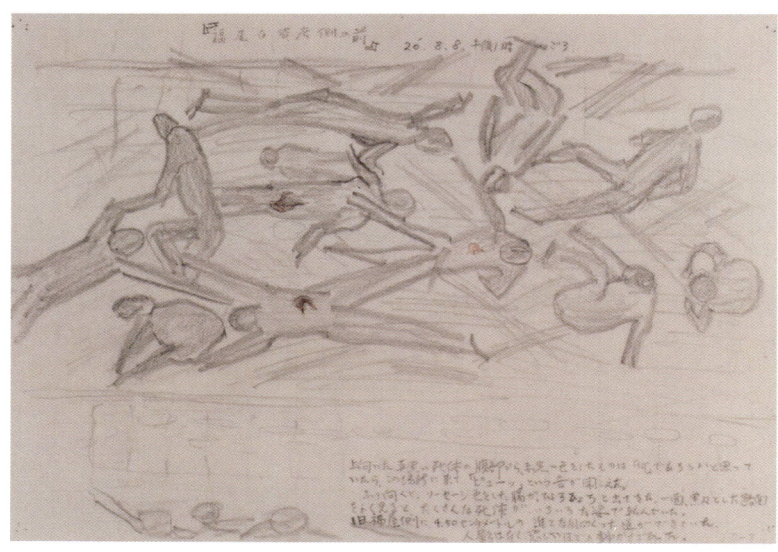

2-A

第3章　いのち

よどみにたまった遺体

らんかんが落ちた三篠橋下の
よどみにたまった、2、30体
の遺体が印象に残る。

8月9日頃
1,470m／三篠橋（4 基町・白島）
前田 正一（32 ▶ 62）

Corpses jammed into a backwater

I remember 20 or 30 corpses jammed into a backwater under Misasa Bridge, the railing of which had fallen off.

Around August 9
1,470m / Misasa Bridge
（4 Moto-machi・Hakushima）
Masakazu Maeda（32 ▶ 62）

1-A

路面に倒れた女学生

歩道のすみに女学生がこもをかぶされて、たおれていました。立札に、女学校名と姓名が焼炭で書かれていました。強い日ざしにかんかんと照らされ、背にやけどをしているのでしょう。血と体汁が一緒にまじって、アスファルト張りの路面に流れ出て、異臭を出していました。

8月12日 午後
太田川べり（近くに大きな屋内変電所）
松永 虎槌（18 ▶ 47）

Girl student collapsed on the road

A girl student had collapsed on a corner of the walkway. Someone had covered her with a rough straw mat and written her name and her school's on a board with charcoal. The fierce sun bore down on the girl, whose back I'm sure was burned. Her blood and bodily fluids emitted a strange smell, mingling as they drained onto the asphalt.

August 12, afternoon
Otagawa riverbank（near the large indoor substation）
Torazuchi Matsunaga（18 ▶ 47）

2-A

103

引いーけ ヨイショ ヒイーケェ ヨイショ

死体処理の兵隊さんの「引いーけ ヨイショ ヒイーケェ ヨイショ」の掛け声が、むなしく耳の底に残っています。建物取り壊し作業の時、家屋をロープで引き倒す時の掛け声であったのですが、死体を引きずることになったのです。

8月10日頃
1,100m／広瀬町（6 十日市・中広）
岡崎 秀彦（18 ▶ 47）

"One-two-three-PULL! One-two-three-PULL!"

I can still hear the lifeless voices of the soldiers calling, "One-two-three-PULL! One-two-three-PULL!" That was the same call they used when pulling down houses for demolition projects — but this time it was bodies being pulled up.

Around August 10
1,100m / Hirose-machi（6 Tokaichi・Nakahiro）
Hidehiko Okazaki（18 ▶ 47）

2-A

第3章　いのち

防火水槽
Fire Cisterns

空襲に備えるため、市内各所に防火用の水槽が置かれた。猛火の中のわずかな水であったが、手記、証言などとともに原爆の絵にも、防火水槽のある光景が多数描かれている。

Fire cisterns were placed around the city for fire fighting in case of air attack. These water supplies were no match for the columns of flame that arose, but they figure in many journals, eyewitness accounts, and A-bomb drawings.

火の海の中
8月6日 午前10時頃
1,650m／鶴見橋付近
（8 比治山・仁保）
道辻 芳子（19 ▶ 48）

In the sea of fire
August 6, around 10:00 a.m.
1,650m / near Tsurumi Bridge
(8 Hijiyama・Niho)
Yoshiko Michitsuji (19 ▶ 48)

A

紙屋町交差点で
8月7日 正午前
200m／紙屋町交差点
（2 紙屋町・本通）
中畑 佐一（37 ▶ 67）

At the Kamiya-cho Intersection
August 7, just before noon
200m / Kamiya-cho Intersection
(2 Kamiya-cho・Hondori)
Saichi Nakahata (37 ▶ 67)

A-◎

105

立ったまま

防火用水槽中の一少女。全く哀れであった。爆心地とも言える地点で、熱いのでとび込んだのか、水を飲むためであったのか、立ったまま完全に死んでいたようである。

8月7日 午後0時30分頃
400m／相生橋西詰
（1 平和記念公園・周辺）
永尾 勝實（42 ▶ 72）

She was still standing.

A young girl in a fire cistern. How pitiful she was! Either to escape the heat or drink water, she had jumped in this cistern virtually at the hypocenter. In death, she remained standing.

August 7, around 12:30 p.m.
400m / west end of Aioi Bridge
(1 Peace Memorial Park)
Katsumi Nagao (42 ▶ 72)

1-A

しかばねの山

あ……8月7日午前9時。娘を探しに修羅の街を通行中に見た、しかばねの山。用水の中に顔を伏せたまま、肩を抱き合って死んでいる姿。あ……水よ水よと叫んだでしょう。胸がいっぱいです。合掌。

8月7日 午前9時
550m／相生橋西詰（1 平和記念公園・周辺）
小松 キクヱ（37 ▶ 67）

Mountain of corpses

Ah.... 9:00 a.m. on August 7. While searching for my daughter through that hell, I happened on a mountain of corpses. Reaching their faces toward the water in the cistern, they had died with their arms around each other's shoulders. Ah.... How they must have screamed for water. I was overcome. I brought my palms together in prayer.

August 7, 9:00 a.m.
550m / west end of Aioi Bridge
(1 Peace Memorial Park)
Kikue Komatsu (37 ▶ 67)

2-A

水を飲むとそのままガックリと

人々は、水を求めて防火用水にむらがった。水を飲むと、そのままガックリと息絶えた。赤絵具を塗るに胸が痛む。

1,300m／天満町電車通り（6 十日市・中広）
小野木 明（15 ▶ 45）

Just as they were when they drank and died.

People wanting water gathered around the cisterns. I found them just as they were when they drank and died. My heart aches as I apply the red color.

1,300m / streetcar street at Tenma-cho（6 Tokaichi・Nakahiro）
Akira Onogi（15 ▶ 45）

2-A

赤鬼のよう

防火水槽の焼死体は、3日目ともなると赤くなり、赤鬼のように見えて思わず顔をそむけた。

8月8日 午前11時過ぎ
250m ／中島本町
（1 平和記念公園・周辺）
小川 紗賀己（28 ▶ 57）

Like red devils

Three days later, the burned bodies in the fire cistern had turned red, like demons. I instinctively turned away.

August 8, just after 11:00 a.m.
250m / Nakajima-hon-machi（1 Peace Memorial Park）
Sagami Ogawa（28 ▶ 57）

2-A

長い黒い髪が水槽いっぱいに

流川の電車通りの北側に置いてある水槽に、長い黒い髪が水槽いっぱいに広がっていました。よく見ると底に人が座っているようでした。思わず身ぶるいしました。

8月9日 午後3時頃
1,100m ／流川電車通り北側
（3 銀山・幟）
近藤 幸子（23 ▶ 53）

A cistern full of long, black hair

I saw long black hair spreading through the water in a cistern on the north corner of the streetcar street at Nagarekawa. Looking more closely, I saw someone sitting on the floor of the cistern. I shuddered.

August 9, around 3:00 p.m.
1,100m / north side of Nagarekawa streetcar street
（3 Kanayama・Nobori）
Sachiko Kondo（23 ▶ 53）

1-A

火葬する
Cremating the Dead

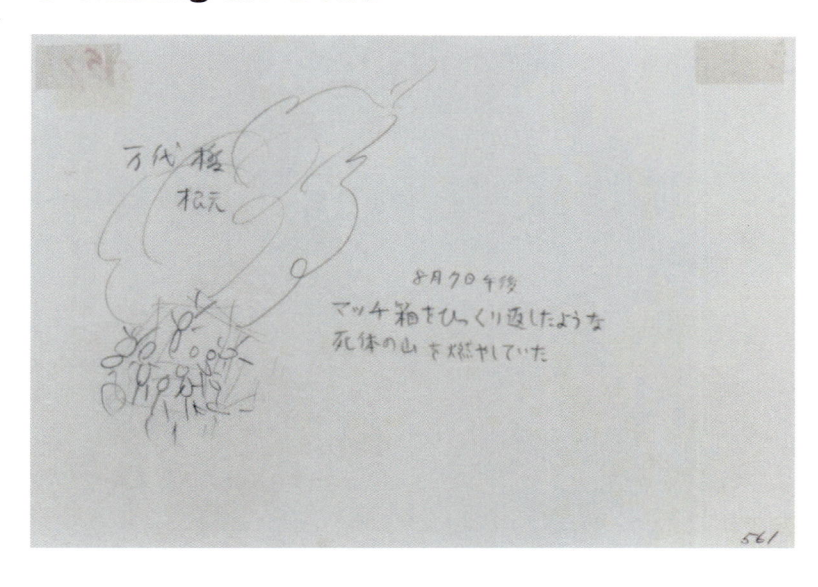

マッチ箱をひっくり返したような死体の山

マッチ箱をひっくり返したような死体の山を燃やしていた。

8月7日 午後
890m／万代橋（5 国泰寺・千田）
室積 淑美（20 ▶ 49）

Corpses piled like matches tossed out of a matchbox

Corpses piled like matches tossed out of a matchbox were being cremated.

August 7, afternoon
890m / Yorozuyo Bridge
(5 Kokutaiji・Senda)
Hidemi Murozumi (20 ▶ 49)

1-A

瓦に遺骨を乗せる

橋のたもとで亡くなった方を、兵隊さんだと思いますが、焼いていました。そして瓦の上に性別・年齢などを書いて、遺骨をのせてありました。思い出したくない光景ですが、今でも時折の夢に出てきます。

8月7日 夕方
1,640m／舟入町観音橋のたもと（10 吉島・舟入・観音）
匿名（13 ▶ 69）

Placing the remains on roof tiles

I believe it was soldiers who were burning the bodies of people who died under the bridge. They wrote the gender, name and other information pertaining to each person on a roof tile then placed bones and ashes on it. This hated memory still appears in my dreams.

August 7, evening
1,640m / under the Kan-on Bridge at Funairi-machi
(10 Yoshijima・Funairi・Kan-on)
Anonymous (13 ▶ 69)

1-B

わしらどうすりゃあえ えんかいのう

大声でこの老人はさけびました。「若い者を皆殺してからに。わしらはどうすりゃええんかいのう」。声を限りにさけびながらどこかへ消えて行かれました。校庭の片すみで若い兵隊さんたちをやいておられ、私はそれを見ながらなみだがとまりませんでした。

2,400m／大芝国民学校校庭
(12 三篠・祇園)
岡本 綾子(31 ▶ 61)

"What're we s'posed to do?"

The old man was shouting, "With all the young people killed, what're we s'posed to do?" He shouted with all his might as he walked out of sight. Young soldiers were being cremated in a corner of the schoolyard. I watched with tears that would not stop.

2,400m / schoolyard of Oshiba Elementary School (12 Misasa・Gion)
Ayako Okamoto (31 ▶ 61)

1-A

黒焦げの人体を道端で焼く

避難の途中、道々に黒焦げの人体をあちこちに見ながら、電車通りを紙屋町へ。そこで、このような場面に出あいました。とうてい、この世のこととは思われませんでした。

8月8日朝
300m／紙屋町電車通り
(2 紙屋町・本通)
横田 ハルヨ(47 ▶ 77)

Burning charred bodies on the roadside

When I was escaping the city, walking down the streetcar street to Kamiya-cho, I saw charred bodies along the way, and then the scene I depict here. It looked like no scene of this world.

August 8, morning
300m / streetcar street at Kamiya-cho
(2 Kamiya-cho・Hondori)
Haruyo Yokota (47 ▶ 77)

2-A

黒こげた荷物

トラックが運動場に入ってきた。黒こげた荷物を積んでいた。近くになり、よく見ると、それは人間の死体である。消防団の人たちがとび口で降ろし、運動場の砂場に積み上げ、まき、わらで囲み、コールタールをかけ、焼き尽くしていた。

8月8日 午前10時頃
3,150m／大河国民学校
（8 比治山・仁保）
山肩 和彦（7 ▶ 64）

Charred luggage

A truck carrying charred luggage drove into the playing field. When it came closer, I saw that it was human bodies. Firemen pulled them off with fire hooks and piled them in the sandbox on the playground. They bundled them in firewood and straw, poured coal tar over the whole pile, and burned them up.

August 8, around 10:00 a.m.
3,150m / Oko Elementary School（8 Hijiyama・Niho）
Kazuhiko Yamagata（7 ▶ 64）

2-B

死体の山

火葬にするため1カ所に集められた死体。50体ぐらいつみかさねられていた。

8月9日
1,750m／横川駅前
（12 三篠・祇園）
塚本 喜三（36 ▶ 66）

Mountain of corpses

Corpses were gathered in this spot for cremation. About 50 were in the pile.

August 9
1,750m / in front of Yokogawa Station（12 Misasa・Gion）
Yoshizo Tsukamoto（36 ▶ 66）

1-A

助けてあげられなくてごめんなさい
"I'm Sorry I cannot Save You."

鷹の橋附近八時二十五分
塀既ニ火災起リ助
ケを求める婦人の
声処し

どうすることもできない

突然女の悲鳴が聞こえその方を見ると倒壊した家屋の二階の窓ぎわに髪をふり乱し両手をあげて助けを呼んでゐるのである。体は梁の下敷きとなり身動きもできないらしい、階下にも「助けてー」という声がする。然しその家屋からは既に火の手が上つてゐてどうすることもできない。生きながらにして焼かれるなんて、何んと言う悲惨なことであろう。此の世の中にこんな地獄の世界があろうとは。(『被爆体験──私の訴えたいこと(上)』NHK中国本部、1977年、37ページから)

8月6日 午前8時25分頃
1,400m ／鷹野橋(5 国泰寺・千田)
伊藤 貫一(40 ▶ 69)

There was nothing I could do.

I heard a female cry and turned around to see a woman reaching out of a smashed window on the second story of a collapsed house. Her hair flew about as she waved her arms and screamed for help. She was evidently pinned under the joist. Below her, another voice screamed for help. But flames were already rising from that house. There was nothing I could do. What an unthinkable fate — to be burned alive! That such a hell can occur on this earth! (Taken from *A-bomb Experiences — What I Want to Say,* Vol. 1; NHK Chugoku Office, 1977, page 37)

August 6, around 8:25 a.m.
1,400m / Takanobashi (5 Kokutaiji・Senda)
Kanichi Ito (40 ▶ 69)

3-A

第3章 いのち

タスケテー

タスケテー
炎に包まれた二階の窓より助けを求める幼女の声
未だに忘れることは出来ぬ

1,500m／広島赤十字病院付近
(5 国泰寺・千田)
佐々木 智佐子(19 ▶ 75)

"Help me!"

"Help me!"
The cries came from a small girl at a window on the second floor of a house enveloped in flames. I can never forget.

1,500m / near Hiroshima Red Cross Hospital
(5 Kokutaiji・Senda)
Chisako Sasaki (19 ▶ 75)

1-B

お父チャンとお母チャンがこの下におるんじゃ！

崩れ果てた屋根瓦の上で「お父チャンとお母チャンがこの下におるんじゃ！ 誰か助けて！」と、叫び泣く学齢前ぐらいの少年。彼の背中でも赤ん坊が泣いていた。誰も少年の手助けができなかった。

8月6日
1,250m／鷹野橋電停付近
(5 国泰寺・千田)
小野山 博子(23 ▶ 80)

"My father and mother are under here!"

A boy not yet of school age stood on a pile of crumbled roof tiles screaming and crying, "My father and mother are under here! Somebody help!" The baby on his back was crying. No one could help the boy.

August 6
1,250m / near the Takanobashi streetcar stop (5 Kokutaiji・Senda)
Hiroko Onoyama (23 ▶ 80)

2-B

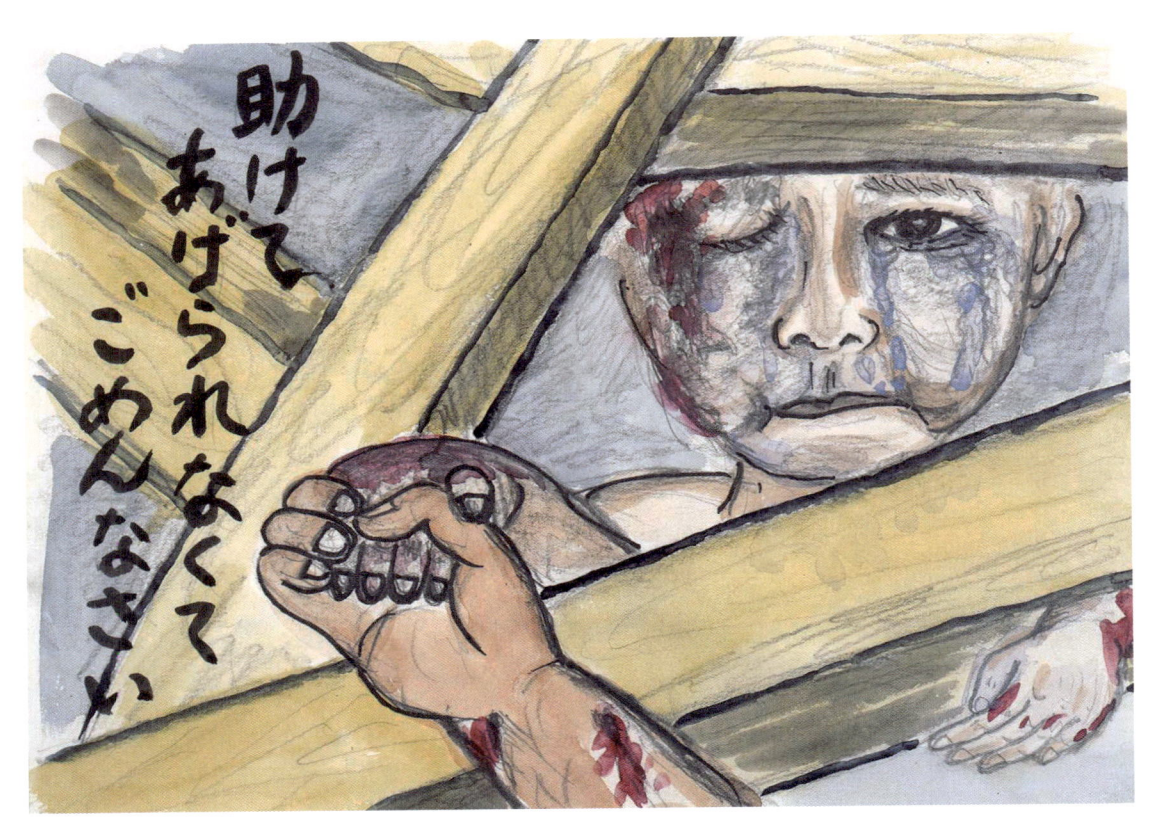

助けてあげられなくてごめんなさい

下敷きになった子供を救助できないまま、校舎は火炎に包まれました。ほおずりをしてあげられるほど、体はほとんど外に出ているのに、片腕が柱と柱に押しつぶされて引き出せなかったのです。「もうすぐ楽になるからね」といって手をあわせました。

8月6日 午前10時30分頃
1,800m ／段原国民学校(8 比治山・仁保)
加藤 義典(17 ▶ 73)

"I'm sorry I cannot save you."

I could not rescue the children trapped under the schoolhouse being engulfed in flames. One little girl was almost out — I could have placed my cheek next to hers and pulled her clear except for the arm pinned under a pillar. I told them in my heart, "You'll be safe from harm soon," and placed my hands together in prayer.

August 6, around 10:30 a.m.
1,800m / Dambara Elementary School (8 Hijiyama・Niho)
Yoshinori Kato (17 ▶ 73)

2-B

第3章 いのち

皮膚はズルリとむけて垂れさがった母親は丸裸の赤ん坊をしっかりと胸に抱き、もう一人の子供は「母ちゃん痛いよう、痛いよう」とかすかに口を動かしていた
子供も母親も死期が近づいていた

死期が近づいていた

ほとんど裸同様の焼けただれた親子を前に、私には何もしてやれることがなかった。赤ん坊はすでにこときれ、子供も母親も死期が近づいていた。この身体で、いったいどうやってここまで歩いてきたのか。私はとてもそこにとどまることに耐えられなかった。歩を移す私の背後に、母親の断末魔の叫び声が鞭打つように響いた。近くからムシロをさがし出し、せめても直射日光を受けないようにと亡骸を覆ったが、空を睨んだ母親の眼が大きく、まるで私の心の底まで刺し通すように感じられた。私には、そのムシロをかける以外にいったい何ができるというのか。私は、声もなく合掌してその場を去った。(『この子らに語りつぐもの』広島平和教育研究所、1977年、147ページから)

池亀 春男（20 ▶ 77）

Their time of death approached.

I could do nothing for this virtually naked family whose skin was coming off. The baby was already dead, and the child and mother were close behind. How on earth had they walked this far in those bodies? I could not bear to stay there. Behind me as I walked away, the dying screams of the mother lashed at me like a whip. I found a straw mat in the area, thinking at least to protect the bodies from the direct sunlight. I felt the mother's large eyes staring at the sky were penetrating the depths of my heart. Was there nothing I could do except cover them with the mat? I wordlessly placed my hands together and left that place. (Taken from *What to Tell the Children*, Hiroshima Institute For Peace Education, 1977, page 147)

Haruo Ikegame （20 ▶ 77）

3-B

なぜトマトを半分にちぎって渡さなかったのか

「お水をちょうだい」と叫ぶ女の子に、青く固いトマトを一つ手渡した。唇は白くむくれ、ただれて開きそうにもなかった。手は両方ともくっついていた。なぜあのトマトを半分にちぎって渡さなかったのか。あの子はどうやってあの手とあの唇であの硬いトマトの汁を吸うことができただろうか。

8月7日 午後1時頃
観音町の土手（10 吉島・舟入・観音）
中津 久子（26 ▶ 56）

Why did I not break the tomato in half before I gave it to her?

I gave the girl screaming, "Please give me water!" a hard, green tomato. Her lips were white and peeling. I didn't see how she could open her mouth. The skin on the fingers of both hands was stuck together. Why did I not break that tomato in half for her? With those hands and those lips, how could she suck the juice out of that hard tomato?

August 7, around 1:00 p.m.
Riverbank at Kan-on-machi (10 Yoshijima・Funairi・Kan-on)
Hisako Nakatsu (26 ▶ 56)

2-A

第3章　いのち

癒えない傷
Wounds that Never Heal

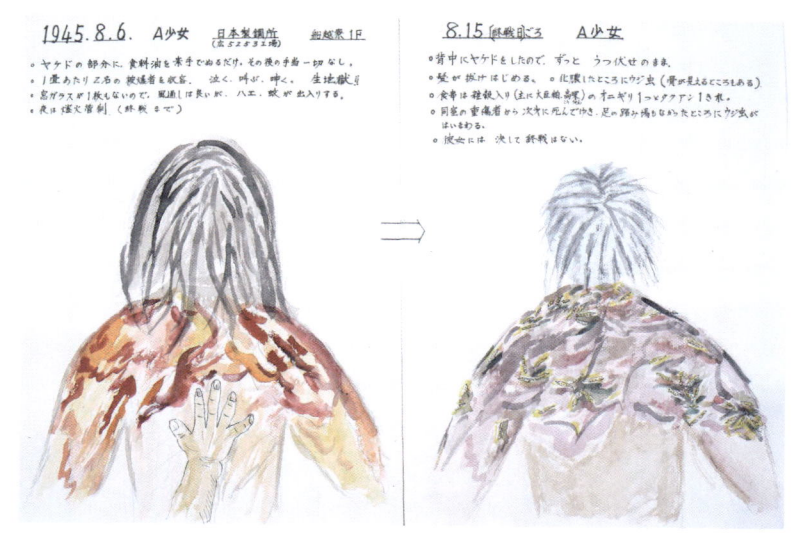

彼女には決して終戦はない

1945.8.6　A少女
やけどの部分に食料油を素手でぬるだけ。その後の手当一切なし。

8.15（終戦日）ごろ　A少女
背中にやけどをしたので、ずっとうつ伏せのまま。彼女には決して終戦はない。

8月6日から15日
6,500m／日本製鋼所の工場寮
田中　陽造（18 ▶ 75）

No end to war for this girl

8/6, 1945; Girl A — All we did was apply cooking oil with our bare hands. No follow-up treatment.

Around 8/15 (end of war); Girl A — Because her back was burned, she lay continuously on her stomach. The war will never end for her.

August 6-15
6,500m / plant dormitory at Japan Steel Works
Yozo Tanaka（18 ▶ 75）

2-B

9月15日ごろ 全部抜ける

8月6日　原爆にあったその時（15歳）
8月10日頃　頭髪一部分抜ける
8月15日頃　2カ所部分的に残る（後ろ向き）
9月15日頃　全部抜ける

8月6日から9月15日頃
親戚の家
竹田　初枝（15 ▶ 44）

It all came out around September 15.

8/6 Just after the bombing (15 years old)
About 8/10 — Some hair fell out.
About 8/15 — Some hair remained in patches. (on the back)
About 9/15 — All hair fell out.

Around August 6-September 15
At her relative's house
Hatsue Takeda（15 ▶ 44）

1-A

一生涯外出できないと泣きました

9月になってから頭の髪が抜けはじめました。束になってグスット抜けるので、心細く不安で泣きました。まゆ毛まで抜けて丸坊主になったので、一生涯外出できないと泣きました。父がセンブリのせんじ汁は毛はえ薬になるからつけてみよと言ったので毎日つけているうちに、6カ月ぐらいしてから産毛が生えてきました。うれしかったのでまた泣きました。

9月
原田 みどり (33 ▶ 90)

I wept to think I would never be able to leave the house again.

My hair began to fall out in September. It came out in clumps, and I cried in fear and helplessness. When I got completely bald down to the eyebrows, I wept to think I would never be able to leave the house again. My father thought we should try a *senburi* (medicinal herb) infusion, which was supposed to help hair grow. I applied it every day, and about six months later, I began to get downy hair. I was so happy I wept.

September
Midori Harada (33 ▶ 90)

1-B

第 3 章　いのち

顔を覆った年ごろの女性

向い側のホームに赤ちんだらけの顔を紙で覆った年ごろの女性。焼け野原の広島の街と共に、一生忘れることはできない。

8月13日
1,750m／横川駅ホーム
（12 三篠・祇園）
杉江 道子（20 ▶ 49）

A young woman hiding her face

On the opposite platform stood a young woman hiding her mercurochrome-painted face behind a piece of paper. I will never forget the sight of her and the burnt plain of Hiroshima.

August 13
1,750m / Yokogawa Station platform（12 Misasa・Gion）
Michiko Sugie（20 ▶ 49）

1-A

あの人は「ピカドン」でやられた人よ

私が小さい時に会った人です。その時、「あの人は広島で「ピカドン」でやられた人よ」と、大人の人が教えてくれました。恐ろしいことと怖いと思うことしかありません。

吉弘 五津美（29 ▶ 86）

"That person was hurt in the *pikadon*."

I met that person when I was young. An older person told me, "That person was hurt in the Hiroshima *pikadon*." I felt only alarm and deeper fear.

Itsumi Yoshihiro（29 ▶ 86）

1-B

ピカドン　Pikadon
廃墟の街で生き残った人々は原子爆弾のことを「ピカドン」と呼んだ。ピカは閃光、ドンは後からきたすさまじいさく裂音のこと。

Those who survived on the burnt plain called the atomic bomb "*pikadon*." "Pika" refers to the flash and "don" to the roar of explosion that followed it.

生きる
To Live

復旧一番電車

乗客は無口な人が多く、「おお電車が動くんか」と驚かれる人。「鉄橋が怖いけんのー」と有難がる人。「火傷の人、斑点が見える人」と、色々でした。「有り難うございました」「済みません」と言い、電車賃の払えない人も多かったように思います。(『電車内被爆者の証言』広島電鉄株式会社、1985年12月15日、112ページから)

8月9日
1,300m から 2,500m ／已斐から西天満町までの路面電車の中
(6 十日市・中広)
堀本 春野 (16 ▶ 72)

The first restored streetcar

A lot of the passengers had nothing to say. Some were amazed: "The streetcars are already running?" Others said, "I'm afraid to cross the rail bridges by myself." People with burns, people with purple spots. Many couldn't pay the fare. "Thank you very much," they said, "I'm sorry." (Taken from *Testimonies by Survivors Exposed in Streetcars*; Hiroshima Electric Railway Co., Ltd., December 15, 1985; page 112)

August 9
1,300m to 2,500m / in a streetcar riding from Koi to Nishi-tenma-cho (6 Tokaichi・Nakahiro)
Haruno Horimoto (16 ▶ 72)

3-B

市内電車の復旧　Restoring the streetcars

懸命な復旧作業により、被爆から3日後の8月9日には、路面電車の一部区間の折り返し運転が行われ、バス2台も広島駅と宇品を結ぶ区間の運行を再開した。しかし、完全に復旧するまでには相当長期間を要した。

By August 9 (three days later), strenuous reconstruction efforts brought the restoration of round-trip streetcar service on parts of routes, and two buses began running between Hiroshima Station and Ujina. Complete restoration took a much longer time.

第３章　いのち

冷たくておいしい

数人の人だかりがあり、近寄ってみると不思議と手押しポンプが生きていて、水が出ているではないか。干天の慈雨と言うべきか、互いにくみあった水は透明ではあったが、ススのようなみじんが漂っていた。これが手茶碗の底に落ち着くのを待って、その上澄みを「冷たくて、おいしい」などと皆で飲みあいながら、町の被害のすごさなどを話し合った。

8月14日 午後3時頃
550m／相生橋西（6 十日市・中広）
香川 嘉久（17 ▶ 74）

"So cool, so delicious."

At the sight of a cluster of people, I walked up and was amazed to see a working water pump — water was gushing out! By the grace of God, there was clear water for people to pump into each other's hands. However, it contained pieces of sooty grit. People waited for these to drift down to their palms, then sipped the clean water on top. They exclaimed, "So cool, so delicious!" as they talked about the horrendous situation in the city.

August 14, around 3:00 p.m.
550m / west end of Aioi Bridge (6 Tokaichi・Nakahiro)
Yoshihisa Kagawa (17 ▶ 74)

2-B

出産

この惨状の中にあっても出産といううれしい出来事もあり、母は懸命にお世話をさせていただいたようです。赤ちゃんは立派に成長され、幸せにお暮らしのことと願ってやみません。

5,200m／青崎国民学校
知久 喜代野（25 ▶ 82）

Giving birth

In the midst of all the horror came a joyous event — the birth of a child. My mother did everything possible to help. I hope with all my heart that the baby grew up healthily and is living a happy life.

5,200m / Aosaki Elementary School
Kiyono Chiku (25 ▶ 82)

2-B

星がきれいでした

父の勤めていた会社の焼け跡に、焼け焦げたトタンやガラクタを拾い集めて父がバラック小屋を建てました。工場の大きな煙突が1本焼け残り、夜はとても恐く感じました。その反面、恐い煙突の辺りにキラキラ輝くたくさんの星がとてもきれいでした。

8月20日頃 夜
1,500m／西観音町の缶詰工場の焼け跡（10 吉島・舟入・観音）
佐々木 澄江（6 ▶ 62）

The stars were beautiful.
My father gathered charred tin sheeting and broken planks and built us a shack over the burnt ruins of his company. One plant's tall smokestack remained standing, and it scared us at night. But the stars glittering all around the scary smokestack were so beautiful.

Around August 20, night
1,500m / ruins of a canning plant in Nishi-kan-on-machi（10 Yoshijima・Funairi・Kan-on）
Sumie Sasaki（6 ▶ 62）

1-B

原子砂漠に灯がともる
9月10日 午後8時
2,100m／比治山山頂（8 比治山・仁保）
田中 儀作（43 ▶ 72）

Lights blinking on in the atomic desert
September 10, 8:00 p.m.
2,100m / top of Hijiyama Hill（8 Hijiyama・Niho）
Gisaku Tanaka（43 ▶ 72）

A

電気の復旧　Restoration of electricity

被爆の翌日8月7日には宇品方面に、8日には広島駅とその一帯に電灯がついた。8月末までには焼失を免れた家屋の3割に、11月末には全戸に送電された。

Electricity was restored in the Ujina area on August 7 and the Hiroshima Station area on August 8. Thirty percent of the surviving houses had electricity by the end of August, and all houses by the end of November.

第3章 いのち

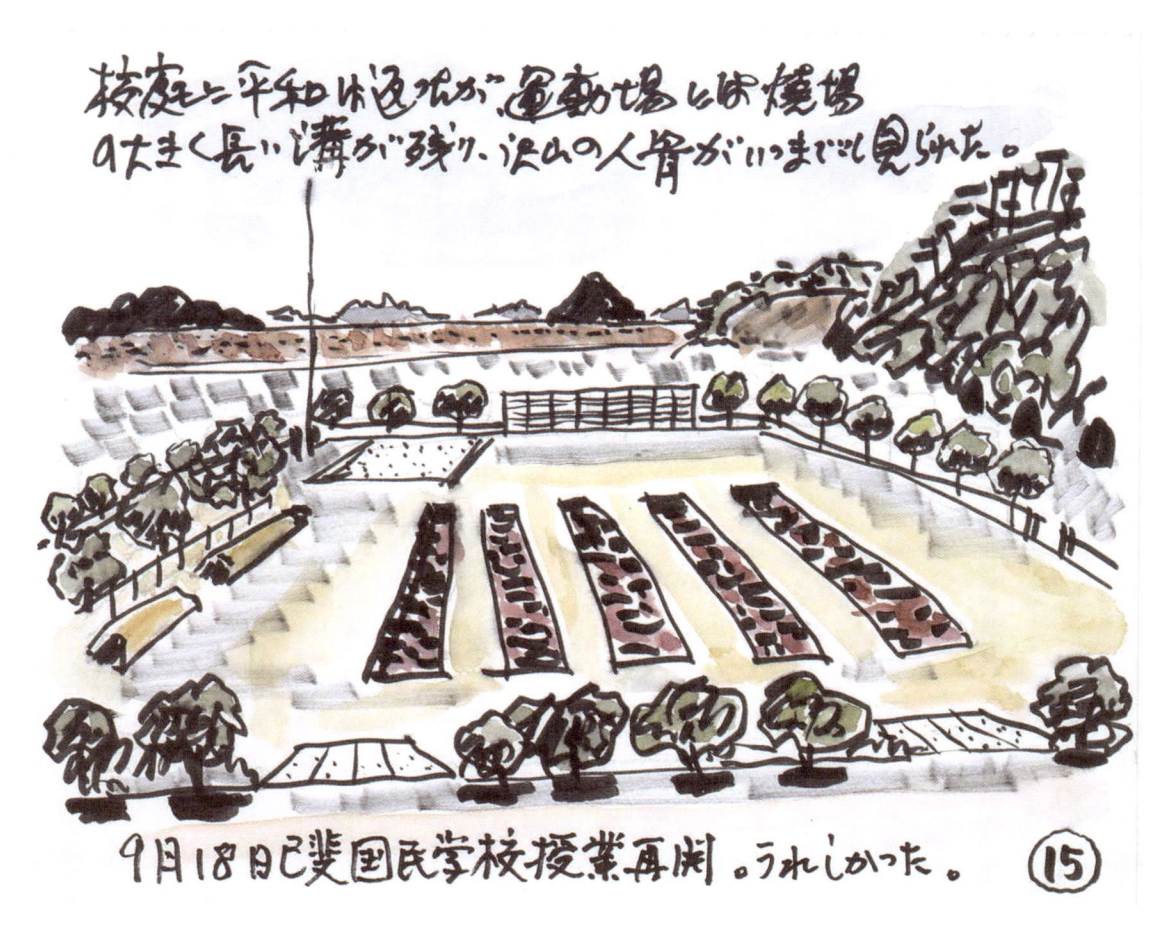

校庭に平和は返ったが……

国民学校の授業再開。うれしかった。校庭に平和は返ったが、運動場には焼場の大きく長い溝が残り、たくさんの人骨がいつまでも見られた。

9月18日
3,050m ／己斐国民学校（11 己斐・草津）
名柄 堯（11 ▶ 68）

Peace returned to the schoolyard, but . . .

My elementary school started up again. I was happy. Peace returned to the schoolyard, but the long ditches in the playground that served as crematoria were still there. We had to look at those bones for a very long time.

September 18
3,050m / Koi Elementary School（11 Koi・Kusatsu）
Takashi Nagara（11 ▶ 68）

2-B

学校の再開　　Reopening schools

9月から学校が再開されることになったが、市内41校のうち、校舎を使用できたのは11校に過ぎず、校庭の木陰にムシロを敷いた「青空教室」が各地に見られた。他校や寺などの建物を借り受けて授業を再開したところもあった。

Schools were expected to reopen in September, but only 11 of the city's 41 school buildings were in usable condition. "Open-air classrooms" held on straw mats appeared under trees in schoolyards. Some schools resumed classes in borrowed rooms in other schools, temples, or other buildings.

似ノ島
◎似島検疫所

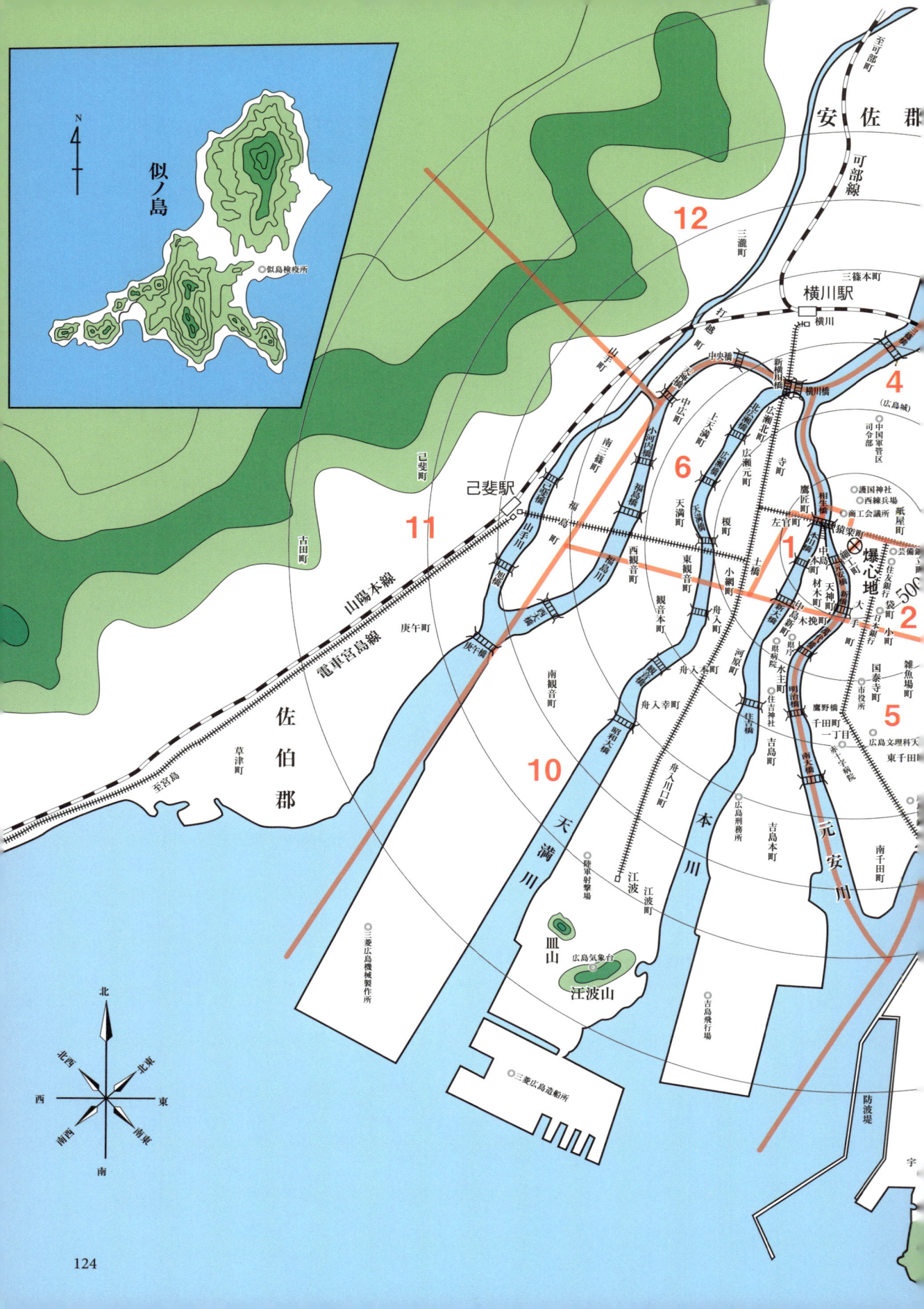

安佐郡
可部線
至可部町

三滝町
三篠本町
横川駅
横川

至芸備

(広島城)
中国軍管区
司令部
護国神社
西練兵場
商工会議所
祇園町
鋳物町
住友銀行
日本銀行
袋町
小町
芸備
爆心地
500
中央橋
新横川橋
横川橋
4
灯籠町
山手町
中広町
上天満橋
広瀬北町
北広島町
広瀬元町
寺町
天満橋
鷹匠町
相生橋
左官町
12
小河内橋
西広瀬橋
福島橋
6
榎町
土橋
中島本町
材木町
猿楽町
大手町
1
南三篠町
福島川
天満町
西観音町
東観音町
小網町
中島
元柳町
2
己斐町
己斐駅
福島町
観音本町
舟入町
河原町
若草
県病院
県庁
雑魚場町
国泰寺町
市役所
山陽本線
電車宮島線
旭橋
舟入本町
住吉神社
住吉橋
明治橋
鷹野橋
千田町
一丁目
南千田町
広島文理科大
新十六大隊
東千田町
5
古田町
庚午町
庚午橋
南観音町
舟入幸町
昭和大橋
舟入川口町
吉島町
広島刑務所
東大橋
11
佐伯郡
草津町
至宮島
10
天満川
本川
三菱広島機械製作所
陸軍射撃場
江波
江波町
皿山
広島気象台
汀波山
吉島本町
吉島飛行場
元安川
南千田町
三菱広島造船所
防波堤

N
北
北西 北東
西 東
南西 南東
南

至宇

広島市街地図
Map of Hiroshima City Neighborhoods

1	平和記念公園・周辺地区
2	紙屋町・本通地区
3	銀山・幟地区
4	基町・白島地区
5	国泰寺・千田地区
6	十日市・中広地区
7	牛田・広島駅周辺地区
8	比治山・仁保地区
9	皆実・宇品地区
10	吉島・舟入・観音地区
11	己斐・草津地区
12	三篠・祇園地区

District	1	Peace Memorial Park
District	2	Kamiya-cho・Hondori
District	3	Kanayama・Nobori
District	4	Moto-machi・Hakushima
District	5	Kokutaiji・Senda
District	6	Tokaichi・Nakahiro
District	7	Ushita・Hiroshima Station
District	8	Hijiyama・Niho
District	9	Minami・Ujina
District	10	Yoshijima・Funairi・Kan-on
District	11	Koi・Kusatsu
District	12	Misasa・Gion

広島港（宇品港）

作 品 一 覧

Other A-bomb Drawings in the Museum Collection

広島平和記念資料館が所蔵する約3,600枚の原爆の絵のうち、本編で161点を紹介した。ここでは、本編に掲載されなかった作者の絵を1人1点ずつ、計1,084点を掲載している。敬称は省略。

- 作者氏名の50音順に掲載し、匿名及び作者が不明なものは最後としている。
- 作者名の後ろに◎印を付しているものは、作者(関係者)の連絡先が不明なものです。心あたりの方は広島平和記念資料館までご連絡ください。

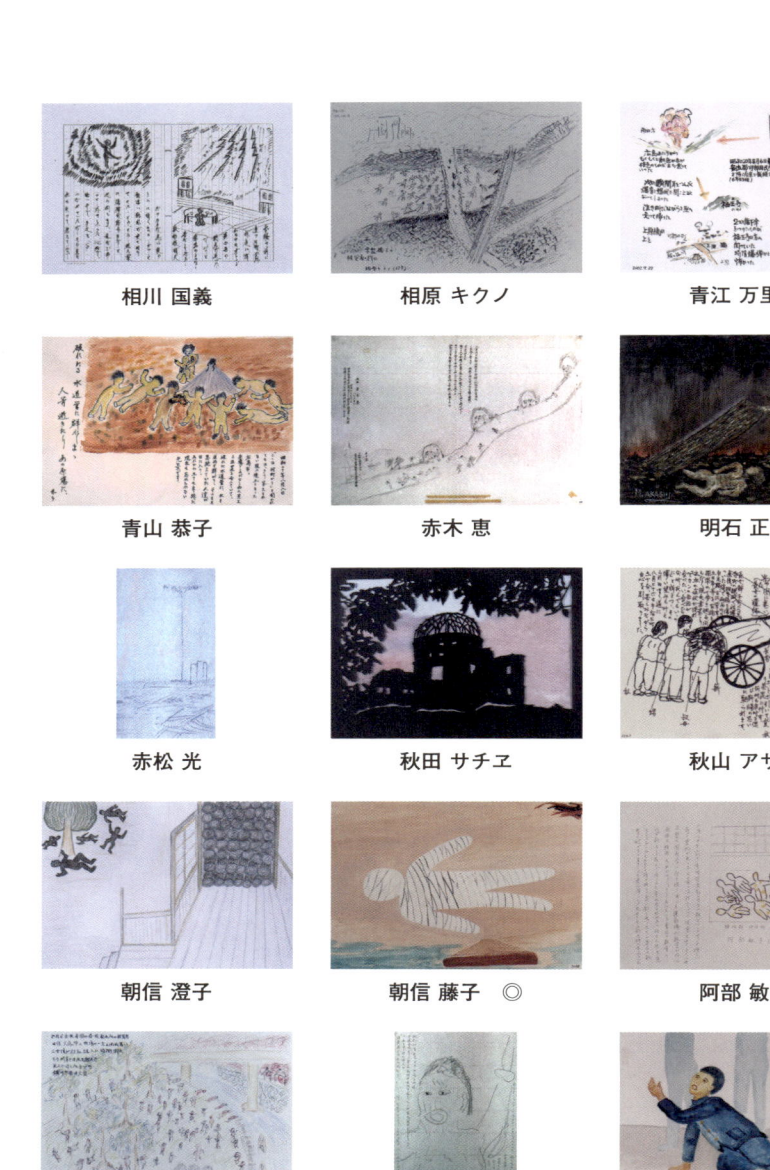

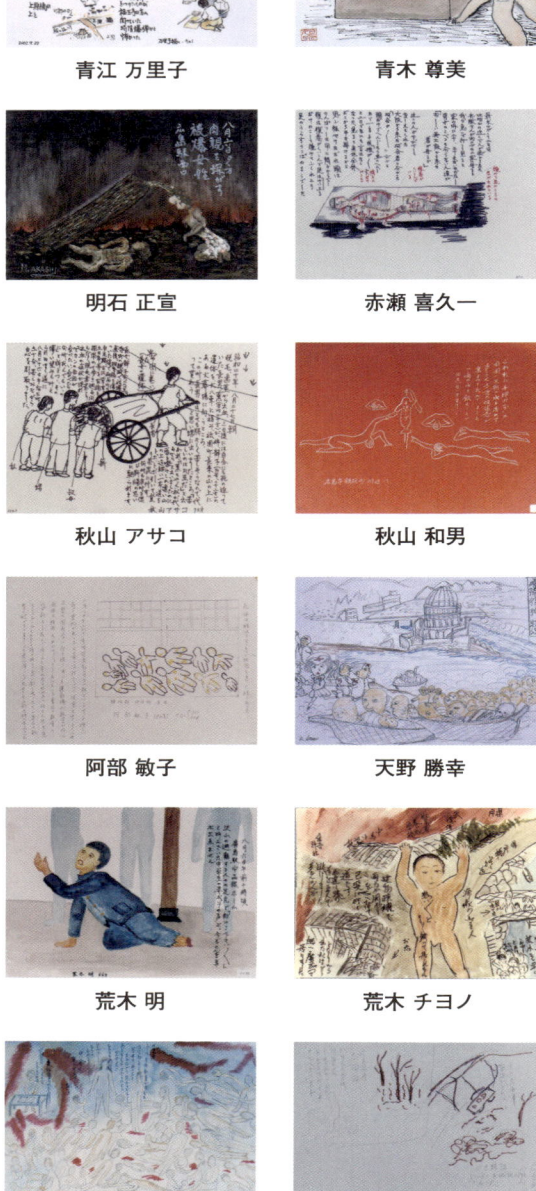

相川 国義	相原 キクノ	青江 万里子	青木 尊美
青山 恭子	赤木 恵	明石 正宣	赤瀬 喜久一
赤松 光	秋田 サチヱ	秋山 アサコ	秋山 和男
朝信 澄子	朝信 藤子 ◎	阿部 敏子	天野 勝幸
天野 忠雄	天野 善郎	荒木 明	荒木 チヨノ
荒木 常市	在川 和磨	有木 絢子	有馬 千代
有馬 元	有村 ひろ子	有村 行夫	有吉 コサダ

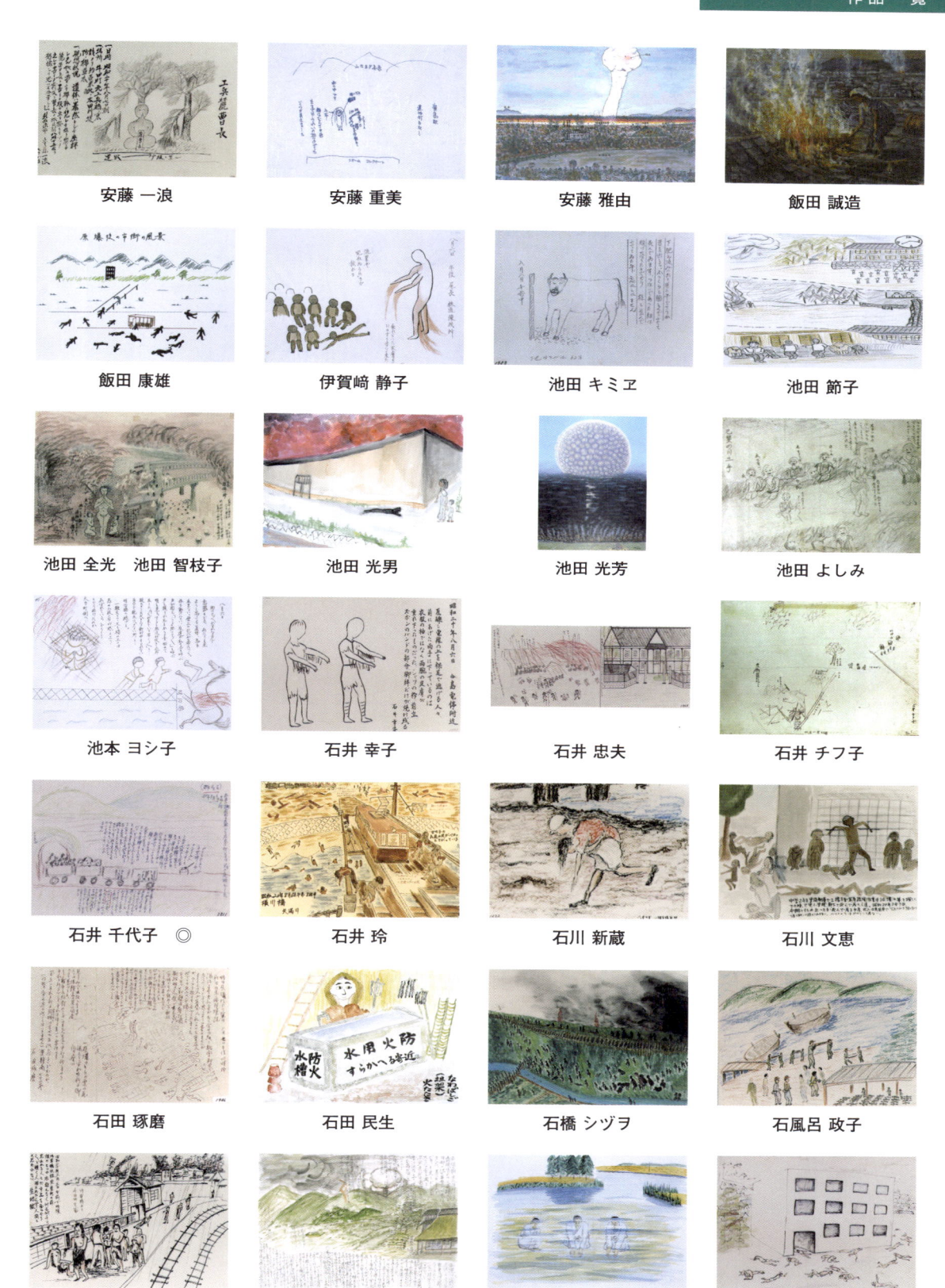

作品一覧

安藤 一浪	安藤 重美	安藤 雅由	飯田 誠造
飯田 康雄	伊賀﨑 静子	池田 キミヱ	池田 節子
池田 全光　池田 智枝子	池田 光男	池田 光芳	池田 よしみ
池本 ヨシ子	石井 幸子	石井 忠夫	石井 チフ子
石井 千代子 ◎	石井 玲	石川 新蔵	石川 文恵
石田 琢磨	石田 民生	石橋 シヅヲ	石風呂 政子
石本 孝雄	伊豆野 キミコ	泉原 寅男	板倉 時重 ◎

129

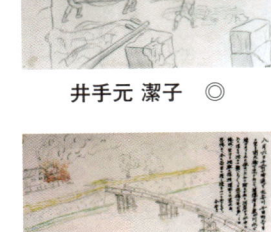

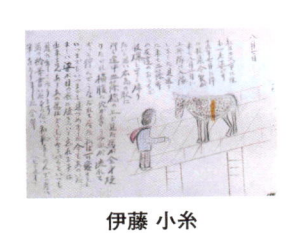

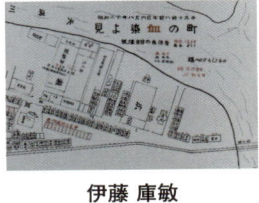

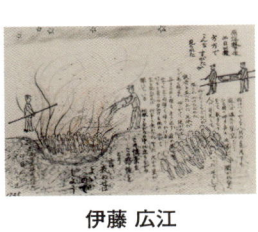

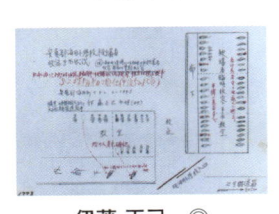

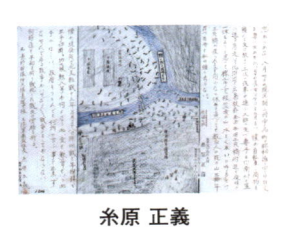

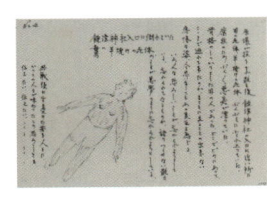

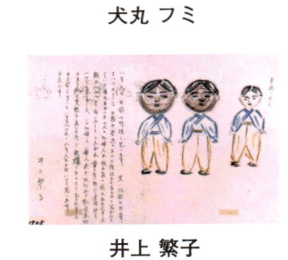

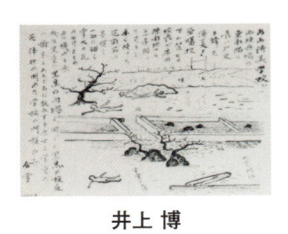

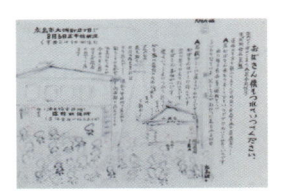

板倉 幸栄	一川 二三 ◎	市田 融慈	市延 美由紀
市場 京子	伊塚 シズノ ◎	井手元 潔子 ◎	井手本 義夫
伊藤 小糸	伊藤 庫敏	伊藤 悟	伊藤 広江
伊藤 正己 ◎	糸原 正義	稲垣 多喜雄 ◎	犬丸 フミ
井上 愛子	井上 イツコ	井上 清	井上 繁子
井上 静雄	井上 田鶴子	井上 ツワノ	井上 博
井上 浩	井上 美恵子	井上 三喜夫	今井 逸二

130

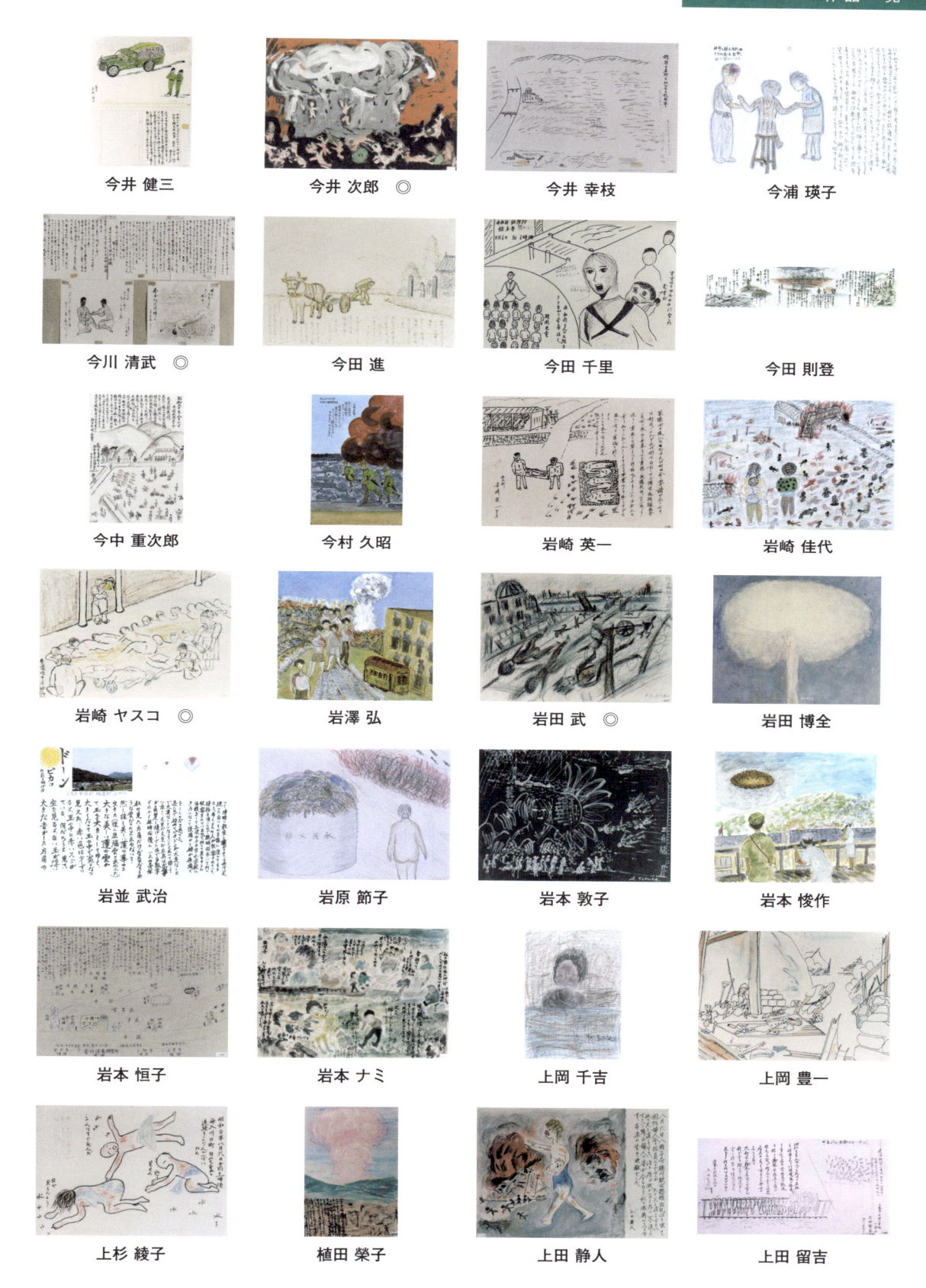

作品一覧

今井 健三　今井 次郎 ◎　今井 幸枝　今浦 瑛子

今川 清武 ◎　今田 進　今田 千里　今田 則登

今中 重次郎　今村 久昭　岩崎 英一　岩崎 佳代

岩崎 ヤスコ ◎　岩澤 弘　岩田 武 ◎　岩田 博全

岩並 武治　岩原 節子　岩本 敦子　岩本 悛作

岩本 恒子　岩本 ナミ　上岡 千吉　上岡 豊一

上杉 綾子　植田 榮子　上田 静人　上田 留吉

131

上田 宏 ◎	上田 富貴代	植田 ミツコ	上田 良三
上藤 軍六	上野 和子	上野 清明	上野 馬左登
上向 静枝	右近 明敏	右近 文子	宇佐川 良
生塩 敏夫	牛尾 富子	宇治原 房代	宇城 フユコ
後田 末美	薄 栄助	打越 嘉子	内田 照彦
内田 豊	内山 新助	内山 純子	内海 昭子
畝 正登	宇野 耕司	馬越 治男 ◎	梅野 栄

作品一覧

梅村 定二	海野 吉郎	益本 ユキミ	江種 茂
恵下 計一郎	江角 隆雄	江村 良雄	煙上 博隆
遠藤 留雄	遠藤 弘	大上 清行	大川 チサ子
大川 哲也	大木 シズヱ	大久保 戒道	大倉 キミヨ
大澤 タカオ	大島 幸子	大杉 寿雄	大杉 好夫
太田 勝子	大谷 勝彦	大藤 誠	大成 徳夫
大西 比呂志	大西 安子	大場 孝子	大本 貢

133

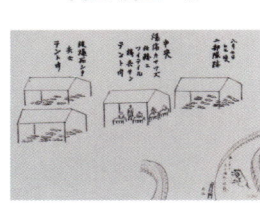

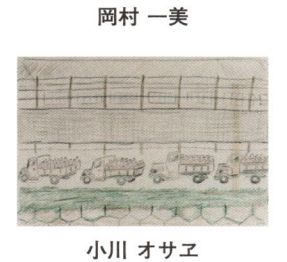

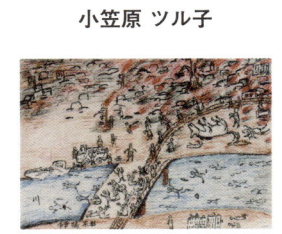

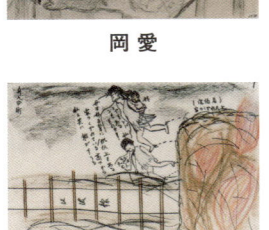

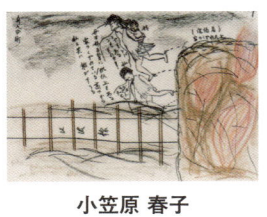

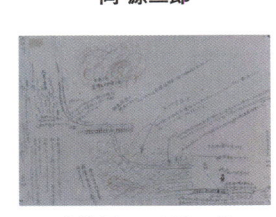

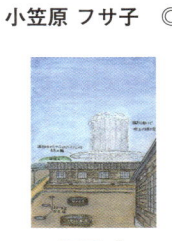

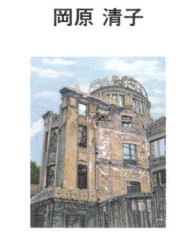

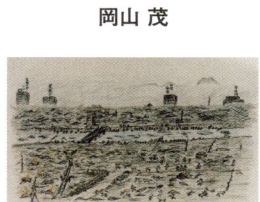

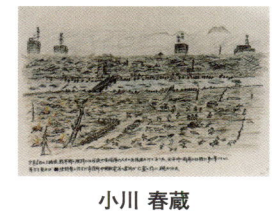

大本 八千代	大山 節夫	岡 愛	岡 源三郎
岡崎 清美	小笠原 ツル子	小笠原 春子	小笠原 フサ子 ◎
岡田 円一 ◎	岡田 佐美子	岡田 政行	岡田 守
岡田 満登 ◎	岡野 哲	岡野 普選	岡原 清子
岡村 一美	岡村 スマノ	岡村 博子	岡山 茂
小川 オサヱ	小川 勝澄	小川 佐智子	小川 春蔵
沖 信枝	沖井 ちか	沖川 保江	沖川 義雄

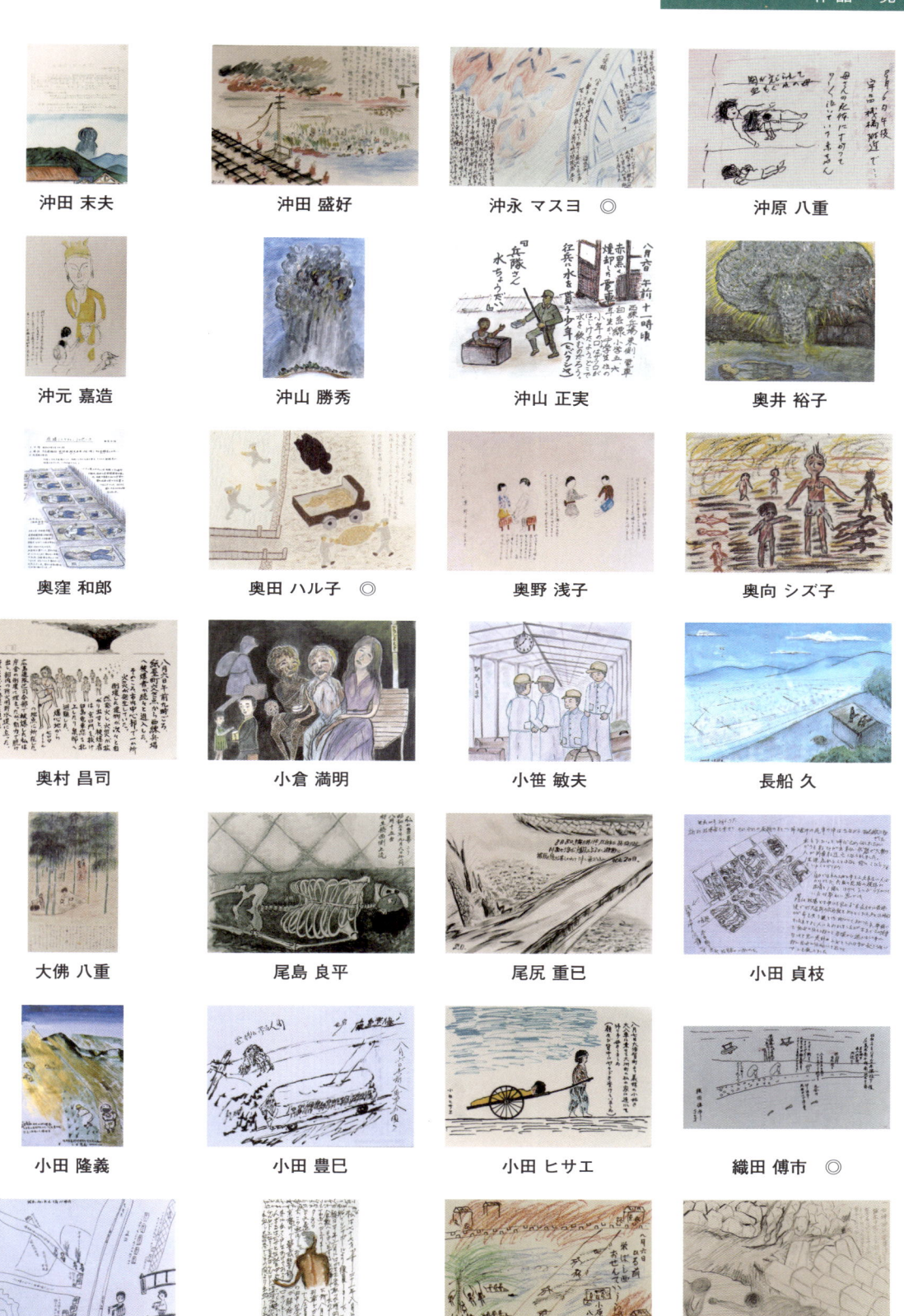

作品一覧

沖田 末夫	沖田 盛好	沖永 マスヨ ◎	沖原 八重
沖元 嘉造	沖山 勝秀	沖山 正実	奥井 裕子
奥窪 和郎	奥田 ハル子 ◎	奥野 浅子	奥向 シズ子
奥村 昌司	小倉 満明	小笹 敏夫	長船 久
大佛 八重	尾島 良平	尾尻 重巳	小田 貞枝
小田 隆義	小田 豊巳	小田 ヒサエ	織田 傳市 ◎
落合 フミコ	小野 照昌	小原 カネ	重谷 喜美江

135

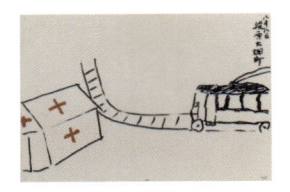

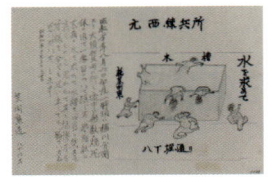

貝川 百合子	香川 勇	香川 喜美恵	香川 清
賀川 里子	賀川 将	香川 千代江	香川 ヒサエ
賀川 博	加川 宏	垣井 文枝	角井 小津美
陰山 壽美恵	笠井 美津子	笠間 勲造 ◎	梶田 瞳
梶谷 俊夫	梶谷 年子	梶野 清子	加島 美重子 ◎
鍛治屋 末美	梶矢 文昭	梶山 アキノ	梶山 繁吉
加瀬 時夫	片桐 サワミ	片桐 豊彦	片山 フジ

作品一覧

勝田 光子	勝田 実	嘉戸 多恵子	加藤 タマエ ◎
香藤 利枝	加藤 久男	加藤 譲　武内 五郎	金川 玲子
金尾 滝一	金子 亘秀	金桝 廣子	金光 德容
金森 マツコ	金行 清香	加納 良三	兜山 年子
神川 巖 ◎	上西 薫	神本 信夫	亀井 五十子
亀好 ヒサノ	加茂 一三	嘉屋 文子	河井 恭子
川合 ミヱ子	川上 喜蔵	川口 富子 ◎	河口 房子

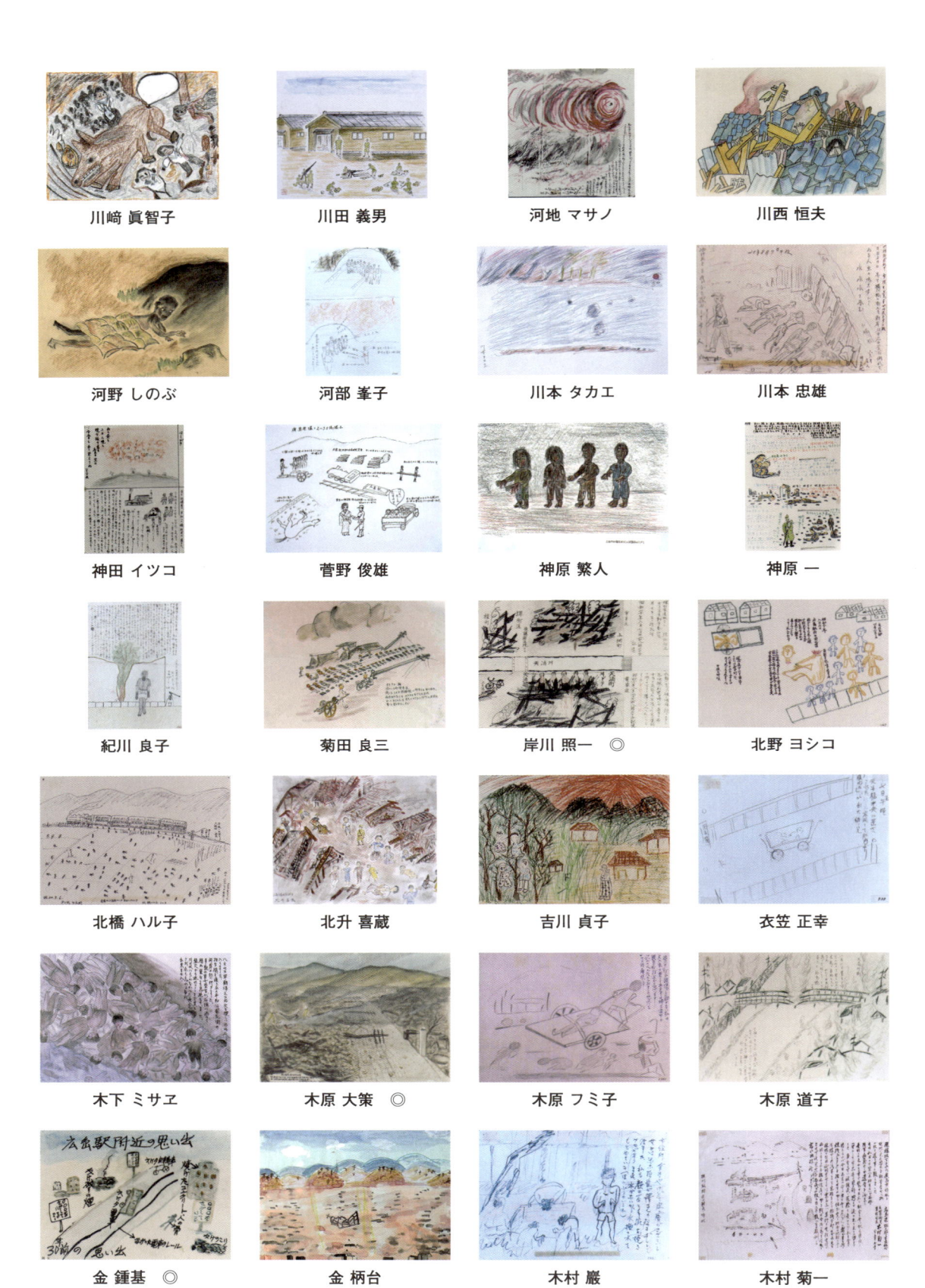

川﨑 眞智子	川田 義男	河地 マサノ	川西 恒夫
河野 しのぶ	河部 峯子	川本 タカエ	川本 忠雄
神田 イツコ	菅野 俊雄	神原 繁人	神原 一
紀川 良子	菊田 良三	岸川 照一 ◎	北野 ヨシコ
北橋 ハル子	北升 喜蔵	吉川 貞子	衣笠 正幸
木下 ミサヱ	木原 大策 ◎	木原 フミ子	木原 道子
金 鍾基 ◎	金 柄台	木村 巖	木村 菊一

作品一覧

木村 幸作	木村 貞子	木村 重治	木村 太矩次
木村 正	木屋 喜勝　田中 虎雄	喜代吉 五郎	久井 一章
久賀 タミヨ	草川 ヨシエ	草田 キヌ	草田 隆夫
草田 正男	櫛 詠子	楠田 フミ子	楠見 ハツエ
工藤 泰弘	國貞 勇	国見 徳雄	國森 平吉 ◎
久野井 聖観	久保 秀子	熊木 久忠	久村 芳男
粂 典之甫 ◎	公文 寿子	蔵本 芳子	栗田 義美

139

黒川 光道	黒崎 昇勝	桑原 寿子	粂本 勝子
桑本 トキコ	慶徳 信子 ◎	K. H.	小泉 越子 ◎
小市 キヨ子 ◎	小出 修	香口 真作	高下 武人
纐纈 隆久	甲田 敏春	江田 法行	河内 政子
河内山 聖	河野 一郎	河野 か津	河野 サダ子
高野 信政	河野 寛治	河野 安夫	河野 洋郎 ◎
神山 晋	神山 幸子	小久保 三好	児玉 宇多子

作品一覧

児玉 武子	児玉 時春	児玉 冨美子	後藤 雅子
小西 トモ子	小西 良子	小早川 浅蔵	小早川 静枝
小早川 泰造	小林 かずゑ	古林 和夫	小林 清子
小林 正男	小林 正巳	小林 みちよ	小林 みつ
小林 豊	小堀 茂	駒田 保	紺田 ヨ子
近藤 最	佐伯 敏子	佐伯 マスノ	佐伯 三枝
佐伯 實	斉藤 敬一	斉藤 安子	才野 マツ子

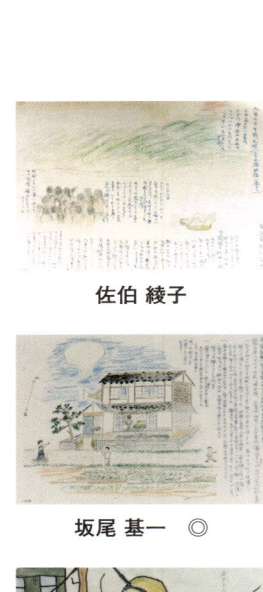

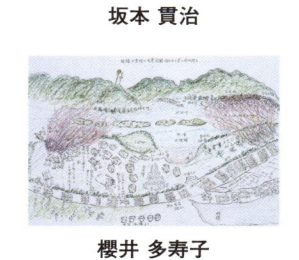

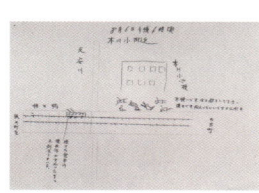

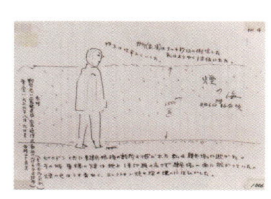

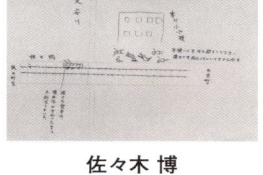

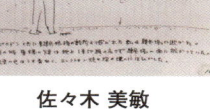

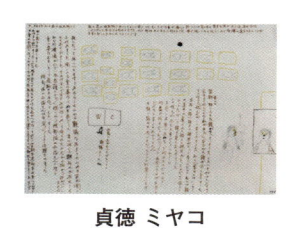

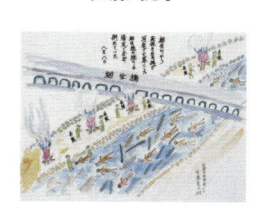

佐伯 綾子	佐伯 千代香	坂井 巖	坂井 武彦
坂尾 基一 ◎	阪田 寛	坂谷 益於	坂本 貫治
先小山 勝	作本 征二	桜井 賢三	櫻井 多寿子
佐々木 悟史	佐々木 肇	佐々木 博	佐々木 美敏
佐々木 ヲシエ	笹口 里子	篠山 益治	貞徳 ミヤコ
貞森 幹夫	佐藤 教	佐藤 健美	佐藤 祝子
佐藤 法行	佐藤 良生	佐藤 芳治	実藤 良三

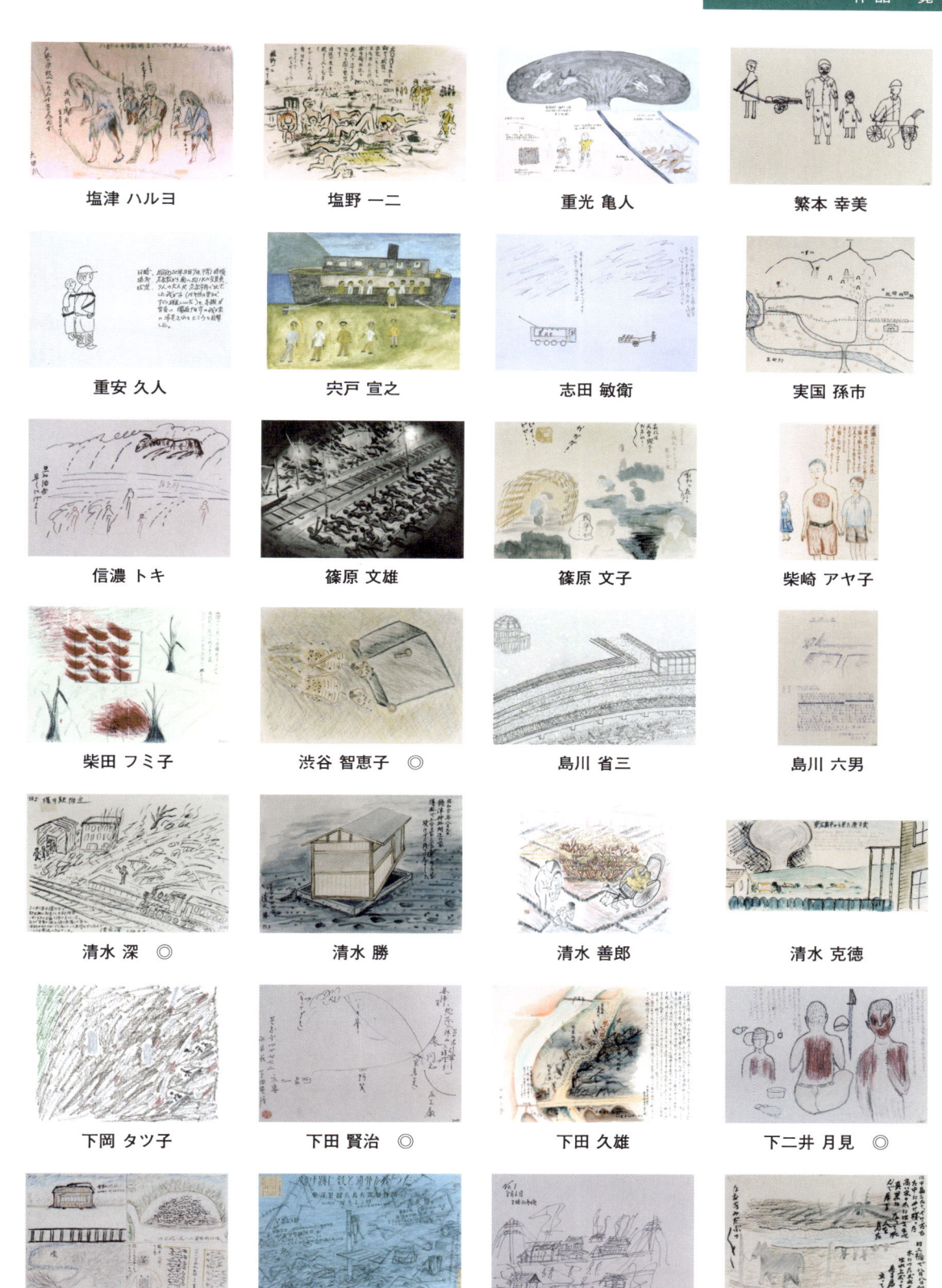

作品一覧

塩津 ハルヨ	塩野 一二	重光 亀人	繁本 幸美
重安 久人	宍戸 宣之	志田 敏衛	実国 孫市
信濃 トキ	篠原 文雄	篠原 文子	柴崎 アヤ子
柴田 フミ子	渋谷 智恵子 ◎	島川 省三	島川 六男
清水 深 ◎	清水 勝	清水 善郎	清水 克徳
下岡 タツ子	下田 賢治 ◎	下田 久雄	下二井 月見 ◎
霜村 喜一	下村 儀三	庄賀 美登	正田 ツネヨ

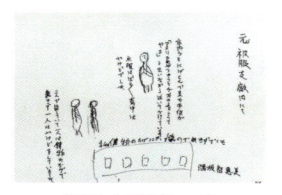

白石 千津子	白川 法光	新谷 幸枝	進藤 不三枝
末国 品吉	末光 五三	菅 敏孝	菅原 盛雄
杉浦 善蔵	杉江 敬一	杉﨑 友昭	杉田 高二 ◎
杉原 悟	杉本 サダ子	杉本 仙	杉本 知佐子
鈴木 旭	鈴木 国勢	鈴木 太三郎	鈴木 恒昭
鈴木 半三	砂田 房子	砂田 フジ子	砂原 福吉
須磨 總子	角 テル	隅坂 智恵美 ◎	住田 和之

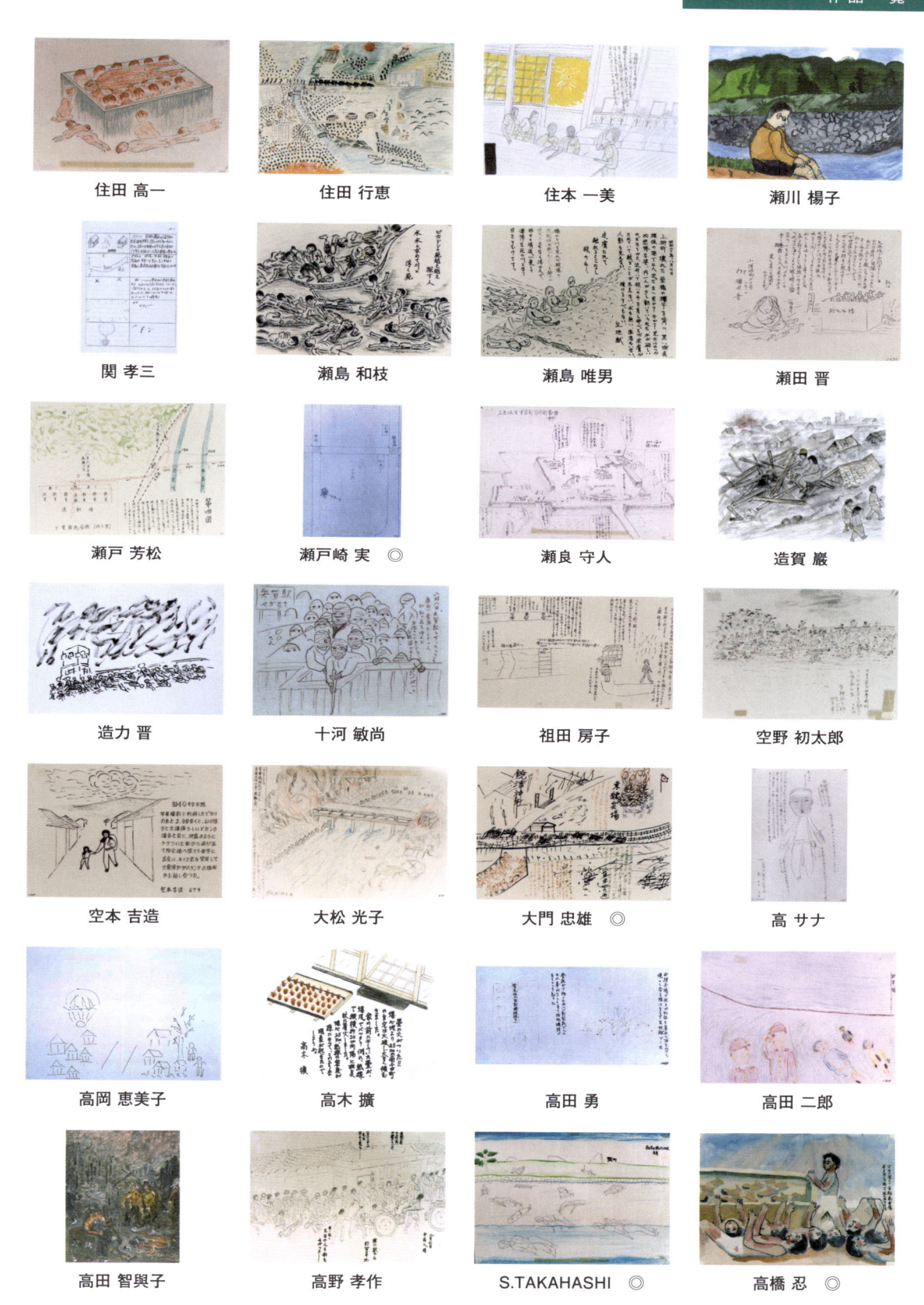

作品一覧

住田 高一	住田 行恵	住本 一美	瀬川 楊子
関 孝三	瀬島 和枝	瀬島 唯男	瀬田 晋
瀬戸 芳松	瀬戸崎 実 ◎	瀬良 守人	造賀 巖
造力 晋	十河 敏尚	祖田 房子	空野 初太郎
空本 吉造	大松 光子	大門 忠雄 ◎	高 サナ
高岡 恵美子	高木 擴	高田 勇	高田 二郎
高田 智與子	高野 孝作	S.TAKAHASHI ◎	高橋 忍 ◎

145

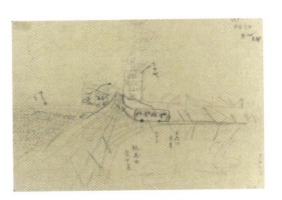

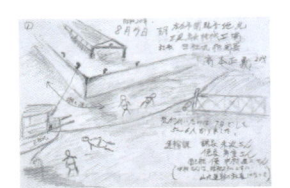

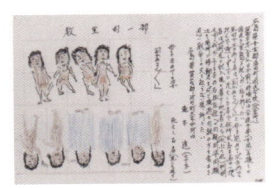

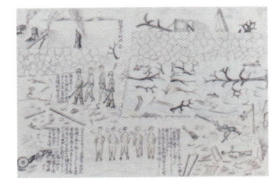

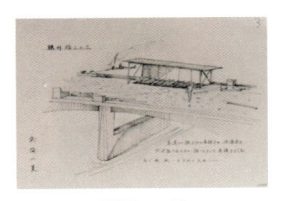

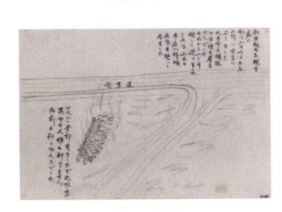

高橋 鉦二	高橋 宏	高橋 正明	高丸 恭仁子
高見沢 安正	高宮 ヨシノ	高本 正義	高安 豊司
瀧川 ヤスコ	滝本 透	田口 清三郎	宅明 香澄
竹内 要 ◎	竹内 只志	竹内 初二	竹腰 宗一
竹下 士郎	武田 明人	武田 一美	武田 益義
武田 靖彦	竹友 忠雄	武永 三太郎	竹中 宝
竹本 重市	竹本 秀子	田阪 古都美	田坂 敏彦

作品一覧

田島 武雄	多田 照子 ◎	多田 藤助	多田 好一
多々良 映子 ◎	辰井 博務	辰岩 秀子	辰岡 綾子
立田 コミ子	田所 久伸	田中 岩夫	田中 暎郎
田中 啓吾	田中 武彦	田中 常正	田中 富安
田中 春男	田中 弓子	田邉 俊三郎	谷 幸太郎 ◎
谷 豪雄	谷内 サミ	谷上 一六	谷川 好枝
渓口 正蔵	谷口 良行	谷峰 アキヱ ◎	胤森貴士・トーマス

147

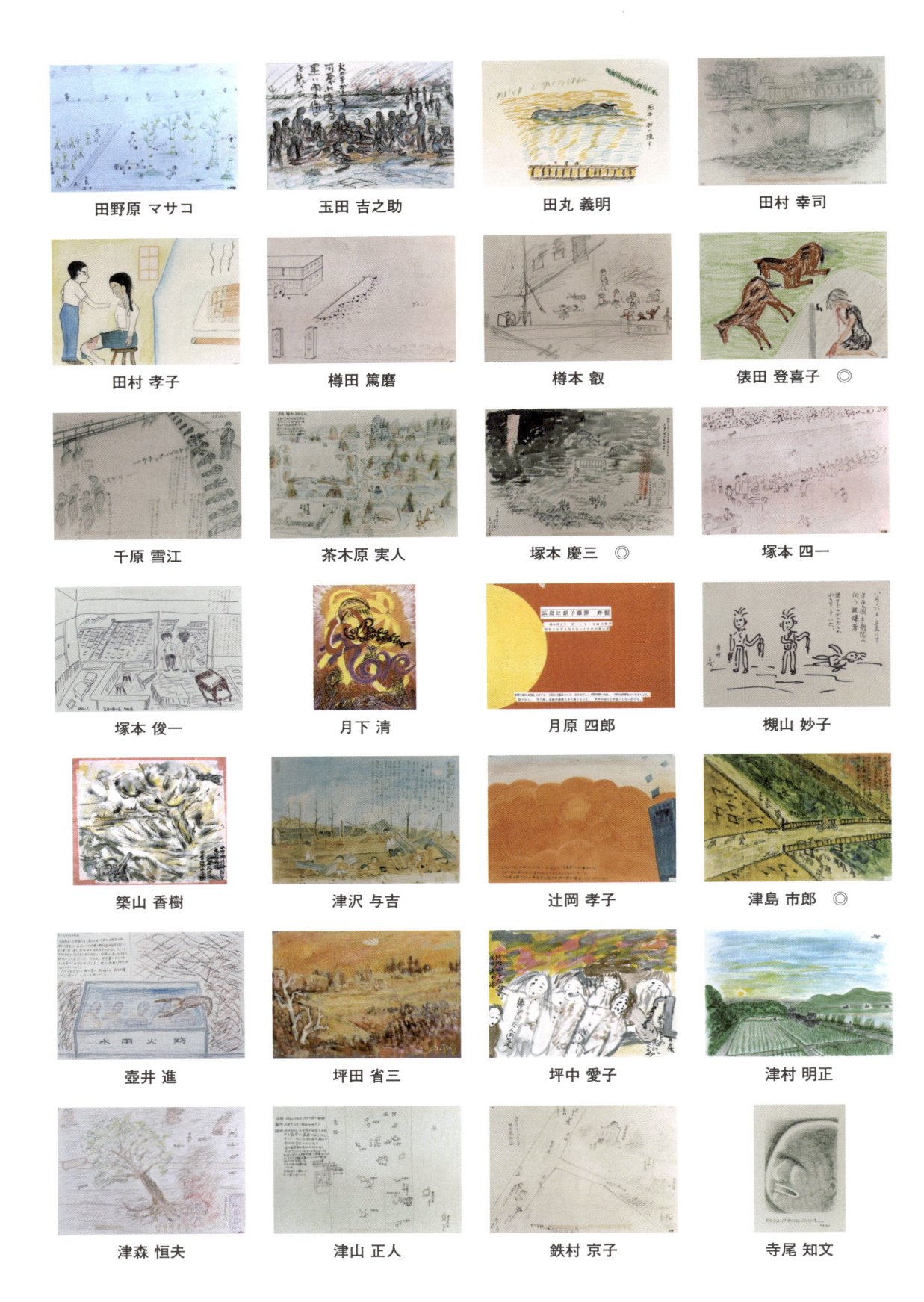

田野原 マサコ	玉田 吉之助	田丸 義明	田村 幸司
田村 孝子	樽田 篤磨	樽本 叡	俵田 登喜子 ◎
千原 雪江	茶木原 実人	塚本 慶三 ◎	塚本 四一
塚本 俊一	月下 清	月原 四郎	槻山 妙子
築山 香樹	津沢 与吉	辻岡 孝子	津島 市郎 ◎
壺井 進	坪田 省三	坪中 愛子	津村 明正
津森 恒夫	津山 正人	鉄村 京子	寺尾 知文

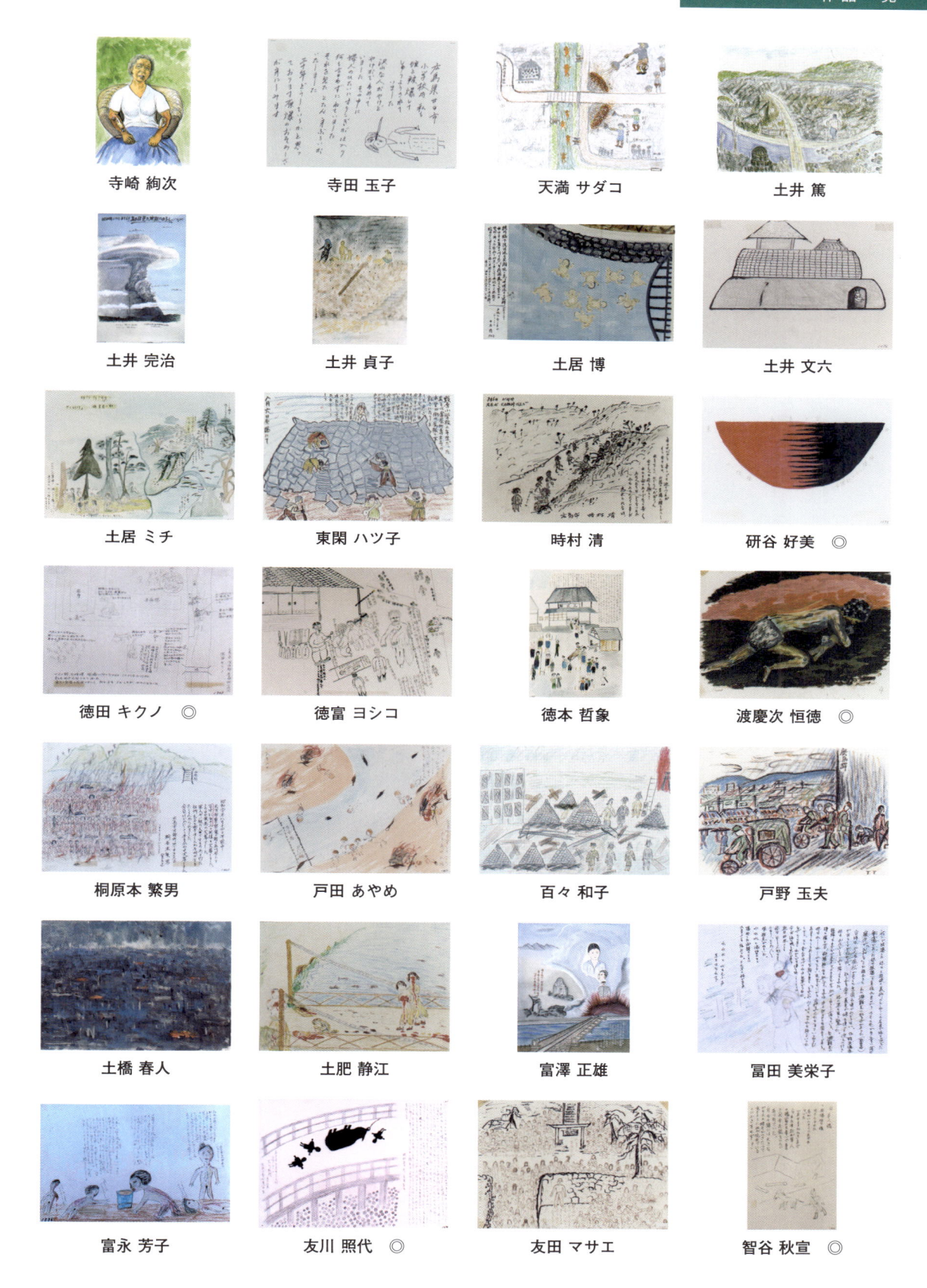

作品一覧

寺崎 絢次	寺田 玉子	天満 サダコ	土井 篤
土井 完治	土井 貞子	土居 博	土井 文六
土居 ミチ	東閑 ハツ子	時村 清	研谷 好美 ◎
徳田 キクノ ◎	徳富 ヨシコ	徳本 哲象	渡慶次 恒徳 ◎
桐原本 繁男	戸田 あやめ	百々 和子	戸野 玉夫
土橋 春人	土肥 静江	富澤 正雄	冨田 美栄子
富永 芳子	友川 照代 ◎	友田 マサエ	智谷 秋宣 ◎

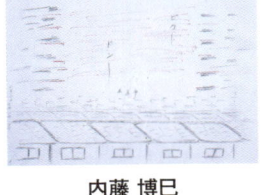

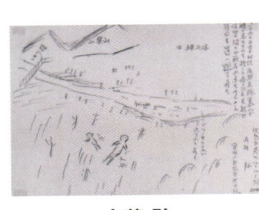

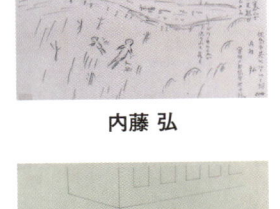

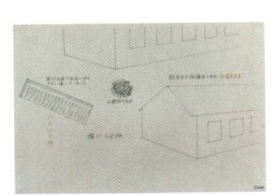

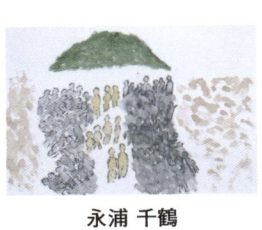

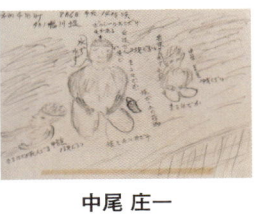

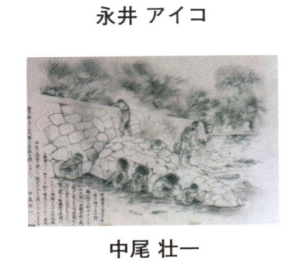

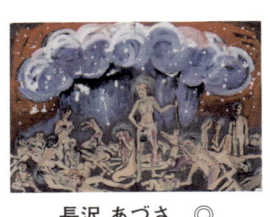

豊田 清史	鳥井 保司 ◎	冨田 実	内藤 弘
内藤 博巳	内藤 正道 ◎	永井 アイコ	仲井 仙之助
永浦 千鶴	中尾 庄一	中尾 壮一	永尾 隆秀
中尾 千代子	中尾 正男	長岡 ワカエ	中川 清
中川 謙	中川 信子	長沢 あづさ ◎	中沢 サワノ ◎
中澤 彪	長沢 由紀 ◎	中島 秋人	中島 和明
中島 ツルヨ	中田 伍一	中田 スエミ	中田 輝子

作品一覧

中田 義明	中谷 昇	中藤 智行	中西 俊佳
仲根 鉄郎	中野 國松	中野 貞治	中野 正英
永浜 初代 ◎	中原 ヤヱコ	中平 武司	長見 英希
中村 嘉作	中村 和三	中村 達吾 ◎	中村 久世 ◎
中村 正子	中村 マサノ	中村 都子	中村 雄子
中本 源次	中本 秀子	名柄 規四郎	名柄 敏子
名原 武子	楢原 裕子	南野 昭美	難波 雪枝

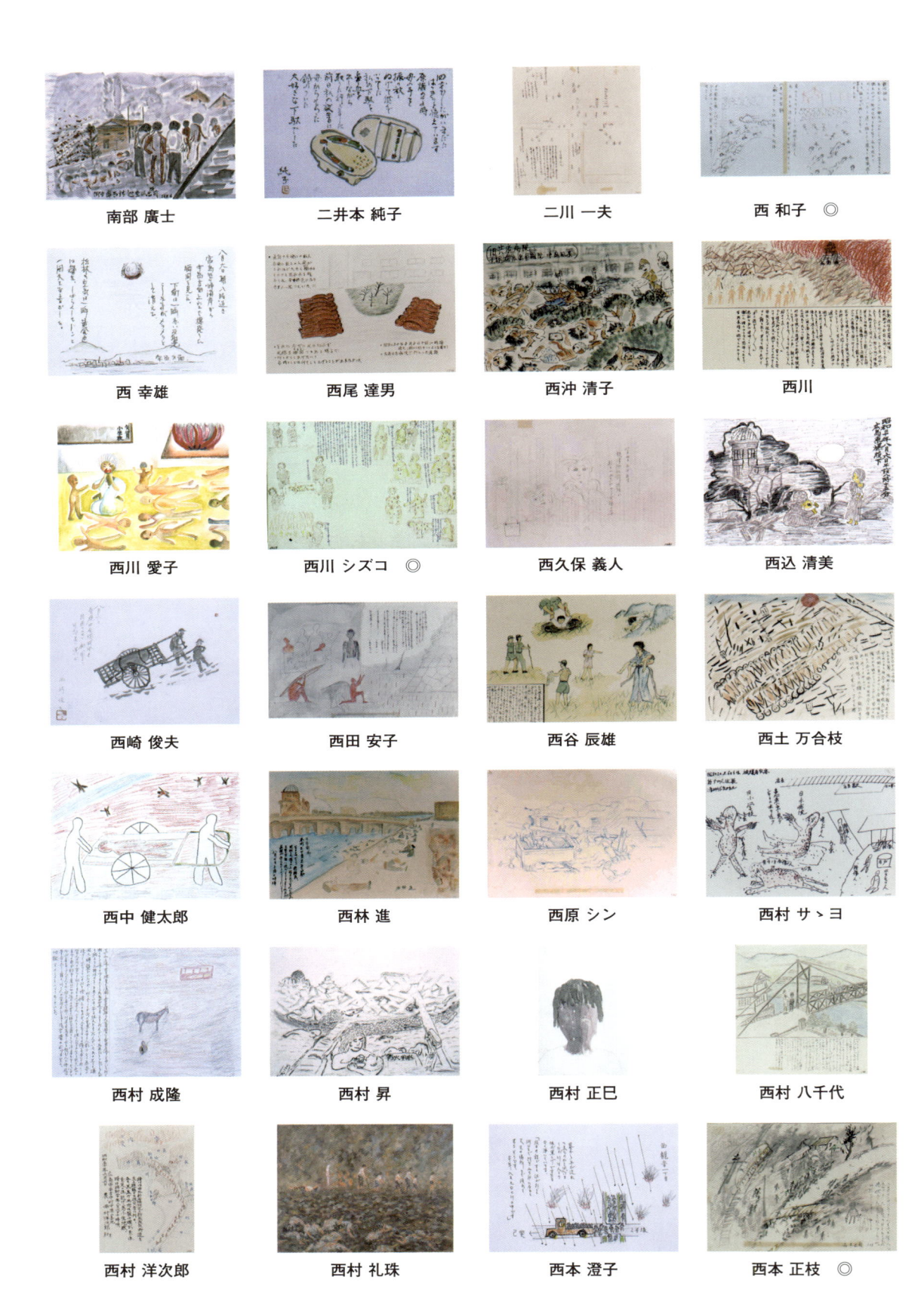

南部 廣士	二井本 純子	二川 一夫	西 和子 ◎
西 幸雄	西尾 達男	西沖 清子	西川
西川 愛子	西川 シズコ ◎	西久保 義人	西込 清美
西崎 俊夫	西田 安子	西谷 辰雄	西土 万合枝
西中 健太郎	西林 進	西原 シン	西村 サヽヨ
西村 成隆	西村 昇	西村 正巳	西村 八千代
西村 洋次郎	西村 礼珠	西本 澄子	西本 正枝 ◎

作品一覧

西本 好子	西山 勝登	西山 吟一	二反田 熊太郎
日山 清実	新田 カツ	丹羽 寿 ◎	沼田 鈴子
根石 福司	根本 小夜子	野崎 和夫	野島 亀太郎
野瀬 佳子 ◎	野村 一雄 ◎	野村 好光	野元 彊
範重 精三	萩原 貞子	橋浜 審	橋本 圭次郎
橋本 健介　高尾 泉	橋本 坂市	橋本 マチヨ	畑 三郎
秦 進一	畑 治良 ◎	畑 ユキコ	畠岡 豊子

153

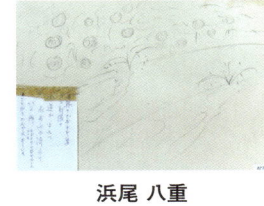

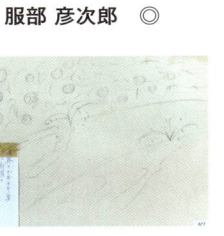

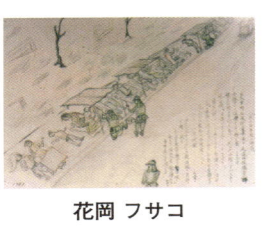

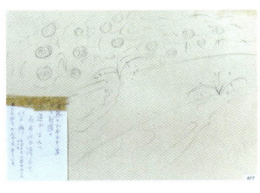

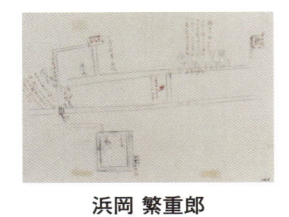

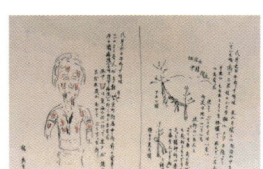

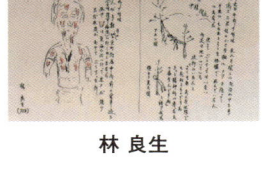

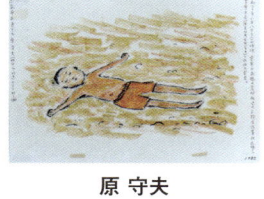

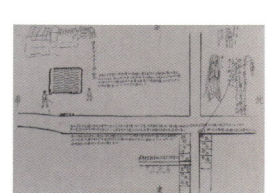

服部 萩	服部 彦次郎 ◎	花岡 フサコ	花岡 ルリ子
花里 儀一	浜尾 八重	浜岡 繁重郎	浜岡 英枝
濱田 佳代	濱田 幸子	濱田 義雄	林 忠之
林 美佐夫	林 良生	原 邦彦	原 達郎
原 敏子	原 守夫	原岡 秋子 ◎	原田 勇
原田 敬二	原田 照美	原田 東雄	原田 安正
原田 ヨシヲ ◎	播本 啓次郎	番 健	檜垣 キミヨ

作品一覧

東 進	東 道代	東 安夫	東谷 トミエ
日南 弘宗	檜山 良子	桧山 義久	平 武士
平井 久仁子	平井 重子	平井 ツルヨ	平川 イトヨ ◎
平川 カツ子	平川 林木	平田 照昌	平田 勝
平野 馨 ◎	平野 鉱三	廣川 越子	廣中 トラコ
廣中 春明	廣本 改次	檜皮 幸子	深川 宗俊
深田 利幸	福井 千代	福岡 光	福田 安次

155

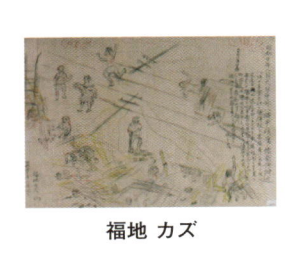

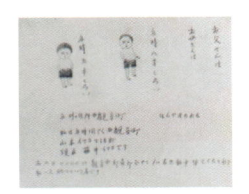

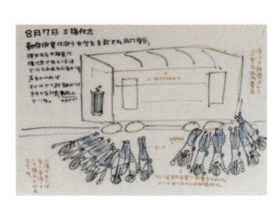

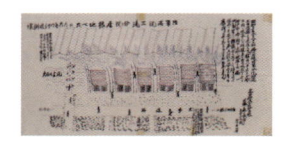

福地 カズ	藤井 イマ子 ◎	藤井 高一	藤井 茂男
藤井千代子	藤井 実	藤岡 澄人	藤岡 久之
藤川 博	藤川 順子	藤重 忠子	藤田 フジエ
藤田 眞喜子	藤田 昌一	藤田 マサコ	藤田 弥生
藤村 光子　藤村 智子	藤本 幸子	藤本 四郎	藤本 仁一
藤本 蔦子	藤本 英雄	藤本 正之	藤本 盛男
藤森 長市	舟越 吉光	布野 正夫	古井 ナツコ

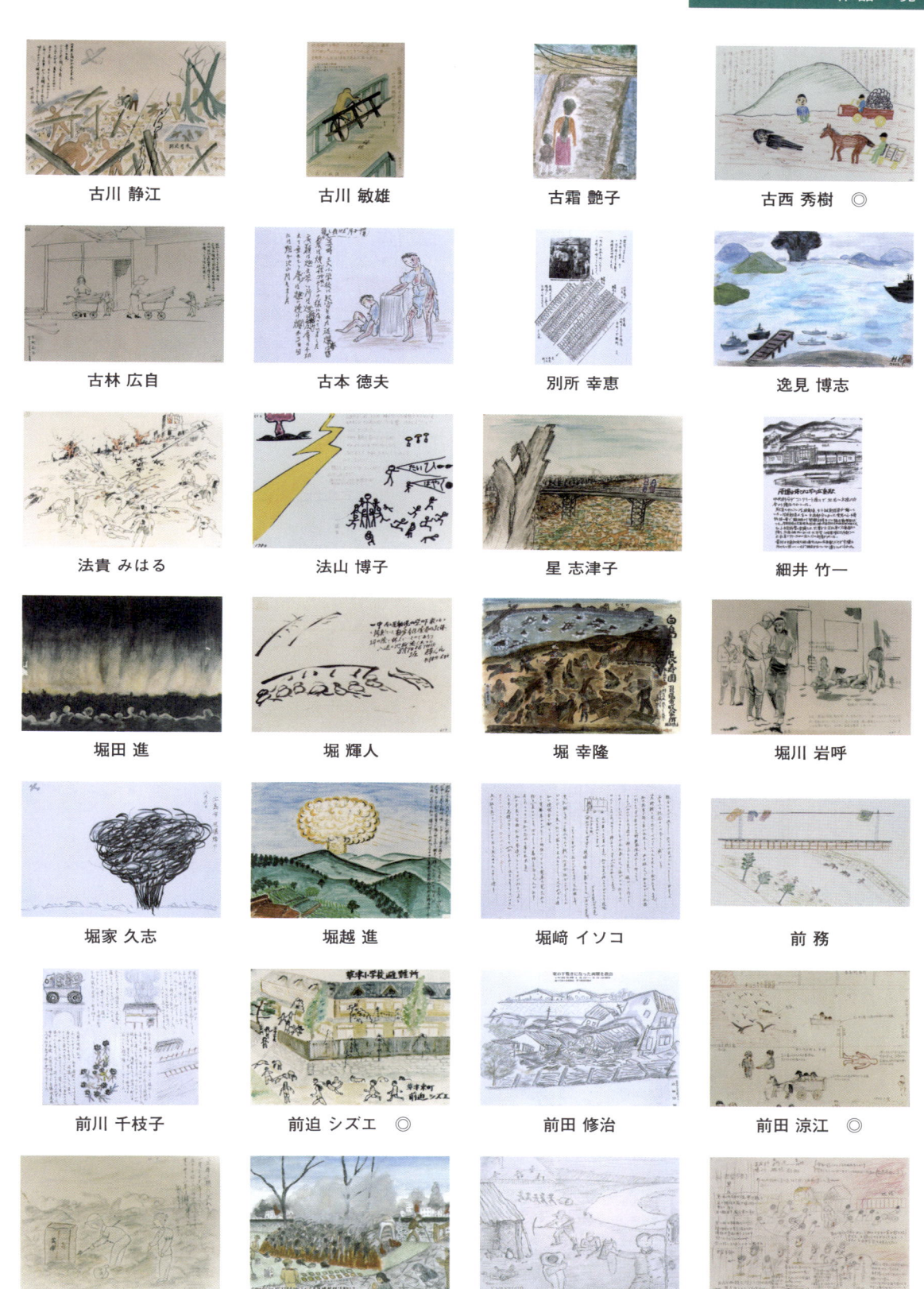

作品一覧

古川 静江	古川 敏雄	古霜 艶子	古西 秀樹 ◎
古林 広自	古本 徳夫	別所 幸恵	逸見 博志
法貴 みはる	法山 博子	星 志津子	細井 竹一
堀田 進	堀 輝人	堀 幸隆	堀川 岩呼
堀家 久志	堀越 進	堀﨑 イソコ	前 務
前川 千枝子	前迫 シズエ ◎	前田 修治	前田 涼江 ◎
前土井 美佐子	牧野 俊介	槙本 喜一	眞志田 シズヱ ◎

157

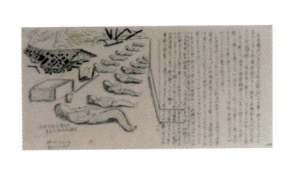

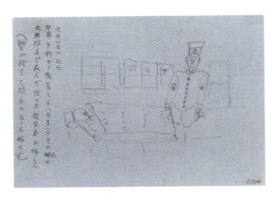

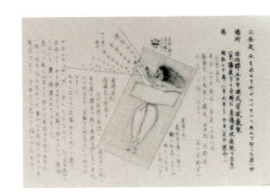

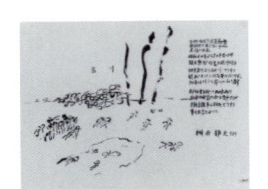

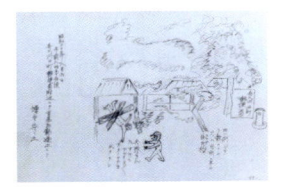

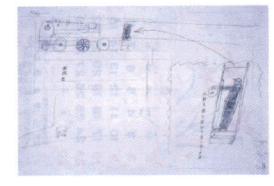

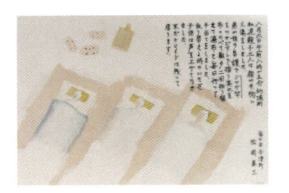

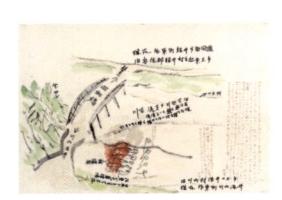

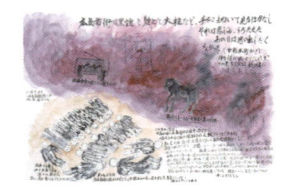

増岡 憲治	升川 貴志栄	増川 昭三	増田 節雄
増田 辰男	増田 ヨシ子	桝原 静夫 ◎	増本 カズヱ
桝本 伸輝	増本 守三	松井 妙子	松井 ます枝
松浦 豊志	松尾 和子	松尾 等 ◎	松尾 政樹
松岡 清徹	松岡 泰三	松下 ハマノ ◎	松島 あや子
松島 要	松島 圭次郎	松島 道枝	松富 光子
松長 静子	松長 雅二	松永 良一	松野 裕

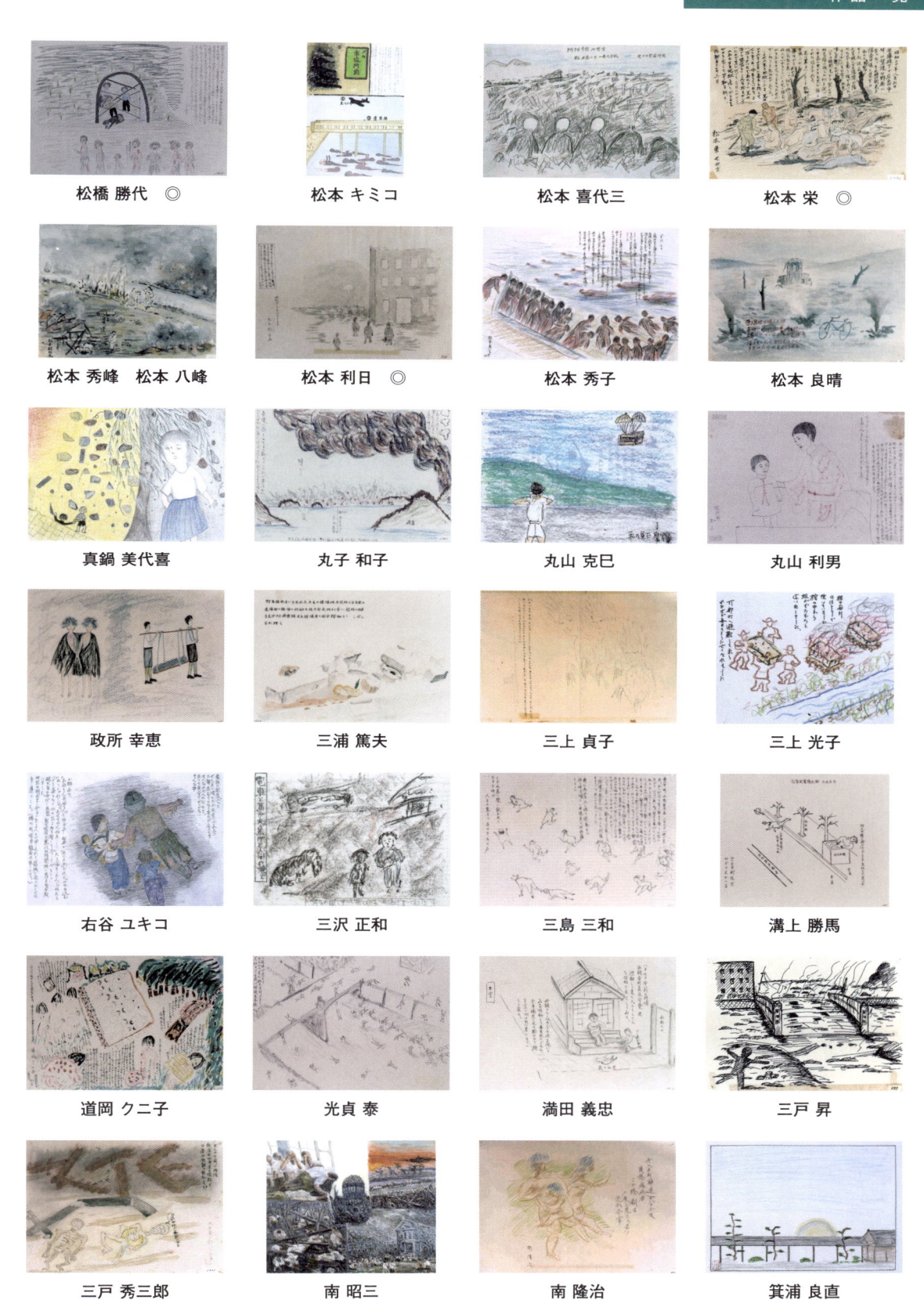

作品一覧

松橋 勝代 ◎	松本 キミコ	松本 喜代三	松本 栄 ◎
松本 秀峰　松本 八峰	松本 利日 ◎	松本 秀子	松本 良晴
真鍋 美代喜	丸子 和子	丸山 克巳	丸山 利男
政所 幸恵	三浦 篤夫	三上 貞子	三上 光子
右谷 ユキコ	三沢 正和	三島 三和	溝上 勝馬
道岡 クニ子	光貞 泰	満田 義忠	三戸 昇
三戸 秀三郎	南 昭三	南 隆治	箕浦 良直

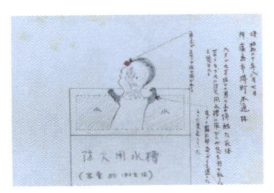

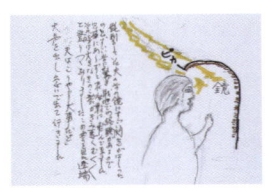

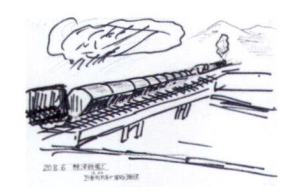

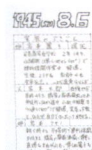

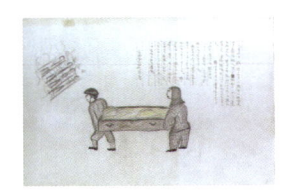

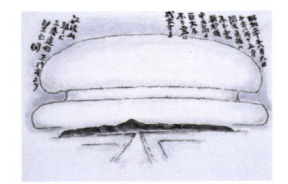

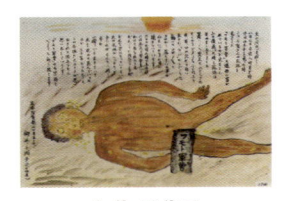

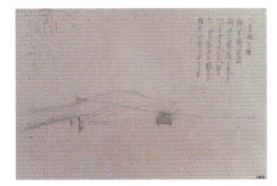

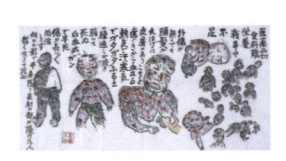

美村 毅	宮内 康子	宮浦 浅登	宮浦 みち子 ◎
宮川 恵美子	宮川 八千代	宮城 タツヨ	宮崎 綾子
宮沢 生駒	宮沢 静一	宮庄 千里	宮原 満男
宮本 鋭	宮本 和人	宮本 勝美	宮本 ゆづみ ◎
明井 吉郎　竹田 初枝	妙見 法彦	三好 茂	三吉 末子 ◎
三次 ハツエ	三好 善昭	向井 千代子	迎林 隆盛
椋 忠六	椋田 行雄 ◎	虫明 とみ恵	宗像 文江

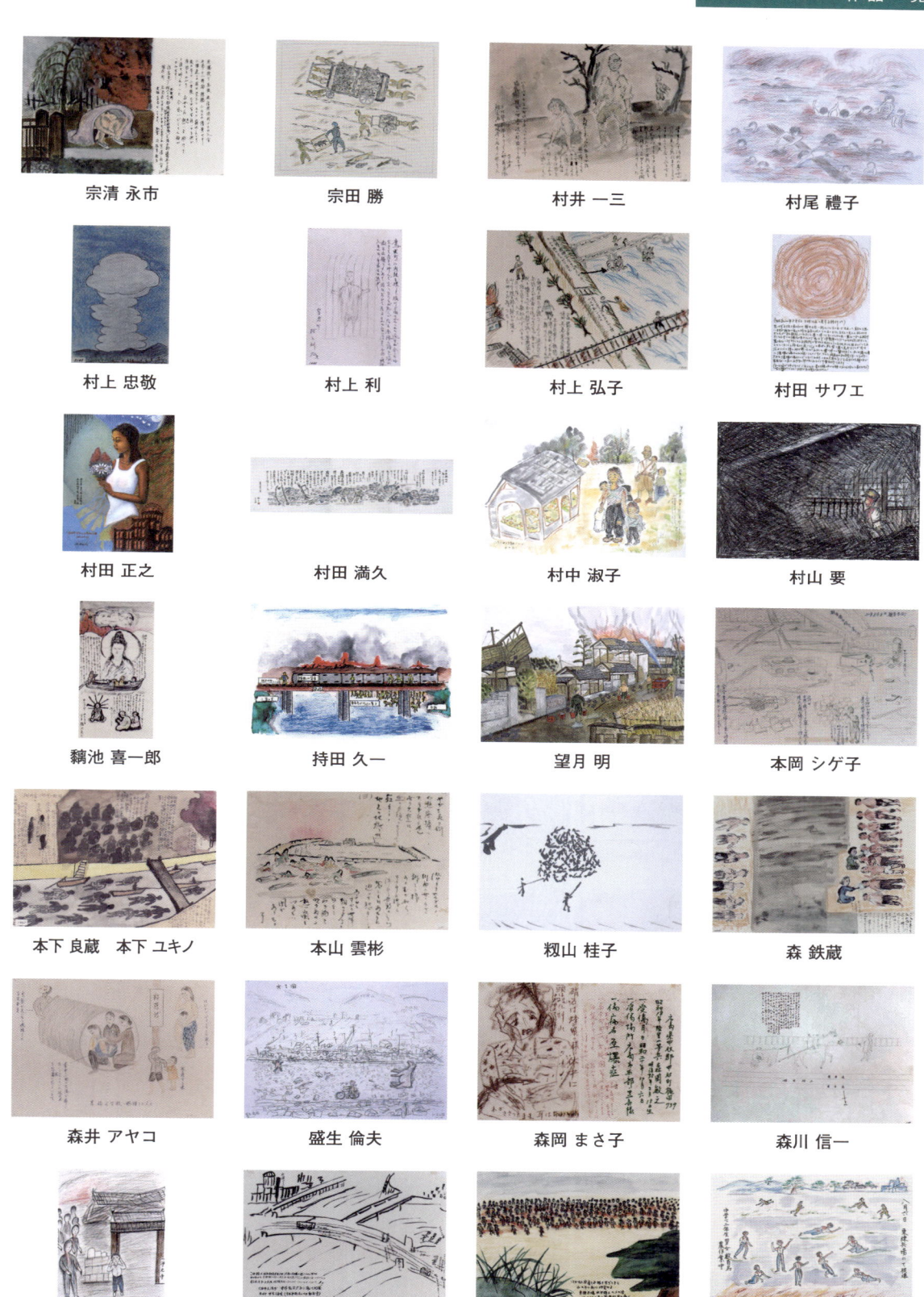

作品一覧

宗清 永市	宗田 勝	村井 一三	村尾 禮子
村上 忠敬	村上 利	村上 弘子	村田 サワエ
村田 正之	村田 満久	村中 淑子	村山 要
藕池 喜一郎	持田 久一	望月 明	本岡 シゲ子
本下 良蔵　本下 ユキノ	本山 雲彬	籾山 桂子	森 鉄蔵
森井 アヤコ	盛生 倫夫	森岡 まさ子	森川 信一
森清 和恵	森重 信夫	森重 美津惠	森田 節子

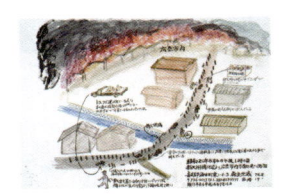

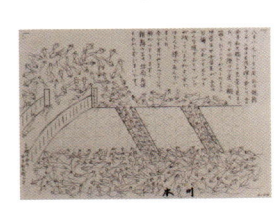

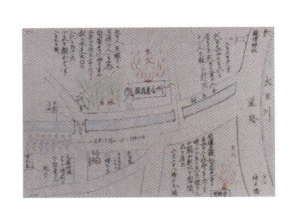

森瀧 澄香	森冨 茂雄	森本 範雄	森矢 光儀
門橋 政子	八木 久子	八木 義彦	八島 猛
安井 勉	安井 信	安国 キミエ	保田 あきの
保田 イサコ	柳本 睦夫	矢野 シゲ子	矢野 盛正
矢野 行夫	八幡 スミ子	矢吹 不二江	山内 正雄
山岡 崇義	山岡 トシコ	山形 明	山県 一枝 ◎
山口 昭治	山口 紀行	山口 藤香	山崎 寛治

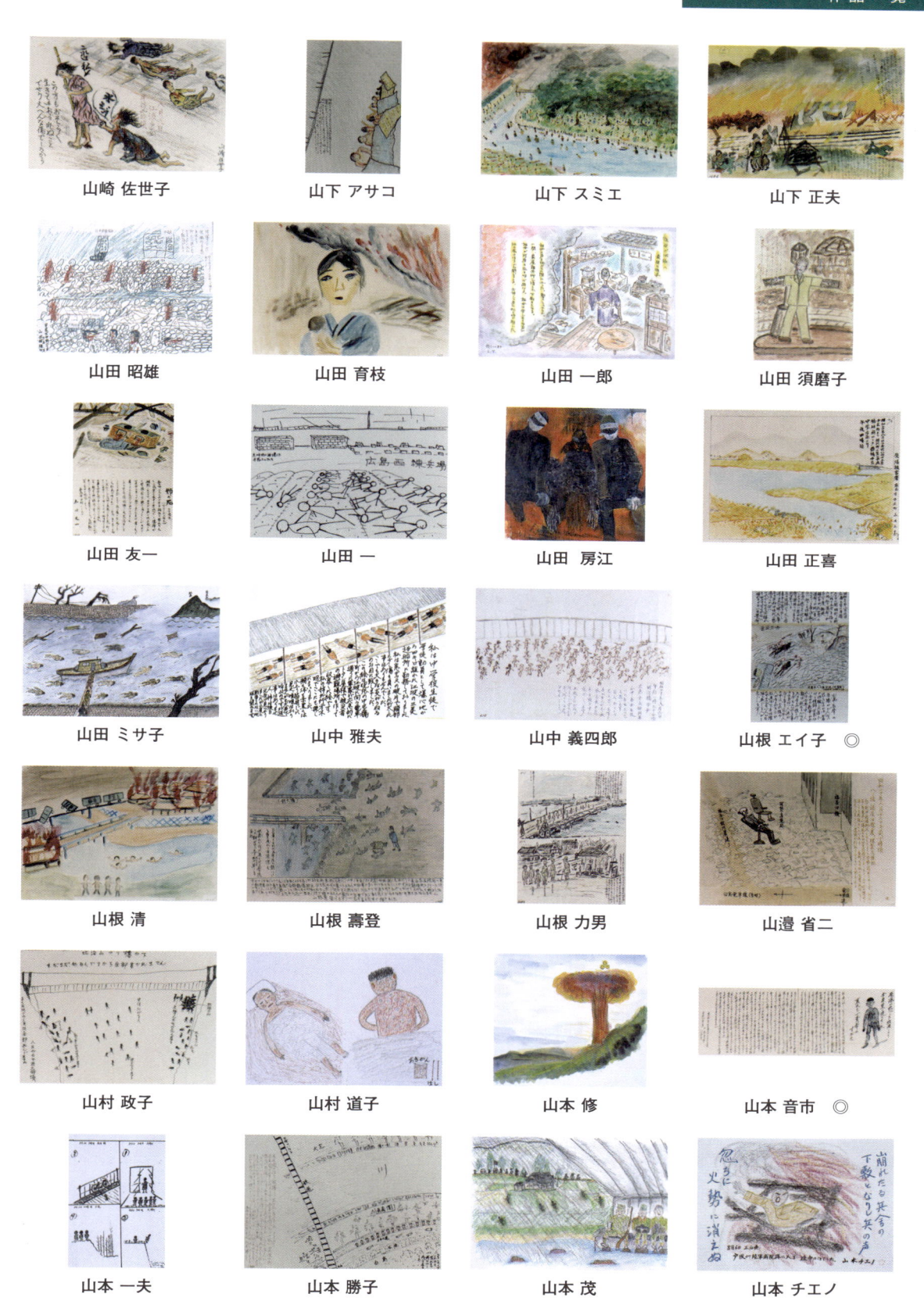

作品一覧

山崎 佐世子	山下 アサコ	山下 スミエ	山下 正夫
山田 昭雄	山田 育枝	山田 一郎	山田 須磨子
山田 友一	山田 一	山田 房江	山田 正喜
山田 ミサ子	山中 雅夫	山中 義四郎	山根 エイ子 ◎
山根 清	山根 壽登	山根 力男	山邉 省二
山村 政子	山村 道子	山本 修	山本 音市 ◎
山本 一夫	山本 勝子	山本 茂	山本 チエノ

163

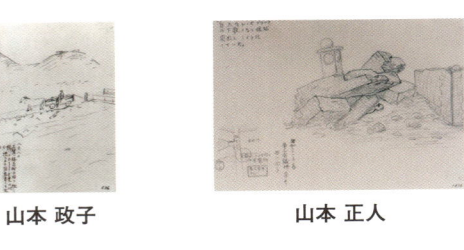

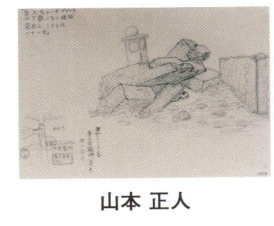

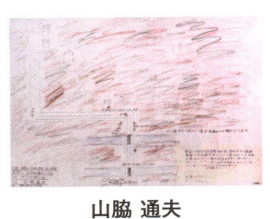

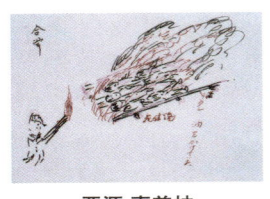

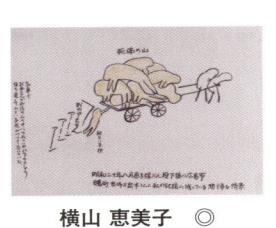

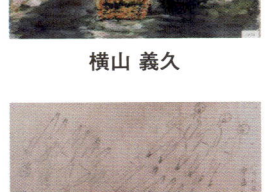

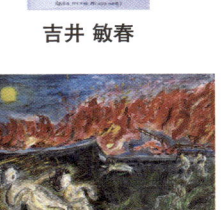

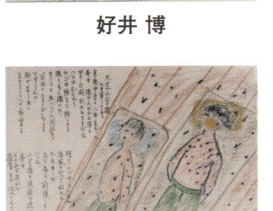

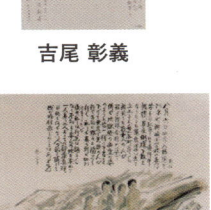

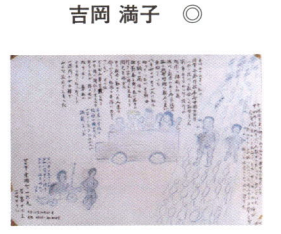

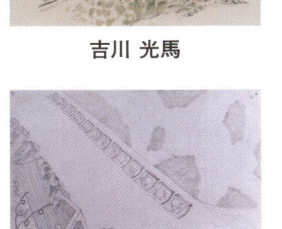

山本 初惠	山本 弘子	山本 政子	山本 正人
山本 満和	山本 八重	山本 康夫	山本 泰正
山脇 通夫	弓場 正荘	要源 喜美枝	横田 俊夫 ◎
横田 勝	横山 恵美子 ◎	横山 十三穂	横山 英子
横山 義久	吉井 敏春	好井 博	吉尾 彰義
吉尾 陸子	吉岡 隆子	吉岡 満子 ◎	吉川 光馬
吉田 弘	吉田 誠	吉富 サワエ	吉長 義唯

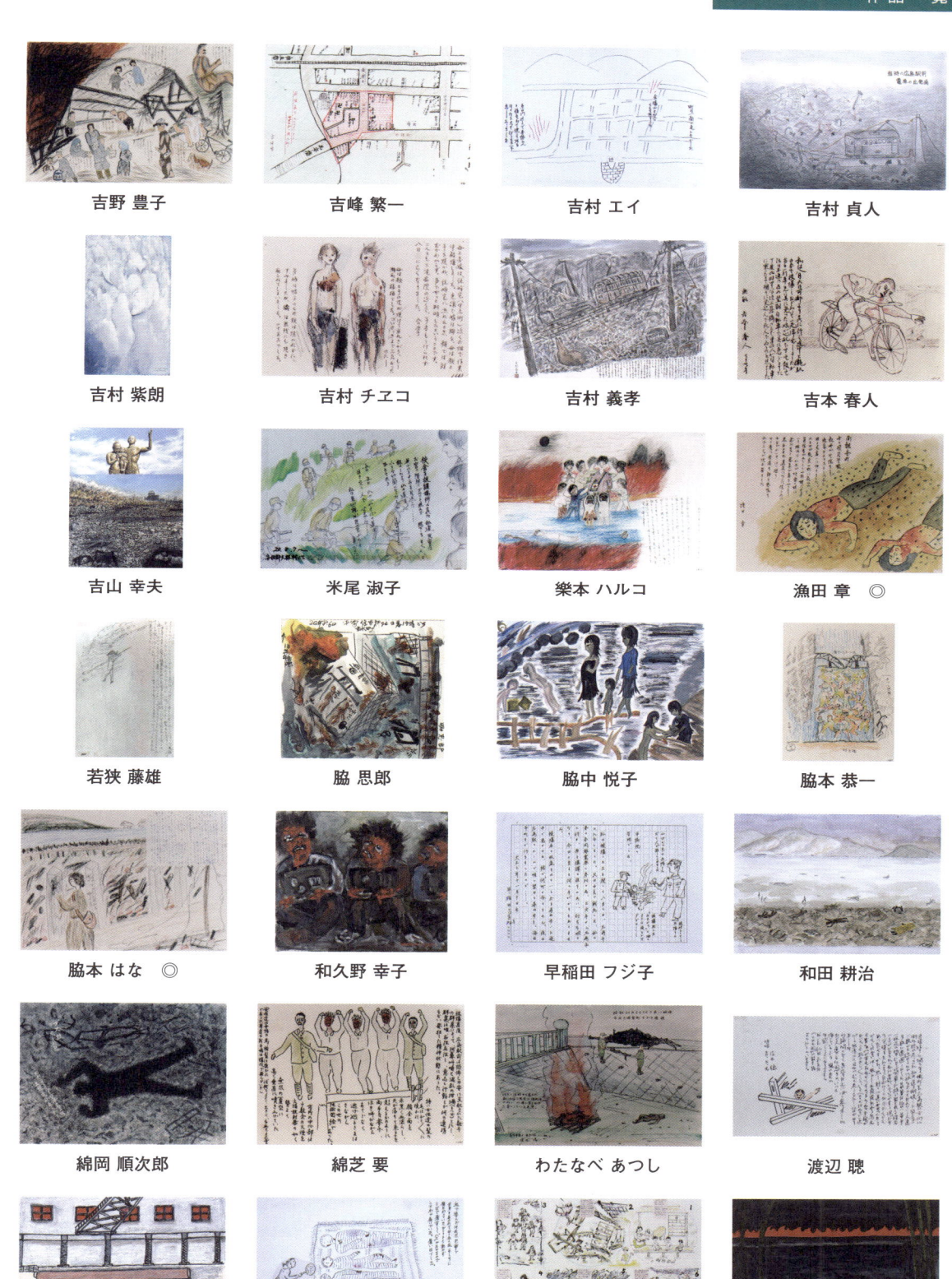

作品一覧

吉野 豊子	吉峰 繁一	吉村 エイ	吉村 貞人
吉村 紫朗	吉村 チヱコ	吉村 義孝	吉本 春人
吉山 幸夫	米尾 淑子	樂本 ハルコ	漁田 章 ◎
若狭 藤雄	脇 思郎	脇中 悦子	脇本 恭一
脇本 はな ◎	和久野 幸子	早稲田 フジ子	和田 耕治
綿岡 順次郎	綿芝 要	わたなべ あつし	渡辺 聰
渡邊 昭三	渡邊 武	渡部 俊典	渡部 治美

165

渡辺 美智子	渡辺 泰 ◎	渡部 芳枝	渡 シズ子
渡 芳子	匿名	匿名 ◎	匿名
匿名	匿名	匿名	匿名 ◎
匿名	匿名	匿名	匿名
匿名	作者不明 ◎	作者不明 ◎	作者不明 ◎

History, Memory & the Legacy of *Hibakusha* Artists

John W. Dower

In 1977, Pantheon Books published an American edition of NHK's early collection of atomic-bomb drawings and paintings by *hibakusha*. The title of the Japanese version was *Gōka o Mita*. In English, this was rendered as *Unforgettable Fire*.

One of the Americans who participated in preparing the translation was the late Howard Schonberger, a professor of U.S. diplomatic history at the University of Maine who had been involved in both the civil rights and anti-Vietnam War movements. Professor Schonberger and I were both in Japan in the academic year of 1974-75, and we encountered the *hibakusha* pictures independently at roughly the same time. He was a Fulbright scholar living for a year in Hiroshima with his wife and two small children. I was on research leave with my family in Kyoto.

Professor Schonberger worked on the translation of *Unforgettable Fire* with people in Hiroshima I never met. My own contribution to the U.S. publication was marginal: I introduced the book to an editor at Pantheon, who immediately recognized the extraordinary window it opened on the true nature of nuclear war. John Hersey, famous for the accounts of six *hibakusha* he published in 1946—first as a rare full issue of *The New Yorker* magazine, and then as the book *Hiroshima*—contributed a send-off statement for the Pantheon edition. *Unforgettable Fire*, he wrote, was "more moving than any book of photographs of the horror could be, because what is registered is what has been burned into the minds of the survivors."

Regrettably, *Unforgettable Fire* has been out of print for many years.

Hersey's observation was incisive. As individuals, we remember intimate events selectively and symbolically by fixing on images and moments that embody the larger experience. Such moments may be happy—reflections of youth, for example, or love or the birth of a child. In

の誕生といった、若き日の幸せな思い出であるかもしれない。ところが、広島と長崎では、人々の脳裏によみがえる瞬間は、恐ろしいものなのである。

　同時に、これらの個人的で象徴的な瞬間というのは、他の人々と共有することができる。それ故、戦争の恐怖、とりわけ核戦争の恐怖を理解しようとする際、他のどの方法よりも、原爆の絵は見る人により強い印象を与えると私は考える。ではなぜこれらの原爆の絵が、写真や映像より迫力をもつのであろうか？　それは、戦争を自分のものとして描いているからである。絵の作者たちは途方もない苦悩を強いられた普通の人々である。名前もある。彼らは、見る人にとって忘れることのできないような生々しい光景を絵に描くことにより、自らの体験を共有しているのである。ヒロシマ・ナガサキについてこれまで書かれてきた言葉を超えた理解の次元を、彼らは作り出している。1945（昭和20）年のグラウンド・ゼロ（爆心地）で起きた出来事を、歴史家よりはるかに痛烈に、力強く、正確に、そして印象深く物語っているのである。

　少なくとも私個人の経験において、初めて原爆の絵を見たときのことは今なお鮮明に覚えている。京都にいたその年のある夜更け、長時間の仕事を終え、ふとテレビのスイッチを入れると、テレビの画像に目が釘付けになった。それは、青い背景に手だけが描かれた素朴な絵で、指がロウソクのように燃えていた。絵の作者に代わって話す女性の声だけが聞こえていた。この手は女性のもので、瓦礫の中から手を天に向け、青い炎を出して燃えていた、そう語っていたのを覚えている。今、想像しているだけかもしれないが、その手が子どもを抱いたかもしれないと思って描いたと語っていたことも覚えている。

　後になってわかったのであるが、その絵は1945（昭和20）年8月当時19歳であった、高蔵信子によって描かれたものであった。その後も、別の原爆の絵がテレビの画面に次々と現れたが、それまで見たこともない絵ばかりであった。

　その後、京都で広島、長崎の原爆投下を扱った小規模な巡回展に出会った。ヒロシマ・ナガサキの写真と並んで原爆の絵が展示されていたのであ

Hiroshima and Nagasaki, of course, the recollected moments were horrendous.

At the same time, these individual symbolic moments can be shared with others. That is what the *hibakusha* drawings and paintings do—more memorably, in my view, than any other way we have of trying to comprehend the true horror of war in general, and nuclear war in particular. Why are these images more powerful in their way than photographs or film footage? Because they depict war as intimately as can be imagined. The artists are ordinary people who suffered in extraordinary ways. They have names. They share their experience through graphic images that often are themselves unforgettable for those who see them. They add a dimension of understanding beyond language per se to what has been written about Hiroshima and Nagasaki. They are certainly more incisive, powerful, accurate, and memorable than anything historians can tell us about what happened in Japan at the nuclear Ground Zeros of 1945.

This, at least, was my personal experience. I still vividly recall the first *hibakusha* drawing I ever saw. Late one evening during that year in Kyoto, at the end of a long day working, I turned on the television at random. The image on the screen transfixed me. It was a rough painting of a hand against a blue background, the fingers burning like candles. The voice of an unseen woman was speaking for the artist. It was a woman's hand, I recall her saying, reaching toward heaven from the rubble, fingers burning with a blue flame. Perhaps I only imagine it now, but I also recall the voice saying she pictured how that hand might have held a child.

The painting, I learned later, was by Takakura Akiko, who was nineteen years old in August 1945. Other paintings and drawings by *hibakusha* followed on the television screen. I had never seen anything like them.

After this, I located a small traveling exhibition in Kyoto devoted to the atomic bombs. This, too, was an education—for the exhibition included photographs from Hiroshima and Nagasaki alongside *hibakusha* paintings and drawings. For me, certainly at that moment, the latter were more powerful—or, perhaps better said, powerful in an entirely different way.

るが、これにもおおいに啓発された。私はそのとき間違いなく、後者の方により圧倒されたのであるが、それはまったく異なる意味で迫力があったという方が正しいかもしれない。

　1945(昭和20)年のグラウンド・ゼロの惨劇を再現するにあたり、写真が中心となることは間違いない。この中には、1960年代半ばまでアメリカ当局に没収されていた、岩崎昶とその撮影班によって被爆後に撮影された記録映画を始め、日本人によって撮影され、米軍が日本の占領を終えた1952(昭和27)年になって初めて公表された写真も含まれる。記録映画の映像やほとんどの写真が白黒であることが、測り知れぬ効果を増している。

　ところが同時に、1970年代になって、そのような1945(昭和20)年8月の写真は、少なくとも反戦・反核運動家たちにとって、慣れ親しんだ光景になってしまった。これらの写真は、おのずと一歩距離を置いたものである。つまり、被爆を体験していない第三者による、破壊と見知らぬ犠牲者の記録なのである。ところが、それらがあまりにも恐ろしいメッセージであるにもかかわらず、あるいはであるが故に、写真による衝撃は「遮断する」ことが可能なのである。つまり、心理的にありがちな、自らを守るための「無感覚の状態」になるのである。われわれの目は、少なくとも頭の中で、ほとんど本能的にそのようなイメージから遠ざかろうとするのである。それは、恐ろしいからでもあり、似たような写真を見たことがあるからでもあり、写し出された犠牲者が、名前も知らない他人であるからでもあろう。

　私の経験では、原爆の絵からそのように目をそらすことはできない。このため私は、あの夜京都でテレビに釘付けになり、さらに、見慣れたヒロシマ・ナガサキの写真と並んで展示されていた原爆の絵から目をそらすことができなかったのである。絵の作者たちには名前があった。1945(昭和20)年8月当時、何歳であったかも記されていた。そこに描かれた経験はあまりに率直であり、具体的であった。色彩には、カラー写真では表現できない、抗うことのできない力があった。描き出された炎は、写真では伝えることができない地獄の炎と化すのである。

　Photography certainly remains central to our ability to recreate the horror of Ground Zero 1945. This includes the documentary film footage taken by Iwasaki Akira and his crew after the atomic bombings, which was censored by U.S. authorities until the mid-1960s, as well as the still photos taken by Japanese and made available only after the U.S. occupation of Japan ended in 1952. That the documentary film footage and most photographs are black-and-white adds immeasurably to their effectiveness.

　At the same time, however, by the 1970s such photo images from August 1945 had become familiar, at least in antiwar and anti-nuclear circles. They were, by their very nature, detached—that is, a record of destruction and of anonymous victims by third-person observers who had not experienced the bombs themselves. Despite or perhaps because of their awful message, moreover, it was possible to "block" the full impact of the photographic record. Psychologically, that is, a defensive "numbing" often occurred. Our eyes, or at least our minds, almost instinctively turn away from such images—partly because they are terrible, partly because we have seen them or their like before, partly perhaps because the victims they depict remain nameless strangers.

　In my experience, it is not possible to similarly turn away from the work of the *hibakusha* artists. This is what drew me in on television that night in Kyoto, and at the exhibition that placed these images alongside more familiar photographs of Hiroshima and Nagasaki. The artists had names. We were told their age in August 1945. The experiences depicted were extraordinarily intimate and concrete. The colors were compelling—in a way that color photos can not replicate. Fire painted becomes hellfire in ways the camera can not convey.

　Additionally, most of these paintings and drawings were interwoven with words in one way or another, sometimes in the form of writing on the pictures, sometimes in the form of accompanying explanatory texts. The familiar lexicon of the atomic-bomb experience assumed an entirely new level of meaning for someone alien to the actual experience depicted, like me—*hellfire, procession of ghosts, black rain, radiation sickness....*

さらに、これらの絵の大半は、さまざまな形で言葉に綴られている。時には絵の中に直接書きこまれていたり、絵に説明文が添えられていることもある。私のような、絵に描かれた体験を直接していない者にとって、「地獄の火」、「幽霊の行列」、「黒い雨」、「放射線障害」といった被爆体験特有の言葉が、まったく新しいレベルの意味をもってくる。

私は、違う形の表現者による被爆体験の描写にも関心をもつようになった。それは、中沢啓治のマンガ『はだしのゲン』のような大衆文化を発見したときと、ほぼ同時期である。また、原爆投下直後に広島に入った丸木位里、丸木俊によって共同制作された力作『原爆の図』などを、紹介された。広島と長崎に通い、1960年代後半から被爆の遺産を記録しはじめた写真家、土門拳と東松照明による草分け的作品があることも、いくぶん遅ればせながら知った。その後間もなく出会った原爆の絵と同様に、1945（昭和20）年8月から20年を経た、被爆者一人一人のきめ細かいポートレートはひときわ感動的である。二人の場合、それぞれの写真が並外れた個性をもち、奥行きのある作品となっている。

1974年から75年にかけて日本に滞在した後、ショーンバーガー教授と私はアメリカに戻り、それぞれヒロシマ・ナガサキに触発された芸術作品について講演会などを開いた。ショーンバーガー教授の話がきっかけとなり、メーン州バンゴアの反核活動家が、市内を流れる川で灯籠流しをし、毎年ヒロシマの記念日を追悼するようになった。当時、私が教鞭を取っていたウィスコンシンでも、これらの生々しい作品に出会い、同様の反応を示した自治体があった。私が、ミシシッピ川岸にある都市、ラ・クロスで行った講演を受けて、平和団体「社会的責任のある医師団」のメンバーである地元の医師たちが、地元民からの熱烈な支援を得て、8月の一夜、アメリカ陸軍工兵隊にミシシッピ川の交通を一部封鎖させ、アメリカ最大の川でも、平和のための灯籠流しができるようにしたのである。この感動的な式典は、数年間続けられた。

これらは、1970年代から80年代はじめにかけてのことで、全米の草の根活動家の政治意識が比

I became interested in other ways that Japanese artists had depicted the atomic-bomb experience. This was roughly the same time that I discovered popular graphic treatments like Nakazawa Keiji's *Barefoot Gen* manga. In a different direction, I was introduced to the remarkable *Genbaku no Zu* and other collaboratively-painted murals by Maruki Iri and Maruki Toshi, who arrived in Hiroshima shortly after the bomb was dropped. Somewhat belatedly, I also became aware of the pioneer work by the photographers Domon Ken and Tōmatsu Shōmei, who returned to Hiroshima and Nagasaki beginning in the late 1960s to document the legacy of the bombs. Like the artwork by survivors that was introduced shortly after this, their extraordinary portraits of individual *hibakusha*, over two decades after August 1945, were especially moving. In these cases, the photography had extraordinary individuality and depth.

After our 1974-1975 stay in Japan, Professor Schonberger and I returned to the United States and independently spent some time giving public presentations based on the Japanese artwork stimulated by Hiroshima and Nagasaki. Under Professor Schonberger's inspiration, anti-nuclear activists in Bangor, Maine, organized to commemorate the anniversary of Hiroshima each year by floating paper lanterns on the river that flows through that city. In Wisconsin, where I was then teaching, there was one similar community response to having encountered these graphic images. Following a presentation I gave in La Crosse, a city on the Mississippi River, local doctors associated with the peace group Physicians for Social Responsibility succeeded—after impressively mobilizing local support—in getting the U.S. Army Corps of Engineers to close a small section of the Mississippi to river traffic for one night in August, so that paper lanterns for peace could be floated there, on America's greatest river, as well. This impressive ceremony was repeated for a number of years.

This was the 1970s and early 1980s, when grassroots political consciousness throughout the United States was still relatively progressive, still influenced by the civil rights and antiwar movements, and still deeply alarmed by the Cold War nuclear arms race. With the collapse of

較的革新的であった時期であり、公民権運動や反戦運動の余波があり、冷戦の核軍拡競争に危機感を募らせていた時期でもあった。1989(平成元)年になってソ連が崩壊し、アメリカの新型核兵器の開発は民衆の意識から遠のき、米国の軍事優先主義への激しい非難も鳴りをひそめてしまった。

9月11日に同時多発テロが起きてから、本来の「グラウンド・ゼロ(核の爆心地)」という概念すら、アメリカでは本質的に消えてしまった。今日、この言葉が何を意味するかと問われると、ほとんどのアメリカ人は、2001(平成13)年に起きた世界貿易センターへのテロ攻撃と答えるだろう。おそらく、核兵器がテロリストの手中に落ちれば、アメリカに何が起こるかということを思い起こさせてくれる以外、ヒロシマ・ナガサキの記憶は希薄なのである。1945(昭和20)年8月に原爆を投下したアメリカの決定が批判されたときに生じる共通の反応は、原爆投下はひどいことかもしれないが、特にサイパン、硫黄島、沖縄での戦闘やカミカゼ攻撃の後では、狂信的な日本政府に勝つ見込みのない侵略戦争をあきらめさせるために必要だったというものであろう。日本の戦争犯罪への懲罰として、原爆投下は仕方なかったという確固とした信念は、アメリカでは今も根強い。では真珠湾攻撃はどうなんだ、原爆投下を擁護する人たちはこう答えるだろう。連合国軍の捕虜に対する残虐行為はどうだ？ 南京大虐殺(アメリカのメディアがよく取り上げるテーマで、とりわけ、中国系アメリカ人社会では厳しい)はどうだ？

反核運動はこうしてほとんど死に体と化し、「グラウンド・ゼロ」という言葉を聞くと、多くのアメリカ人は9月11日を思い、アメリカ人が犠牲になったことを考える。世界貿易センターへの攻撃では、多数の外国人が犠牲となったが、広島、長崎で被爆した韓国人が、日本人の意識から大きく切り捨てられているのと同じように、そのことは、今日、ほとんどのアメリカ人の心を苛む被害者意識からは、大きく切り捨てられている。アメリカの中東政策が、反米感情の高まりを生み、より精巧な大量破壊兵器の開発への固執が、他国の軍備の増強を煽っているというのに、これらの開発に対する草の根運動家の批判は力を失い、結

the Soviet Union in 1989, the U.S. development of new nuclear weapons has essentially dropped out of public consciousness—as has, indeed, serious criticism of U.S. militarism itself.

In the wake of September 11, even the original concept of "Ground Zero" essentially disappeared in the United States. Asked what these words mean today, almost every American will reply: the terrorist bombing of the World Trade Center in 2001. There is scant recollection of Hiroshima and Nagasaki—except, perhaps, as reminders of what might happen to the United States if nuclear weapons fall into "terrorist" hands. If the U.S. decision to drop the atomic bombs in August 1945 is mentioned critically, the common response is that this may have been terrible, but—especially after Saipan and Iwo Jima and Okinawa and the *kamikaze*—it was necessary to force the fanatical Japanese government to abandon its unwinnable war of aggression. Firm belief that the bombs were deserved retribution for Japanese war crimes also remains strong in the United States. What about Pearl Harbor, those who defend the use of the bombs respond. What about atrocities against Allied prisoners of war? What about the Rape of Nanking (a popular subject in the U.S. media, and especially in the highly vocal Chinese-American community)?

The anti-nuclear movement is thus largely moribund now; and when Americans hear the words "Ground Zero," they think of 9-11 and how Americans were victimized. Even though hundreds of non-Americans died in the attacks on the World Trade Center, they are largely excluded from the victim consciousness that gnaws at most Americans today—much like the Korean victims of the Hiroshima and Nagasaki bombs are largely excluded in Japanese consciousness. And even though U.S. policies in the Middle East contributed to the rise of anti-American sentiments there—just as the unrestrained development of ever more sophisticated weapons of mass destruction persists in the United States today and incites other nations to expand their own arsenals—grassroots criticism of these developments remains weak and fragmented. Identity politics, patriotism, nationalism, neo-nationalism, victim consciousness all impede critical

束することはない。国粋主義政治、愛国心、ナショナリズム、ネオ・ナショナリズム、被害者意識などすべて、近代に巣くう病理に関する問題意識の妨げとなっている。

実際、2003（平成15）年にブッシュ政権がイラクに戦争をしかける準備に奔走していたとき、政府やメディアはこぞって「衝撃と畏怖」という言葉を口にした。大量のアメリカ軍の襲撃がイラク人に衝撃を与え、すぐにアメリカの侵略への黙従へと追い込むという考えである。「衝撃と畏怖」というのは、実は、アメリカの国防界における公式戦術教義であり、ヒロシマ・ナガサキの成功例とあからさまに関連づけられている。

アメリカや日本はもとより、世界中の多くの若い世代にとって、第二次世界大戦の惨劇は、大昔の出来事として捉えられている。あるいは、戦争がヒーロー物語や、テレビ・ゲームになったり、抽象化されている。戦争や大量破壊は依然貪欲な野獣のように暗雲となって垂れ込めているというのに、アメリカにおける一般的な反応は、さらに高度な兵器システムの開発であり、日本でもその声は高まっている。戦争で解決を図るこの固定観念はそもそも狂気の沙汰であり、軍国主義や戦争の成れの果てを忘却へと追いやる。

だからこそ、直接体験した「記憶」を、赤裸々に、次の世代へと継承できる数少ない好例である、原爆の絵のような迫力ある作品が、ますます重要になってくる。ただし、継承が効果的に行われるために重要となるのが、その展示の形式である。アメリカでは、これにはいくつかのことが必要であると考える。概念的には、これらのイメージは、日本人が加害者であり、被害者でもあった、アジア太平洋戦争の全戦域で発生した、より大きな範囲の恐怖の一部として紹介されると、最も効果的ではないかと思う。私の経験では、簡潔なテーマによって展示するのも、より効果を高める。つまり、被爆体験における「普遍的」テーマを掲げて、ヒバクシャ各自の体験をまとめあげる内容にするのである。そのようなテーマとして、たとえば、「家族」、「母と子」、「火災」、「のどの渇きと水にまつわる死」、「変わり果てた姿」、「黒い雨」、「乏しい治療」、「被爆後茶毘に付す」、「生存と死」、

thinking about the pathology of our modern times.

Indeed, as the Bush Administration geared up for its war of choice against Iraq in 2003, one of the most popular phrases in governmental and media circles was "Shock and Awe"—the notion that a massive U.S. military assault would shock Iraqis into quick acquiescence to the U.S. invasion. "Shock and Awe" was in fact a formal tactical doctrine in U.S. defense circles—and was explicitly associated with the positive example of Hiroshima and Nagasaki.

Almost everywhere in the world—certainly in America as in Japan—the horrors of World War Two are largely ancient history to younger generations. Or else that war is romanticized; or turned into some form of digital game; or rendered abstract in some other way. Although war and mass destruction still loom over us like an insatiable beast, the common response in the United States, and increasingly in Japan as well, is to develop ever more sophisticated weapon systems. There is an inherent madness in this fixation on militaristic solutions—and a terrible forgetfulness of how militarism and war eventually come home.

This is why powerful artwork like the *hibakusha* pictures has become more important than ever, for there are few better examples of how intimate, first-hand "memory" can be passed from generation to generation. What is now required for such transmission to become effective, however, is a *structure* of preservation and presentation. In the United States, I think, this requires several things. Conceptually, these images are most effective when presented as part of the larger horrors that took place in all theaters of the Asia-Pacific War—where Japanese were victimizers as well as victims. In my experience, they are also most effective when presented in some kind of concise *schematic* format—in a context, that is, that integrates the unique experience of each *hibakusha* with certain more "universal" themes in the atomic-bomb experience. Such themes would include families, for example, mother-and-child, fire, thirst as well as death by water, disfiguration, the black rain, the absence of medical care, cremating the dead after the bombings, survival as well as death, the guilt of survivors....

「生き残ったヒバクシャの自責」などがあるだろう。

　中学校から大学まで各学年のアメリカ人の若者の大半は、そのような構成で紹介されれば、熱心な反応を示す。絵の大半が1970年代に描かれているものの、被爆当時、作者の多くは若く学生であったという原爆の絵の特質に対する反応は良い。たとえ日本人でなくても、今日の学生は、これらの絵に共鳴できるのである。さらに、絵は死を告げている一方で、各自の生存のあかしでもある。心理的に、心に残りやすいのである。これらの平凡な作者たちが、語り伝えることに道義的責任を感じていることも、若者が見習うべき教訓である。

　今日の若者は、もはやあまり本に頼ることをしない。このことは、障害ではなくむしろチャンスと考えるべきである。なぜなら、原爆の絵は、バーチャル世界でとりわけ活用できるからである。コンピュータやネットワークの領域では、これらの絵は、テーマの構築が可能となり、教師の指導や教材をともなって、具体的に再生され、広く、自由にアクセスされるのである。「Web」には、教室の内外での教育を可能にする、未来の「公教育」の姿があると私は信じている。

　私が所属するマサチューセッツ工科大学でも、これを検討しはじめたところであり、まったく予想外ではあるが、京都で30年前にテレビで原爆の絵を初めて見た時から、一つの目処を迎えた。当校では先ごろ、「Visualizing Cultures（文化の視覚化）」というオンライン・プロジェクトを導入したところであるが、われわれの関心を引いた現代の多くの「文化」の一つが他でもない「戦争の文化」であった。最初の単元の一つは「Ground Zero 1945（1945年のグラウンド・ゼロ）」と名づけられ、広島平和記念資料館所蔵の原爆の絵を紹介している。そこには高蔵信子の燃える手も含まれている。

＊ジョン・W・ダワーは、マサチューセッツ工科大学歴史学フォード・インターナショナル教授。同大学の「Visualizing Cultures」プロジェクトの共同ディレクターである（http://visualizingcultures.mit.edu）。

Most young Americans at every level from middle school through university respond attentively to such structured presentations. They also respond well to one of the special features of the *hibakusha* pictures: the fact that, having been done mostly in the 1970s, many of the artists were young and in school when the atomic bombs were dropped. Students today—even non-Japanese—can identify with this. While the pictures tell of death, moreover, they are also testimonies to individual survival; psychologically, this makes it easier to stay with them. That these ordinary artists feel a moral responsibility to speak out is also a lesson that young people can be encouraged to emulate.

What young people today do not do is rely so much on books anymore. This is less an obstacle than an opportunity, however, for the *hibakusha* artwork is particularly adaptable to the virtual world. In cyberspace, these pictures can be given conceptual structure, reproduced in detail, accompanied with teacher's guides and other pedagogic material, and made widely and freely accessible. The Web, I have come to believe, is where the future of "public education" lies—education, that is, both in and outside the classroom.

We have begun to pursue this at my own university, M.I.T.; and in an entirely unexpected way, this has brought me full cycle to that time over thirty years ago when I first saw the *hibakusha* artwork on television in Kyoto. We recently introduced an on-line project called "Visualizing Cultures," and one of the many "cultures" of modern times that interests us is the culture of war itself. One of our first units is titled "Ground Zero 1945" and based on *hibakusha* drawings and paintings from the Hiroshima Peace Memorial Museum. It includes Takakura Akiko's burning hand.

＊ JOHN W. DOWER is the Ford International Professor of History at the Massachusetts Institute of Technology. He is co-director of the "Visualizing Cultures" project at M.I.T. [http://visualizingcultures.mit.edu].

［監修者紹介］

浅井 基文（あさい もとふみ）
広島市立大学広島平和研究所所長。
1941年愛知県生まれ。1963年東京大学法学部中退、外務省入省。25年間の勤務の後、1988年文部省出向（東京大学教養学部教授）。1990年外務省退職。日本大学法学部教授、明治学院大学教授を経て、2005年4月から現職。
専攻は国際関係論、日本政治外交論。
主な著書に『日本外交　反省と転換』（岩波新書、1989年）、『新保守主義』（柏書房、1993年）、『中国をどう見るか』（高文研、2000年）、『集団的自衛権と日本国憲法』（集英社新書、2002年）、『戦争する国　しない国』（青木書店、2004年）など。

横山 昭正（よこやま あきまさ）
広島女学院大学・大学院教授。
1943年広島県福山市生まれ。1972年から75年までフランス政府給費生としてルーアン大学に留学。1976年広島大学大学院文学研究科博士課程を単位取得退学し、同年、広島女学院大学講師。同大学助教授、教授、リヨン大学客員研究員を経て、1995年4月から現職。
専攻はフランス文学。
主な著書・論文に詩集『夢の錨』（思潮社、1978年）、『石の夢――ボードレール・シュペルヴィエル・モーリヤック』（渓水社、2002年）、『現代日本文学のポエジ――虹の聖母子』（渓水社、2004年）、『スタンダールと視線のロマネスク』（広島女学院大学総合研究所、2005年）。"*La symbolique animale chez Baudelaire*, Bulletin d'Études parnassiennes et symbolistes"（Lyon、1995年）、『広島の被爆建造物――被爆45周年調査報告書』（共著、朝日新聞社、1990年）、『ヒロシマの被爆建造物は語る――被爆50周年・未来への記録』（共著、広島市、1996年）など。

直野 章子（なおの あきこ）
九州大学大学院比較社会文化研究院准教授。
兵庫県西宮市出身。高校卒業後、米国のアメリカン大学に入学。大学卒業後、米学生が広島で原爆について学ぶ特別講座を同大学に創設。スミソニアン博物館での原爆展論争を受け、被爆50年の夏、アメリカン大で原爆展を開催。カリフォルニア大学大学院にて博士号を取得。その後半年間、ソウルの高麗大学に語学留学。日本学術振興会特別研究員を経て、2005年4月から現職。
専攻は社会学。
主な著書・論文に『ヒロシマ・アメリカ――原爆展をめぐって』（渓水社、1997年、第三回平和・協同ジャーナリスト基金賞奨励賞受賞）、『「原爆の絵」と出会う』（岩波ブックレット、2004年）、"Searching for grandpa in the Hiroshima memoryscape, under the shadow of the bomb"（Inter-Asia Cultural Studies、2003年）など。

広島平和記念資料館

原爆による被害の実相を世界中の人々に伝え、核兵器廃絶と世界恒久平和の実現に寄与するために、1955（昭和30）年に開館した。被爆者の遺品、被爆の惨状を示す写真や資料を収集・展示するとともに、広島の被爆前後の歩みや核時代の状況などについても紹介している。
平和記念資料館本館は国の重要文化財で、資料館が建つ平和記念公園は国の名勝である。

〒730-0811　広島市中区中島町1-2
TEL：082-241-4004　FAX：082-542-7941
E-mail：hpcf@pcf.city.hiroshima.jp
ホームページ：http://www.pcf.city.hiroshima.jp/

図録 原爆の絵 ヒロシマを伝える

2007年3月27日　第1刷発行
2025年1月24日　第10刷発行

編　者　広島平和記念資料館
発行者　坂本政謙
発行所　株式会社　岩波書店
　　　　〒101-8002　東京都千代田区一ツ橋2-5-5
　　　　電話案内 03-5210-4000
　　　　https://www.iwanami.co.jp/

印刷／製本・大日本印刷

© The City of Hiroshima 2007
ISBN 978-4-00-022765-0　　Printed in Japan

増補版 敗北を抱きしめて[全二冊] ――第二次大戦後の日本人	ジョン・ダワー 著 三浦陽一／高杉忠明／田代泰子 訳	A5判上製カバー 上巻・四一二頁 定価上三九〇〇円 下巻・四七六頁 定価下三三〇〇円
原爆体験と戦後日本 ――記憶の形成と継承	直野章子 著	四六判上製・二九〇頁 定価三五二〇円
なぜ原爆が悪ではないのか ――アメリカの核意識	宮本ゆき 著	四六判並製・三四〇頁 定価三一九〇円
新版 1945年8月6日 ――ヒロシマは語りつづける	伊東壮 著	岩波ジュニア新書 定価九二四円
広島平和記念資料館は問いかける	志賀賢治 著	岩波新書 定価九四六円

――― 岩波書店刊 ―――
定価は消費税10％込です
2025年1月現在